Cultural Heritage in Transit

PENNSYLVANIA STUDIES IN HUMAN RIGHTS

Bert B. Lockwood, Jr., Series Editor

A complete list of books in the series is available from the publisher.

Cultural Heritage in Transit

Intangible Rights as Human Rights

Edited by

Deborah Kapchan

PENN

UNIVERSITY OF PENNSYLVANIA PRESS

PHILADELPHIA

Published by
University of Pennsylvania Press
Philadelphia, Pennsylvania 19104-4112
www.upenn.edu/pennpress

Printed in the United States of America
on acid-free paper

10 9 8 7 6 5 4 3 2 1

Library of Congress Cataloging-in-Publication Data
Cultural heritage in transit : intangible rights as human rights / edited by Deborah Kapchan. — 1st ed.
p. cm.—(Pennsylvania studies in human rights)
Includes bibliographical references and index.
ISBN 978-0-8122-4594-3 (hardcover : alk. paper)
1. Cultural property—Protection—Law and legislation. 2. Intellectual property. 3. Culture and law. 4. Group identity. 5. Human rights. I. Kapchan, Deborah A. (Deborah Anne) author editor of compilation. II. Series: Pennsylvania studies in human rights.
K487.C8C86 2014
323.1—dc23 2013046746

Contents

Introduction

Intangible Rights: Cultural Heritage in Transit

Human rights. Are they universal?

Our immediate response is "yes, of course." However that simple affirmation assumes agreement about definitions of the "human" as well as what a human is entitled to under law, bringing us quickly to concepts such as "freedom," "property in the person," and the "inalienability" of both.[1]

The assumption that we all mean the same thing by these terms carries much political import, especially given the fact that different communities (national, ethnic, religious, gendered) enact some the most basic categories of human experience (self, home, freedom, sovereignty) differently. This is why when organizations such as the United Nations draft charters, like the Universal Declaration of Human Rights (UDHR), a great deal of time is spent choosing the language (Groth 2012). Indeed, in the very preamble of this document we find a key concept of the notion of rights as what is "inalienable," that is, unable to be separated from the self: "Whereas recognition of the inherent dignity and of the equal and inalienable rights of all members of the human family is the foundation of freedom, justice and peace in the world."

There is a debate in political philosophy about what, if anything, is inalienable in the human being (Pateman 2002, 1988). The term is associated with "property in the person," a concept that for much of American history was applied to free male subjects who (unlike slaves) owned first and foremost themselves as well as other alienable objects, including their wives and children (Pateman 1988). Personal freedoms were defined against the negative benchmark of human chattel. Thus defining the human as possessing "property in the person" assumes that one can do what one likes with that "property," including alienating its own labor (a sovereign person can conceivably contract her- or himself into servitude). Carole Pateman thus calls the notion of "inalienable rights" a "political fiction,"[2] for although one cannot actually sever one's mind from one's laboring body, the ability to contract one's labor to an employer demonstrates that human labor *is* in fact alienable as a value (1988). I will not review this debate here; however I mention it to forefront the fact that legal parameters of the "person" are not now and have never been unproblematic, yet they undergird the most basic discussions of human rights.

That the Western subject has been defined as a property owner has deep implications. It associates sovereignty and freedom with private property and its tangible possession (see article 17 of the UDHR, for example).[3] However what is "private" has also undergone serious transformation in light of innovations in virtual media, cyborg realities, and the posthuman, as have the parameters of the human it/her/himself (Haraway 1985; Hardt and Negri 2000; Coole and Frost 2010). Indeed, studies in the philosophy of the emotions, as well as what Patricia Brennan calls "psychoneuroendocrinology," demonstrate that rather than being separate until proven coextensive with others (in "liminal" experiences such as religious ritual, art, music, and sexual union), people are actually together (in intangible but measurable ways) until their separateness is consciously enacted through gendered, cultural, and institutional education (Brennan 2004). "Property in the person" can no longer circulate as a general definition of the self, if it ever legitimately could, and is certainly not a universal category. What's more, this political fiction is a very dangerous one, especially when we recognize, following Michel Serres, that property ownership goes hand in hand with one's the ability to pollute (Serres 2011).[4] The rational and sovereign Western subject not only presides over himself (I use the masculine pronoun, as historically the unmarked political subject was assumed to be male), but has deeply misrecognized the rights of other life forms, objectifying and dominating land, animals, plants, and other forms of biological life, and rendering them fodder for capitalist consumption and the detritus it produces.

Tangible Intangibilities

As we inquire further into the relation of "property in the person" and human rights we inevitably land in the territory of the cultural and the everyday practices that compose it. Definitions of a legal entity (a person) as one who is able to determine his or her own destiny often contradicts what we know about how cultural practices overdetermine the subject, limiting his or her agency by creating (unconscious) desires and motivations that collude with the state or other hegemonic systems (Boddy 1989; Foucault 1972, 1977). We appear to have, for example, unlimited freedom to consume—at least in the West—but less freedom to opt out of consumption (Hardt and Negri 2000) While there are copyright laws protecting the creations (i.e., the property) of the individual, as well as corporations, it is much more difficult to insure the rights of the community. Can we even think in terms of "property in (the) common"? In a postsecular era, when religious communities are reforming around affective and aesthetic practices, it is perhaps time to do so. But where would be its bounds and its defenses? What's more, the current ability to patent and copyright forms of nature, such as seeds, as well as other genetic material further skews our intuitions about the limits of the human and what belongs to whom. Indeed the ethics (or the unethical "nature") of biopolitics provide the most pressing studies in rapidly transforming notions of self, nature, and nation (see Scher, this volume).

Political fictions are the stuff of human rights. The discourses that circulate about alienability, sovereignty, and agency create our social unconscious and manifest in the material world as the "way it is," our "natural" and inalienable rights as individuals. What's more, these fictions produce our phenomenological experience of our own bodies and communities. These are necessary and often worthy fictions that do important political work, but we must recognize that discourses of universalism are also political fictions, or what Gayatri Spivak called "strategic essentialisms" (Spivak 1999; cf. Jakobsen and Pellegrini 2005; Mahmood 2004; Tsing 2011).[5] They are motivated. They work for some, and not for others.

The notion of property in the person insists on the presence of a body and its effects. Implicit in this historical formation, however, is the idea of a rational owner, one who possesses the property and can dispose of its values and attributes. This focus on the discrete rational actor is no longer sufficient to account for the many factors that contribute to social change and creativity, particularly when it comes to intangible culture, which is, after all, inextricable from practice: singing, dancing, storytelling, feting. Are the people who enact these practices their "owners"? Is it sufficient to practice them to possess them? What are the claims that history and precedent make? And how do our political fictions about the subject and its community collude to produce particular sociopolitical formations, especially in the realm of the heritage industry?

Defining anything as "universal" is politically charged. It is often done by hegemonic authors writing a particular kind of subject and culture into historical consciousness. The universal rights of humanity—to health, clean water, energy—too often translate into the privilege of some over the oppression of others. As Jacques Rancière notes, "if those who suffer inhuman repression cannot exercise the Human Rights that are their last recourse, then it is up to others to inherit these rights and exercise them in their place. The name for this is the 'right to humanitarian interference'" (Rancière 2010: 74). Elsewhere he calls this the "right to invasion" (62).

While we can all agree that violence is an abrogation of human rights, definitions of cultural rights are less clear. Where it gets murky is in the domain of possession. Who owns the intangible? Who owns the ephemeral? How, for that matter, distinguish between ownable matter and freely circulating and ungraspable energy like sound, light, or even water? As soon as we concentrate on the materiality of the invisible and the virtual, or contrariwise, on the vibration of matter, the distinctions between these realms seem to melt, skewing notions of agency and the subject in the process (Bennett 2010; Whitehead 1948). Asking these questions is like asking who owns sound in the ether; however, the answers we give have real material and political consequence—in the lives and practices of people and communities. Claims to universality are in fact only effective when they can be instrumentalized at the local level and made "vernacular" (Merry 2006).

In this book we explore the "intangibilities" of human rights in the realm of heritage production, focusing not only on ephemeral culture and its "holders," but on the ambiguities and intangibilities of the idea of cultural property in general—who it belongs to, who may use it, who "should not," but does. These are not easy problems to solve. We might all agree that a Jackson Pollock is a Jackson Pollock, and that the market demands millions for each painting. However, who owns songs? Who owns the spoken word? Who owns the gestures associated with a particular national form of dance? We might say that the people who create them do. But even creation becomes a contested issue when aesthetic forms arise from shared visions, intersubjective imaginations and intertextual citations. What is public domain? The modern icon of the lone artist inhabiting the margins of society in order to better reflect upon it no longer works. We have cycled back to a very different form of Renaissance studio, one in which collaborators work virtually and often not explicitly, yet collectively.[6] Just as notions of God have changed since the Renaissance, so have notions of the person (Luhrmann 2012). Yet most protectionist agencies are working on models of the sovereign rational subject that no longer correspond to rapidly transforming paradigms of the self and the way plural selves collectively create the world.

The World International Property Organization (WIPO) was created to grapple with some of these issues and to protect culture bearers. But the debates surrounding WIPO have not really touched the basic assumptions of the rational and autonomous subject that underlies its bylaws. Nor have they engaged with the critique of "universalism" and alienation.[7] Definitions of the human are changing more rapidly than the laws designed to protect them. These are the conundrums of intangible cultural heritage.

It has become a truism that the production of heritage creates local, national, and international hierarchies that often oppress the very tradition bearers who either make the crafts, sing the songs, dance the dances, or otherwise represent or are responsible for the objects and events that make up tangible and intangible heritage (Noyes 2006; Hafstein 2004a; Kirshenblatt-Gimblett 1998a; L. Smith 2006a). Not only are the webs of administrative red tape entangled at ever more complicated levels, as heritage is displayed, museumized, put on stage, and otherwise commodified, but the artists and artisans of intangible and tangible culture lose their freedom to invent, transform, and add to their art in order that it remain recognizable to the tourist, who expects to encounter a known and consumable object or event.

To whom does culture belong? Who can lay claim to it? Who has the right to profit from it? Where are the limits of the public domain when the notion of privacy is fast retreating into history books and when laws of community ownership and definitions for communities themselves do not exist? The supreme irony of the protectionist polices of international organizations such as UNESCO is that they cannot help but infringe on the rights of some in their intention to protect the rights of others, especially when those rights are adjudicated through the state. As Valdimar Hafstein asks in this volume, "When is protection *not* a means of dispossession?"

The Race for Heritage: Cultural Rights and the Intangibilities of Everyday Life

In this volume we focus on the circulation and transformation of intangible culture, the role of the heritage industry in these "transitions" and the implications for human rights violations—particularly in the fuzzy area of cultural rights, which are inextricable from the right to imagine, to identify, to sense, and to feel. Because culture is always embodied, it is transmitted in sensate practices, in the repetitive habits of both everyday life and extraordinary performance. Insofar as folklore is both marked and unmarked in its cultural contexts (that is, it may be set apart from the quotidian environment or indistinguishable from it), both the performances as well as the practices of everyday life become material for the production of "intangible cultural heritage" (ICH). It is in fact the availability of all aspects of cultural experience for recycling in the heritage industry that demands a sensitive analysis of cultural rights.[8] When performances once deemed "private"—whether culinary arts,[9] lullabies, or religious rituals—become codified and reified materials for heritage production, their reascription as heritage transforms the practices as well as the attitudes that surround them. This, we assert, bears on the cultural rights of individuals and communities. Creating "heritage" in these circumstances acts to "reform" everyday life as actors reevaluate their practices and change their performances as a result (Klein, this volume).

How then define the rights of a community? Do definitions of community arise organically from within or are they imposed from without? Who will advocate for women and minority interests? And is advocacy necessary, or even desirable? In short, what are the political fictions that drive the race for heritage?

One place to look for answers to these questions is in the domain of endangered languages and the communities who speak them. As Jane Hill notes (2002: 120), there are three themes that characterize the literature on endangered languages—that of "universal ownership" (this language needs to be preserved for the benefit of "humanity'), that of "hyperbolic valorization" (this language is a "priceless treasure" and thus must be saved), and that of "enumeration . . . of alarming statistics" (this language has only three speakers left, or this language is one of thousands of languages on the brink of extinction). These discourses do not normally help save anything nor do they empower the communities in question. What's more, they participate in what Barbara Kirshenblatt-Gimblett has called "eleventh hour ethnography"—that is, anxious research undertaken because tomorrow it will be too late (Kirshenblatt-Gimblett 1992). Just as Hill reminds us that the imposition of an official national language does not necessarily contribute to the disappearance of a local one, likewise, it is not to be assumed that all local knowledge disappears simply because some aspects of these traditions are commodified as heritage and others are not. In drawing attention to the changing hierarchies caused by the heritage industry, it is easy to paint with a large brush, but this is not always helpful.

That said, advocacy for the rights of communities is more difficult than protecting the rights of an individual. Are the boundaries of a community defined by language? If so, what of Native Americans who don't speak their native tongue? By bloodline? What of communities like the NeoPagans who claim an ancestry impossible to prove (Magliocco, this volume)? Are communities defined by the state? If so, what of communities like the Sámi who find themselves in several countries (Kuutma 2008; Kuutma and Jaago 2005), or the Roma who travel across borders (Silverman, this volume)? Like any identity, the notion of "community" is produced in the discourses from which it emerges and does not exist apart from them (Foucault 1970, 1972), but conflicting discourses produce different definitions of community. When the official definition of the state conflicts with more local definitions, claims to human rights are invariably at play.

The Price of Heritage/The Rights to Heritage: The Example of the Gnawa

Official recognition of Intangible Cultural Heritage (ICH) is often the catalyst not only for changing definitions of community but for the practices that compose them as well. An example will serve. The Gnawa are musical and ritual specialists in Morocco who heal the possessed through all-night trance-inducing ceremonies that propitiate the spirits (Kapchan 2007). The Gnawa came to Morocco as slaves from different regions of West Africa primarily in the fifteenth and sixteenth centuries, but their practices, while known and recognized, remained somewhat clandestine and marginal to mainstream Moroccan society, at least compared to their popularity today. It is fair to say that the possession rituals of the Gnawa were in part what was indeed inalienable since their forced migration to Morocco, and today those rituals have become the icons of their racial and ethnic identity. In postindependence Morocco (1956), the Gnawa became known for their ritual knowledge as well as their musical style.[10] The Gnawa "aesthetic" entered the public canon, as the Gnawa "beat" as well as the strong pulsing bass became iconic of a Moroccan style of music that later would be dubbed the "blues" of Morocco, both because of its pulsing rhythms and because, like in the United States, the music emerged from a culture of slavery (El Hamel 2013). Today there is an annual international Gnawa Festival in Morocco that attracts hundreds of thousands of people. It takes place in Essaouira, a former Portuguese port city (originally called Mogador), which was a stop in the cross-Atlantic slave trade, but also a historically Jewish enclave. Essaouira is classified as a UNESCO world heritage site for reasons of both its architecture and its history (Kapchan 2005). As many as 300,000 to 400,000 spectators are said to attend the Essaouira Gnawa Festival of World Music annually. While the crowds are surely lured by famous "world-beat" musicians like Omar Sosa and Archie Shepp—to say nothing of the city itself—they are perhaps even more entranced by the mystique of the Gnawa who are masters of not just the musical world, but the world of the spirits. Their music is, in fact, an inducement to trance, and the audiences at the festival are willing subjects.

The Essaouira Gnawa Festival of World Music is now in its sixteenth year. While the festival did not create the Gnawa aesthetic in the world music market (Gnawa musicians in Morocco, France, and the United States had CDs before the festival began), it has contributed greatly to the awareness of Gnawa music and its role in healing the possessed. So much so, that it has spawned an association for the intangible culture of the Gnawa—Yerma Gnawa. As the website states,

> The creation in 2009 of the Yerma Gnaoua Association aims at preserving and enhancing the status of the intangible heritage of the Gnaoua. The Yerma Gnaoua Association is a vehicle for disseminating information about Gnaoua culture in Morocco and throughout the world, in addition to respecting and keeping its traditions. As well as being a contemporary creative body, the association also undertakes social responsibilities.
>
> The Association is committed to the continuation of the Gnaoua and World Music festival (a genuine showcase for Gnaoua art) and inspires Gnaoua musical creation through artists' residencies and partnerships with foreign festivals and musicians.[11]

That the Yerma Gnawa Association is an outgrowth of the Essaouira Gnawa Festival of World Music is not accidental. It is largely the festival that has brought international attention to Gnawa music and culture. Indeed festivals are one of the primary ways that states create both heritage and nationalist sentiment (Guss 2001), but more and more they are international in scope, bringing audiences and foreign currency into local sites such as Essaouira. The

Essaouira Gnawa Festival of World Music joins the Fes Festival of World Sacred Music in Fes, Morocco, as well as a myriad of other festivals in Morocco and around the globe in creating what I have elsewhere called the "festive sacred"—a transnational capitalization of sacred aesthetics that contributes to the reenchantment of the postsecular world (Kapchan 2008). The festive sacred inculcates religious or spiritual affect in audiences who are drawn to festive events by the promise that aesthetics—and particularly music—can translate culture to culture more easily than words and ideology.

That the Gnawa festival is as popular as it is speaks to a complex set of desires, including those generated by the heritage industry to iconize aspects of folk culture and turn them into tourist productions (Kirshenblatt-Gimblett 1998a). Yerma Gnawa stresses the artistry of Gnawa culture, yet the term *fanan* (artist) is not the usual term of discourse for Gnawa musicians. Rather, some are called *mu'allemin* (ritual masters), others simply Gnawa. They are ritual healers, spirit appeasers, but "artist" is a new label. It is clear that the festivalization of sacred ritual domesticates what is otherwise unruly, unpredictable, and uncontrollable (spirit possession ceremonies), while both creating and responding to an international fascination with trance (see Noyes, this volume). The festive sacred is a complex socioeconomic phenomenon as well, and trance-as-heritage is now a niche market in which ritual specialists have become artists, ritual knowledge has been replaced with savvy in regard to the world music market, and local economies are infused with global currency (Essaouira now boasts several four- and five-star hotels and a much-boosted economy, at least in June, due to tourist revenues).

What's more, now that the music is a recognized practice of intangible heritage, the community of practitioners and devotees has changed shape. Whereas historically the women in the Gnawa community have been just as important if not more important than the men as both ritual specialists (*muqaddamat*, overseers; *shuwafat*, clairvoyants) and trancers (*majdubat*) (Paques 1991; cf. Willemont 2011), they are now no more than an ornament on a male-dominated stage, swinging their heads in time to the music. Not only is heritage "conservative" in this regard (upholding the values of patriarchy), but it infringes upon the cultural rights of women in the tradition whose power has been diminished, if not erased, and who cannot even afford to pay for a ceremony (the men being able to charge more for "secular" or staged performances and thus less willing to provide ritual services).[12] The women that need the services of the Gnawa to perform propitiation ceremonies still know each other, but their complaints hold them together as much as their practice (Wilce 2003). What was once a community of somatic intersubjectivity is now a discursive community of witness.

The male community has also transformed. No longer simply local (the Gnawa of Fes, of Marrakech, Casablanca, or Essaouira, for example), the Gnawa are symbols of the nation, as well as recognized international stars. There are Gnawa fusion groups in Paris and in Spain and there are Gnawa "masters" in New York, California, and New Jersey, some who have never undergone any initiation at all (that is, they are self-proclaimed "masters"). The members of this male community know each other, though often as competitors for a piece of the world music pie, at festivals and in concerts at college campuses. While preconcert talks often revolve around the past oppressions of slavery, the powers of the music to heal, and the ubiquity of trance in different parts of the world, the untold story is that of a community whose practices have been fractured from within due to competition and the desire to please new audiences who are not initiates but spectators.

For audiences who attend sacred music festivals like the Gnawa Festival in Essaouira, music holds the promise of affective communion[13] and ultimately of peacemaking (whether the promise is fulfilled or not—and it usually is not). Festive performances of musical heritage also create alternative and hybrid identities for local youth as well as international elites—identities that transcend nationality—while creating revenues for local and national corporations. And though there are economic benefits for the state, the most important benefits are symbolic. For Morocco (a Muslim country whose king claims descent from the Prophet Muhammad), sacred music festivals create an image of a neoliberal nation comprised of and open to diversity. Working through the power of the aesthetic, the festive sacred is an instrument inspired by intangible religious and ritual culture that plays a neoliberal and enchanting global song (Curtis 2002).

If, as Hafstein notes (this volume), the conservation of intangible heritage is actually the construction of communities that are aware of themselves yet subject to the state and its power, then the Gnawa are performing an important function of the state—that of a minority community, which, because of their racial and cultural differences, makes visible the functioning of democracy in Morocco (Appadurai 2006). In their performance of heritage, the Gnawa both reflect on themselves and are reflected *as* the minority that stands for the heterogeneous nation (the blues musicians of Morocco, black Africans in North Africa). In this scenario, the name of a community is safeguarded more than the practices that inhere in it, although it is a fractured community from which women are mostly excluded, a community that reiterates the paternalistic values of the Moroccan nation-state (Hammoudi 1997).[14]

It is in this way that the official category of Intangible Cultural Heritage becomes an instrument of reform: as ritual life turns into spectacle for mass consumption, ethics and affect are also transformed and the cultural rights of the community are abrogated or at least subtly eroded; in this case, the rights of the community *to imagine* itself as comprising both male and female ritual specialists, *to identify* as ritual healers and not solely as "artists," and ultimately (because the ritual life of Gnawa music is ceding to a spectacular and staged performance) the right *to sense* the spirits and *to feel* the healing and relief that results from the intimacy of spirit propitiation ceremonies, including the olfactory experiences brought on by the use of incense, the contact and movement repertoire of entranced bodies, and the music as it is transmitted in intimate ritual circles. In other words, the embodied knowledge passed on somatically in ritual ceremonies is, if not absent, then forever transformed when it is enacted on the stage for audiences who are not initiates. Heritage purports to be a designation that gives value to traditional practices and identities, but is in fact a kind of simulacrum of value: the desire to transform practice into heritage is already a profound transformation of that practice into something other than itself, namely, a display that effects a permanent change in the ritual sensorium and its hierarchies (Kirshenblatt-Gimblett 1992).

Between UNESCO's recognition of the city of Essaouira, the Yerma Gnawa Association's consecration to the preservation and continuity of intangible culture, and the efforts of Gnawa artists themselves to represent and often codify the repertoire (see Kapchan 2007), Gnawa music has become so iconic of Morocco in general that travelers can buy Gnawa refrigerator magnets at the Casablanca airport. What all this media hype means is that more and more Gnawa aspire to recording contracts, while the ritual knowledge is overlooked in lieu of a young Gnawa's aspiration to musical stardom. Style has taken precedent over content. The meanings of the rituals have been reinterpreted. The musicians now have "Gnawa" marked on their state identification cards. What's more, the role of women in the culture—once pivotal—has declined as men take to the stage and the festival circuit (Kapchan 2007). The absence of women in the mass production of Gnawa heritage on stage and in a nongovernmental organization like Yerma Gnawa is symbolic of a host of absences that the presence of heritage creates, and these changes are felt most profoundly in the transformations of embodied practices in everyday life.

The Heritage Event and the Ironies of the Present

> Global flows and articulations work in contradictory as well as complementary ways. (Kratz and Karp 2006: 6)

UNESCO understands the power it wields in its designation of World Heritage Sites. Indeed, the relation between heritage and human rights is acknowledged explicitly by UNESCO, an organization whose genesis in the wake of World War II was a response to the infringement of human rights worldwide: "Spurred on by France and the United Kingdom, two countries that had known great hardship during the conflict," their website notes, "the delegates decided to create an organization that would embody a genuine culture of peace. In their eyes, the new organization must establish the 'intellectual and moral solidarity of mankind' and, in so doing, prevent the outbreak of another world war."[15] Yet UNESCO cannot help but create new human rights infringements in its very advocacy. Setting down a law, a category, a designation, drawing a boundary, always creates some kind of cultural violence.

The authors in this book neither reify nor codify traditions either as they are practiced or as they are displayed. Rather, we track the effects of the heritage industry as it is deployed in different cultural contexts and by different governmental and nongovernmental agencies, trying to unweave the invisible threads between cultural rights and human rights writ large. The contributors describe different "heritage events" and the way these events participate in creating new social, political, and aesthetic materialities, including inequities and hierarchies that did not exist before. Events, like performances, are singular happenings that nonetheless contain within them the influences of the past and the potentialities of the future (Derrida 1972). An event can be repeated, but never in the same way. Indeed, in the repetition of events, it is the emergent aspect—the part that comes into being at a particular historical moment and in a particular way—that has interested most scholars focused on creativity and social transformation (Bauman 1977, 1986; Kapchan 1996, 2005).

By focusing on the performance of the heritage event—that is, on the intangible and processual rather than the static and material aspects of heritage production—we call attention to how heritage is brought into public being and awareness, how it responds to past contexts and actively creates future possibilities (or impossibilities). Indeed Laurajane Smith goes so far as to say that all heritage is intangible, by which she means that it is produced through public discourses of varying degrees of hegemony (2006: 4–5). What she calls the "authorized heritage discourse" is always in tension with counterdiscourses or "dissonant heritage" (Tunbridge and Ashworth 1996; L. Smith 2006: 4–5, 80). The authors in this volume examine the performance of these global tensions. Such emphasis on the performative aspects of heritage production is not new (Kirshenblatt-Gimblett 1998a; L. Smith 2006). In this volume we build on a nascent literature on heritage and human rights, attending particularly to the ironies of heritage production (Slyomovics 2005).

How do heritage events produce irony?

First off, the ironies of the heritage event are not intentional, nor are they comic. Irony here serves to call attention to contradiction, to the often unintended and almost always unofficial consequences of heritage production, such as the forced acceptance of the Western property principle in order to protect natural and cultural resources in places where the notion of culture as personal property has not existed before (Yudice 2003: 2; see also Tsing 2004).

Some examples from this volume will serve:

• As local songs, dances, and stories become the property of "humanity," the very people who possess these traditions are disempowered (Hafstein, Chapter 1). The process of making a practice a masterpiece undermines the very local traditions it was intended to protect.

• The reification and regulation of bodies in state-controlled performances of intangible heritage permanently transforms the identities of cultural actors, altering people's sense of self and value (Scher, Chapter 3; Silverman, Chapter 5).

• Verbal artists are silenced because their art does not "fit" the UNESCO genre designations for verbal artists (in particular, storytelling). What's more, the very carnivalesque festivity that provides the "value" necessary for its designation as a World Heritage Site is eclipsed in the regulation of its production as a "masterpiece" (Kapchan, Chapter 7).

• The music and cultural contributions of the Roma to national heritage go unacknowledged because they, also, do not or cannot claim state identity (Silverman Chapter 5).

One major irony of heritage production is the way it redefines categories of the cultural and transforms public affect. Dorothy Noyes shows us how, in a neocolonial and perhaps newly imperial world, heritage becomes a way of control. Noyes makes the distinction between heritage, legacy, and zombieism. Culture, in this global scenario, is chaos—an unknown and threatening terrain that must be categorized and contained. Heritage, she says, is "what you freeze cryogenically at the point of death; legacy is what you keep on life support because you can't afford to kill it off; and zombie is the thing that you try to kill but can't: it keeps coming back to life and attacking you" (Noyes, Chapter 2). While there is obviously a lot of play in Noyes's use of these categories, they remind us that heritage is always linked to a "passing away" that gives value to a practice that must be mummified in order to be recognized. Culture, when it is unruly, is quickly labeled a legacy to be reckoned with and managed, or it is made into heritage so that it can be contained and controlled. "Heritage," notes Noyes,[16] "cuts a practice or an environment or a community loose from its moorings in the world and fixes it in a dedicated frame deemed capable of containing it," in effect, cutting it off from its roots in the sensate lifeworld. Examining the ironies produced in the wake of the heritage event, the authors in this volume gauge the barometer of human and cultural rights infringements.

The Language of Culture/The Language of Law

Human rights discourse is usually a juridical one—changing or creating the law so that changes in circumstance (oppression, exploitation, suffering) may follow. Because legal language is necessary for the public recognition and institution of human rights, analysts of human rights discourses are obliged to understand the language of law and to address themselves to policymakers in a similar language. While there are plenty of examples of deliberately ambiguous and obtuse legal language—often in court and other oral forums—lawmakers strive for the "purity" of abstraction in written documents, even though they must admit to the inexactness of language at certain points (Tiersma 1999: 38). In written form, legal language is (at least ideally) a language of disambiguation, of categories, of distinct boundaries and meanings.[17]

Whether or not such clarity is achievable, legal language seeks above all to exclude and/or diminish ambiguity. The language of art and sometimes of religion, however, relies on ambiguation, especially when religion or aesthetics is most subject to exegesis by "specialists." How do the rights of nations interact with the rights of individuals and communities when legal designations such as World Heritage Site or Masterpiece of World Intangible Heritage come to constitute the public value of artistic creations, as well as artists themselves? What are the ethical issues at stake?

The Universal Declaration of Human Rights was written in an attempt to avoid conflict and violence by acknowledging the basic foundations of human dignity. Drafted just a few years after the foundation of UNESCO, the 1948 document states that "it is essential, if man is not to be compelled to have recourse, as a last resort, to rebellion against tyranny and oppression, that human rights should be protected by the rule of law." In cases of disputed territory, however, as in the Thai/Cambodia example where the UNESCO ruling actually spurred violence over contested territory, the rule of law may or may not protect human rights.[18] Likewise, in the codification of Gnawa heritage, the role of women is neither recognized nor valorized. Whose rights are then protected? As Lisa Hajjar (2000) has noted in regard to the Palestinians, in the context of occupation the law of state sovereignty—which is that recognized by UNESCO and other international agencies—may actually contradict the law of human rights.

There is no question that some human rights must take priority over others. Torture, hunger, homelessness, and discrimination must be obliterated in order for "cultural" rights to flourish. And yet, all of these very serious issues are deeply cultural. Political and cultural rights are not necessarily of equal magnitude, but they are linked. Indeed, cultural practices often mask human rights violations—as in the case of culturally sanctioned female genital mutilation, forced sterilization, or the unfair distribution of allocated resources due to particular forms of cultural hierarchy that give men in power more than women and children (Bahar 2000). Child mortality rates themselves, as well as definitions of disease and wellness, are hard to separate from the cultural contexts in which they are embedded; what looks like starvation to some may be considered a disease of *nervios* by others (Scheper-Hughes 1992; Low 1994). Cultural practices (and the arguments of cultural relativity they spawn) may deflect criticism in the name of cultural rights.

On the other hand, the abrogation of cultural freedoms is usually a sign of the degradation of human rights writ large, as when women are no longer allowed to dress as they like or participate in public and civic community in Afghanistan. Indeed, the confiscation of musical instruments by the Taliban is a particular example of this. Veronica Doubleday (2007) has noted that little by little women and children are beginning to sing to the accompaniment of makeshift percussion instruments—pots, pans, and kitchen utensils—but that there are still severe consequences for such demonstrations of cultural and gendered freedom. In China, the crackdown and torture of the Falun Gong violates their freedom of expression—religious, bodily, and artistic (because improvised and ecstatic). While the torture of these practitioners is the most egregious abuse of human rights, simply suppressing their meditative practice should be enough to alert us to the violation of human rights (cf. Ots 1994). It is necessary, in other words, to understand human rights violations in their cultural contexts, not only to define them in abstraction.

Culture and cultural rights are often messy, ambiguous, and disputed. In the realm of artistic copyright, numerous stories circulate about well-known Western artists who appropriate the repertoire of others to make a fortune, as is allegedly the case with the song "Mbube," claimed by South African artist Joseph Shambalala (Erlmann 2003), or Paul Simon's appropriation of the genre of *isicathamiya* music on his *Graceland* album (Meintjes 1990; cf. Feld 1994). The cultural rights of folk and indigenous artists have been violated over and over again in the popular music industry. But the issues extend farther than concerns with big money and exploitation of the artists of former colonies. Questions about who can lay claim to "tradition" define not only particular artists but also ethnic groups and entire countries (Hafstein 2004a: 8–11; Klein, this volume). There are many layers to the commodification of heritage. In these scenarios, heritage is often made to represent a moral good that is used (or abused) by groups and nations, often spurred by anxieties related to increasing diversity within national borders. Who is included and excluded from ethnic and national categories, who is silenced, and whose voice predominates are central themes in the discussion of intangible rights (Silverman, this volume). The country of Bolivia brought attention to these issues in 1974, for example, when it claimed that the appropriation of the Andean folk song "El Condor Pasa" by Simon and Garfunkel, and its subsequent attribution to the country of Peru, was a form of cultural theft (Hafstein 2004a: 8–11; and this volume).

The effects of such (mis)representations of cultural identity are not superficial; indeed (imposed) changes in the symbolic identifications of individuals, groups, and gendered and ethnic communities have far-reaching historical consequences. Both the Seto in Estonia and the Sámi in Scandinavia, for example, are undergoing radical redefinition as a result of UNESCO designations and heritage policies, creating anxieties about endangered cultures (Kuutma 2012, 2007, 2008) and what Hafstein (2004a) calls "transculturation," the destruction of culture by its free appropriation and circulation under other names. The Roma people in the Balkans have virtually been "erased" from a ritual tradition in which they have been central, leading them to create alternative definitions of authentic tradition (Silverman, this volume). And the voices of Balkan women at war tribunals make us very aware of the ambiguous and dangerous power of naming, blaming, and testifying when human rights violations are publicly acknowledged (Noyes, personal communication).

In general, women suffer dearly from human rights violations, once as objects of the state, and again as objects of patriarchal oppression. The circulation and commodification of cultural heritage appropriates practices from women's worlds that are then claimed as symbols of the (male-identified) nation (Goodman 2005). Exceptions to this are found in reinventions of tradition that invoke ancient matriarchal culture as a symbol for the (new age) nation (see Magliocco, this volume). Who has the right to redefine history and what are the effects of such revisions? How categorize a cultural expression so that it may be protected from extinction? How represent a particular group through only one or two of its cultural symbols or metaphors? How define the rights of groups as well as individuals? How define intangible rights?

Intangible Rights

Certainly there is no extricating culture and cultural aesthetics from issues of human rights. Indeed scholars like Merali and Oosterveld note both the impossibility of keeping categories such as "political" and "cultural" rights separate and the necessity of making the links between them explicit. Our intention in this volume is not simply to exemplify, through detailed ethnography, the deep interrelation and mutual dependence of cultural, social, and human rights, but to advocate for the importance of aesthetics and performance in human rights discourse. Human rights are and must be performed—that is, they are created in the bodies and voices of those affected by their absence (Slyomovics 2005).

The ambiguities of culture are most apparent at the boundaries of cultural and legal representation. This volume thus takes a close look at the effects of the culture and heritage industry, including but not limited to UNESCO's legislation about tangible or intangible heritage. The authors in this volume demonstrate that cultural expressions may be essential barometers of human rights. Cultural expressions, we assert, are not epiphenomenal. Rather songs that circulate on the world market, festivals that capitalize on a particular ethnic or regional identity, reform movements that use the words "tradition" and "authenticity" as moral compasses (Klein, this volume) are all indicators of larger movements that change not just local relations, but international landscapes of power. As the culture wars of the 1980s in New York demonstrated, censorship, the withdrawal of state funding, and the silencing of voices are part of larger trends that have serious consequences for civil liberties and human rights (Gates 1993; Yudice 2003). Indeed, the cultural wars may be seen as precedents to the actual wars that followed—in Iraq, in Afghanistan, and elsewhere—and that led to the breaches in constitutional law and human rights that have ensued.

Because culture and politics are intertwined, it is important to read the aesthetic as well as the political signs of human rights violations. It is thus that the authors in this volume attend to the necessity of defining intangible rights. Intangible rights are those human rights that remain under the radar often because they are inked into the fabric of aesthetic life and feeling. These include the right to sense and feel, the right to imagine, and the right to identify. When any of these intangible rights are eclipsed, the more tangible consequences of human rights violations are not long to follow.

Feeling Right and Human

Sensory worlds are changing, not only because pollution is causing climate change, or because Monsanto is patenting most varieties of seeds and taking them off the market, making the consumption of genetically modified foods unavoidable, but also because what seems like more—in terms of consumption and promises—is often less: less choice, less variety, less synaesthesia, less human contact. While "globalization," urbanization, pollution, and general consumption practices are usually blamed for these changes, there are also legislative acts that, sometimes with the best intentions at cultural preservation, transform the sensorium of communities permanently.

How might a reconfiguration of the senses be conceived as a human rights issue? In Susan Slyomovics's book (2005) we learn of young female political prisoners in Morocco who communicate through touch—tracing the letters of words and sentences onto each other's palms. This is a response to surveillance and forced silence—a reduction of one's sensory liberties. When does a change in the sensorium constitute a breach of human rights and how is this effected? There is, in fact, no abrogation of human rights that does not work through the senses. Indeed, "power is a thing of the senses" (Stewart 2007:

84). The performance of heritage, the actual embodiment of heritage—in festivals, dances, historic recreations, interactive museum exhibits, storytelling, music listening[19] and production—thus takes on political force. For insofar as performances inculcate identity through mimesis and repetition, evoking and creating memories henceforth associated with heritage, the heritage event creates the very body of the "inheritee," transforming the social sensorium in the process. Philip Scher (this volume) makes these connections clear in his analysis of how Jamaicans' sense of themselves necessarily transforms through their obligatory participation in and performance of narratives of nationalist heritage that satisfy both the state's and the tourist industry's conceptions of Caribbean identity. While the global may produce the local (Kirshenblatt-Gimblett 2006a: 36), there are many levels and connections in between. Evoking Foucault's notion of "biopolitics," Scher brings home the very complicated relation between the global, the nation, and the individual body and its senses, reminding us that heritage events are "not only physical experiences of 'doing,' but also emotional experiences of 'being'" (L. Smith 2006: 71). Indeed, the senses are incontrovertible attestations of presence that play into and may be appropriated as heritage but that refuse to be contained. Inevitably, the body returns (Noyes, this volume).

But whose body is it? Scher notes that the "state, increasingly limited under neoliberalist regimes, finds what appears to be its proper role in the stewardship of the tangible and expressive cultural activities of its citizens" (this volume). What is disturbing here is that the performances of everyday life become fodder for the cultural tourism industry of the state. Not only are marked performances like dance, music, and festival subject to objectification and commodification but the state has an interest in commuting the process of change in these forms so they may be codified and controlled. What's more, these performances (inherently changeable, but artificially stultified) extend to "potentially public behaviors of all kinds such as fishing, selling in the market, driving a taxi, dancing in a public place, and so on." This reification of local difference works to counter what Scher has called a "'no-culture' shock, or the disorienting feeling of having traveled in search of novelty only to be confronted with sameness." He demonstrates that biopolitics not only serves to produce ethical and moral subjects as items for heritage display, but creates new bodies in the process, re-formed into images that reflect a national and static character, at least insofar as these bodies remain docile. Caribbean citizens must "play their part" if they are to court tourist dollars.

Thus does the commodification of cultural heritage become a program of national reform (Klein, this volume), not only of institutions, but of individual performances that are highly personal, emotional, and yet somehow subject to public definition and scrutiny. Heritage production works through a re-signification of everyday life, and this is most effective, and most insidious, when the body and its sensorium are changed from within.

The Right to Imagine

Modernity has sometimes been equated with an excess of imagination in the social world (Augé 1998; Ivy 1995; Russo 1995; Stewart 2007 cf. Anderson 1991), but excess does not negate a possible impoverishment of imagination (Chittick 1989; Jameson 1994). When does a surge in individual and social imagination signify liberty, and when might it indicate a more totalitarian expansion and curtailment of intangible rights?

In Jmaʿ al-Fna—the famous performance square in Marrakech, Morocco—the right to perform is also the right to a kind of social and plebeian chaos, a deliberate decentralization of focus. For most, it represents the epitome of the grotesque and the carnivalesque (Bakhtin 1984), a frothing of imagination without control. The verbal artists are often bawdy and even the spatial placement of the performers seems to be willy-nilly. But "saving" this site of intangible heritage from being razed and turned into apartment complexes has involved some strange ironies, including the regulation of this space of freedom and a reconceptualization of the place of the carnivalesque in capitalist society (Kapchan, this volume). If "tradition" must be translated into a commodity that is "owned" by a "community" (represented as a "person") in order for it to be universally recognized and "protected," that tradition is of necessity transformed—sometimes unrecognizably—in the process. What's more, the equation of such translatability with a state of "modernity" both hastens these changes and makes them inevitable. Even those cultures that commodify a premodern aesthetic, such as the performances in Jmaʿ al-Fna, are modern by virtue of turning it into a consumable item.

The control of the imagination is one aspect of heritage production. The creation of an imagined heritage (sometimes ex nihilo) is another. Both processes involve the augmentation and hyperbolizing of some cultural practices and the erasure of others.

The Right to Identify

Sabina Magliocco's chapter brings us to the heart of debates around heritage, one found at the crux of identity politics, namely, that of the right to imagine one's identity, to imagine oneself and one's community differently, to imagine one's sovereignty. Magliocco refers to this as the "freedom of imagination—the right to imagine one's relationship to the past and construct a sense of identity based upon it." And indeed, all the groups that share a culture or lay claims to a heritage must construct themselves in relation to an imagined past. This is, in effect, an essential aspect of shared identity. As soon as we acknowledge that genealogies may be constructed in several ways, that is, when we recognize that historical accounts are always interested and, in some senses, partial, then we must also come to terms with the fact that rights to imagine the (cultural) identity of some groups will come into conflict with the identifications and imaginations of others.

The Neo-Pagan movement challenges the notion of human rights and heritage in several ways. Unlike the Seto and the Sámi, unlike the Roma and other groups that define themselves through bloodline (blood right) and language, the Neo-Pagans have a tenuous blood connection at best to their "ancestors" the Druids, the Heathen, and other pagans of the past. Although there may be a genealogical connection, it cannot be proven through family trees and cannot be claimed. What is at issue here is not who can claim this identity, but who chooses to. Who is free to choose their identity? Who has the freedom to identify?

The inability to prove bloodline as a claim to heritage has, in part, led to the development of national laws for the respectful unearthing and storage of human remains. The "intangible rites" of ancient people, reinterpreted by modern self-defining communities, are still at odds with the "intangible rights" developed by the Church of England and English Heritage (Magliocco, this volume). Intangible rites—that is, spiritual practices—and not genealogy, are the basis for ancestry in this regard.

The Sound and Sense of Cultural Rights

The authors in this volume are keenly aware that the rights to determine and define heritage are about who has the authority to write and rewrite history. But there are also nonnarrative means of representation that somehow escape or exceed the limits of discourse and therefore challenge and skew attempts to close down meaning. Music is one such example (Kapchan 2008; Noyes, Scher, Silverman, this volume). As an art form that travels quickly, irrespective of national borders, music has a special status in heritage production. It is invasive and pervasive (Deleuze and Guattari 1987; LaBelle 2010). When it is charged with carrying the weight of heritage, music is both threatening in its unwieldiness and potent in its effectiveness. In both narrative and nonnarrative forms, however, the right to sense and feel, the right to imagine, and the right to identify are touchstones for intangible rights, sticky points of contact (see Tsing 2005) between the artificial separation of political, economic, cultural, and social rights.

This volume gives ethnographic density and detail to the legal language of human rights, providing examples of how social and cultural rights are integral to a discussion of human rights more generally. Further, we open a discussion about the tangibility and intangibility of human rights. For if heritage is about the past, it creates the discourses and communities of the future, erasing cultural memory and replacing it with new collective imaginaries and identities—largely through transformations of experience, in festivals and other sense-based practices. Yet while the authors in this volume stress the importance of recognizing the aesthetic dimension of human rights, we do not advocate an "aestheticization" of human rights discourse. An abrogation of safety and human dignity with torture and subjection is not comparable to an abrogation of festivity. We are not advocating a free-for-all in discourses of human rights. Rather, we elucidate the links between tangible and intangible rights, where they exist, making the links between cultural, political, and economic rights explicit. The essays in this volume expand our ideological perspective so that a legal one might follow, giving meaning to cultural rights by delineating the ambiguity of cultural rights in ethnographic examples, "humanizing" the tangible effects of cultural mediation and globalization, and making the intangible legible.

PART I

Redefining Cultural Rights

Chapter 1

Protection as Dispossession: Government in the Vernacular

Valdimar Tr. Hafstein

The Convention for the Safeguarding of the Intangible Cultural Heritage was a long time coming. Within UNESCO it is customary to speak of three decades of negotiation, from 1973 to 2003. The latter is the year UNESCO's General Conference adopted the convention; the former refers to a letter addressed to its director general. Conventionally taken to have inscribed folklore on the international agenda, the letter serves as a bookend, marking the beginning of decades of documents and reports on the international protection of folklore.

It opens with a place and a date: La Paz, April 24, 1973. It was sent from the Ministry of Foreign Affairs and Religion of the Republic of Bolivia. "My ministry," the letter begins, "has made a careful survey of existing documentation on the international protection of the cultural heritage of mankind," and it has found that all existing instruments "are aimed at the protection of tangible objects, and not forms of expression such as music and dance, which are at present undergoing the most intensive clandestine commercialization and export, in a process of commercially oriented transculturation destructive of the traditional cultures" (Republic of Bolivia, Ministry of Foreign Affairs and Religion 1973).

At the time of writing, the folk revival may have been past its peak, but its effects were widely felt and well beyond the "West," often in dialogue with Western fashions and currencies. In a memorandum accompanying his letter to UNESCO, the Bolivian minister made the case for the urgency of action, noting that "The current revalorization of folk arts due to their notable invasion of the consumer market is currently giving rise to the de facto situation of which the following examples afford a rundown." The examples follow, three in number:

> In the musical sphere, there are instances of melodies being wrongfully appropriated by persons unconnected with their creation who register them as their own compositions to secure to themselves the benefits conceded by copyright regulations. This leads, amongst other things, to the debasement of the folkishness of the piece.

"In the sphere of the dance," the minister continues, folk dances are

> appropriated by other countries wholly unconnected with their genesis to be passed off by them, even in international competitions, as folk dances of their own. In the particular case of Bolivia which, owing to its geographical situation, suffers greatly from depredations of this kind, certain organizations from neigbouring countries go so far as to send here [for] complete sets of costumes for the main Bolivian folk dances, and engage "embroiderers," "mask makers" and even choreographers (of peasant "folk" origin) to organize this switching or deliberate non-spontaneous transculturation process which amounts to the filching and clandestine transfer of another people's culture. In this way the creator peoples gradually lose their folk art assets, while others, with better financial facilities, present as their own what was never a part of their tradition. The themes may, in some cases, be similar, but the décor and choreography are usurped.

The third example is crafts. "In the realm of popular art," writes the minister,

> which likewise forms part of national folklore and which has, at present, a large consumer market, there are similar filchings, as in the case of countries which reach the point of industrializing themes and techniques from the traditional patterns of the cultures of particular population groups and offering them at cut prices on the international markets with no statements of origin—a process which, in addition to lowering the quality of the objects, means the "submarginalization" of

> large population groups who often depend for their livelihood on this paying work.

Note the plaintive vocabulary of misappropriation in the minister's letter and memorandum. It is there in every other sentence: "Export," "invasion," "appropriation," "depredation," "switching," "filching," "clandestine transfer," "loss," "usurpation," and (my personal favorite) "deliberate non-spontaneous transculturation process."

Export is one: the problem is foreigners. This is a national problem—a challenge to national culture—and therefore also an international problem, because borders are permeable and no one patrols the circulation of culture across them. The term *invasion* makes clear that we are faced here with acts of aggression, even if that aggression is commercial in motives and means.

Filching, usurpation, depredation: so many ways to name a thief. The colorful lexicon of theft in the minister's letter emphasizes ownership. It goes to support the minister's main point, namely that folklore should be considered cultural property controlled by states, on the model of UNESCO's 1970 Convention on the Means of Prohibiting and Preventing the Illicit Import, Export and Transfer of Ownership of Cultural Property, adopted two and a half years before the letter was drawn up:[1]

> The international conventions drawn up by UNESCO now provide protection for anonymous works in the domains alike of archeology and of the plastic arts, but it has only been thought fit to do this in respect of tangible objects, and not of forms of artistic expression transitory in time and space, such as music and dance, but nonetheless, works of art which are, today, subject to the most intense clandestine commercialization and export, despite the fact that they form part of States' cultural heritage.

Consider the actors and owners here, the states. According to the Bolivian letter, these artistic expressions form part of "States' cultural heritage." This is no slip of the pen, as the following paragraphs make clear:

> the Bolivian Government, by Supreme Decree No. 08396 of 19 June 1968, has proclaimed State ownership of the folk music (anonymous, popular and traditional) of its territory, of the music currently being produced by unidentified composers in peasant and general folk

> groups and of the music of Bolivian composers deceased 30 or more years ago.
>
> Legislation extending the application of these measures to folk dance, popular art and traditional literature is in process of enactment.
>
> The Government of Bolivia, in informing the Director-General of UNESCO of these decisions taken in the exercise of its legitimate authority and of its ownership of expressions of folk art, ancient or modern, which have grown up or become traditional on its territory, of anonymous works at present performed by ethnic or folk groups, and of works by composers deceased 30 or more years ago, would indicate that the national registers of these forms of cultural property are scientifically checked by specialist researchers.

Stories we tell about ourselves sometimes reveal more than we would like. As noted, this letter serves as the opening salvo in UNESCO's own etiological account of the Convention for the Safeguarding of the Intangible Cultural Heritage of 2003. In some of its variants, there is an interesting prelude to this account that explains the motivation for the minister's request for international cooperation (e.g., Albro 2005a: 4; Honko 2001; Sherkin 2001: 54 n. 13). Three years before the Bolivian letter was delivered by diplomatic courier in 1973, Paul Simon and Art Garfunkel released the album *Bridge over Troubled Water*. On one of the tracks, Simon and Garfunkel perform "El Condor Pasa," accompanied by the Peruvian group Los Incas, whom they had heard performing this song at a concert in Paris. "El Condor Pasa" is an indigenous folk song from the Andes, arranged and incorporated into a larger composition in 1913 by Peruvian composer and folk-song collector Daniel Alomía Robles. In Alomía Robles's version, the song commemorates an indigenous revolt against white oppressors who abuse the native population, while the condor flies above, ruler of the skies and spirit of the Incas. *Bridge over Troubled Water* won the Grammy award for the record of the year and instantly reached the number one spot on Billboard's pop album chart, where it sat for six weeks. It is still one of the highest-selling albums of all time.

Perhaps the American artists were showing solidarity with poor, oppressed peoples in performing "El Condor Pasa." Whether or not that was their intention, however, there was no jubilation in the Andes. On the contrary, as seen from the Andes this must have looked less like a celebration of indigenous music and more like exploitation. Rich Americans had ransacked the musical tradition of poor people in the Andes and made millions of dollars, while not a dime was returned to the rightful "owners"—a pattern not unfamiliar from colonial expropriation, though this time around even the condor was siphoned off, a symbol of native pride. The whole affair left a bad taste in many mouths and, according to this etiology, the Bolivian letter to UNESCO's director general in 1973 is a political expression of this bad taste (López 2004; Moreno n.d.; Sherkin 2001: 54 n. 13).

That is the way the story is told, and its appeal is not hard to recognize in the way it sets international diplomacy in the context of pop music history. Reading against the grain, however, the story only gets more intricate. Consider its political backdrop. The government that sent this letter was a military dictatorship, led by General Hugo Banzer Suárez who came to power by coup in 1971. He banned opposition parties, suspended trade unions, and shut down universities. Not surprisingly, Banzer's regime also had strained relations with indigenous groups. The Aymara and the Quechua lived in abject poverty in the highlands and towns of Bolivia, their lands confiscated and their identities suppressed in a "transculturation" rather different from the one Banzer's minister complained about (Ströbele-Gregor 1996; Hylton and Thomson 2007). Meanwhile, the military regime celebrated their expressive culture and appropriated it as the national-popular culture of Bolivia (on the emergence of "transculturation" as national-popular master language in Latin America, see G. Williams 2002: 23–70). Banzer was in power during the golden age of the folkloric spectacle, which celebrates traditional costume and music and dance in colorful performances of national pride and harmony; indeed, the folkloric spectacle was a favorite form of entertainment under dictators, from Franco's Spain and Salazar's Portugal to Pinochet's Chile and Banzer's Bolivia (cf. DaCosta Holton 2005; Ortiz 1999).

It is important to understand, then, that the Bolivian government's efforts to protect an indigenous Andean folk song hide the real oppression of indigenous peoples within Bolivia in this period. This is especially insidious because "El Condor Pasa" is a song of resistance, but through Supreme Decree 08396 it was nationalized, as the Bolivian government proclaimed state ownership of the folk music of its territory, and subsequently of "folk dance, popular art and traditional literature."

As a matter of fact, the South American dictators of the 1970s also appropriated the condor, converting a symbol of defiance to a symbol of compliance enforced at gunpoint: along with Pinochet and others, Banzer was one of the ringleaders in Operation Condor, essentially an intergovernmental murder ring coordinated by intelligence agencies to quash dissent (McSherry 2005).

The lesson of "El Condor Pasa" thus extends beyond the transnational flows of culture. This story explains how folklore came to be inscribed on the international agenda, but it also sheds light on the uses of folklore in hegemonic strategies within states, how folklore is instrumentalized in subject formation under conditions of internal colonialism. What is more, these are difficult to disentangle; invoking a threat from the outside—"the most intensive clandestine commercialization and export"—the government's measures for protection in effect serve as means of dispossession.

We speak always of ourselves, and the lexicon of theft in the minister's letter—of appropriation and depredation, of filching and usurpation—reflects critically back on his regime and its cultural policy. Beyond Bolivia's borders, however, this story leaves us with a question, one that is suddenly very current as we hear stories from various parts of the world about the implementation of UNESCO's intangible heritage programs, from Catalonia (Noyes 2006) to Marrakech (Kapchan, this volume) to Kerala (Lowthorp 2007) and beyond, where some local actors complain that they are losing control over their cultural practices because of the conversion of these practices to intangible cultural heritage; because an administrative grid has been superimposed on these practices in order to safeguard them; because, they claim, they no longer have as much of a say in the work of representation. The question concerns the relationship between communities and states, between empowerment and subjection, between heritage and governmentality. It is a question that is as crucial to theorizing intangible heritage as it is to writing it into policy and putting it into practice. Namely, when is protection *not* a means of dispossession?

My contribution to *Intangible Rights: Cultural Heritage in Transit* explores this question, in particular as it relates to the empowerment and subjection of communities through their intangible heritage. One of the major controversies in the Intergovernmental Meeting of Experts that drafted the Intangible Heritage Convention concerned the relationship between this heritage and the communities that practice it, in particular the role of those communities vis-à-vis that of states. In what follows, I examine that relationship with reference to the convention and its pivotal concept, focusing on how intangible heritage and community constitute one another and set the stage for "government in the vernacular." Drawing on debates within and outside UNESCO and juxtaposing these with the literature on heritage and governmentality, I argue that intangible heritage permits a relocation of culture in communities and of communities in a matrix of organized diversity.

Deterioration, Disappearance, and Destruction

There had been signs of concern for folklore at the international level before the Bolivian letter of 1973. The first coordinated attempt to provide folklore with international legal protection was at the Diplomatic Conferences of Stockholm in 1967 and Paris in 1971 for the revision of the Berne Convention for the Protection of Literary and Artistic Works. However, the diplomats at these conferences found themselves unable to elaborate legal principles for folklore protection; they cited conceptual and definitional difficulties surrounding this topic as an insurmountable obstacle. The only legislative trace of their attempt is article 15(4) of the Berne Convention, which makes possible the international protection of "unpublished works where the identity of the author is unknown, but where there is every ground to presume that he is a national of a country of the Union."

In such cases, national laws may specify a competent authority to represent the unknown author. The framework of authorship employed here translates communities (whose traditional expressions this clause targets) into individual authors. Their identity, however, is lost in translation; because they do not conform to conventional notions of authorial subjectivity, they must of necessity remain unknown. They are therefore subsumed under the state as presumed "nationals of a country of the Union" and the state speaks on their behalf or appoints a "competent authority" to do so—in effect excluding communities from the work of representation.

Moreover, as early as 1971—two years before receiving the letter from Bolivia—UNESCO administrators prepared a study on the "Possibility of Establishing an International Instrument for the Protection of Folklore" (UNESCO 1971). This document made no specific policy recommendations, but stressed that the situation of folklore was "rapidly deteriorating" and insisted that further efforts for its protection were "of the utmost urgency" (Sherkin 2001: 44).

This sense of urgency has animated international negotiations for four decades, but it has a history going back to the twin ages of European Enlightenment and Discovery. The rapid deterioration of popular tradition has been part and parcel of the concept ever since doctors and priests began to record "vulgar errors" in the European countryside while attempting to eradicate them, and since the days when missionaries and colonial administrators recorded the supposedly moribund customs of colonial populations they were charged with civilizing. For better or worse, folklore and its synonyms have never quite shaken off connotations of decline and disintegration, and this alarm of the eleventh hour has always fueled both research and policy debate (Dundes 1969; Kirshenblatt-Gimblett 1996; Bauman and Briggs 2003).

Irrespective of the initiatives from 1967 and 1971, seldom cited in UNESCO documents, the better-known 1973 request from the government of Bolivia appears to have been a catalyst for the inscription of folklore on the international agenda. After decades of deliberations, it is extraordinary to consult the letter from 1973 and to find how closely the work still being conducted follows its formulation and how little the problems seem to have changed, despite dozens upon dozens of expert meetings, workshops, roundtables, consultations, and fact-finding missions. The "process of commercially oriented transculturation" is still cited as a major threat requiring immediate attention from the international community, though it now tends to be spoken of in terms of globalization. Thus, part of the rationale for the Convention for the Safeguarding of the Intangible Cultural Heritage, cited in its preamble, is "that the processes of globalization and social transformation, alongside the conditions they create for renewed dialogue among communities, also give rise, as does the phenomenon of intolerance, to grave threats of deterioration, disappearance and destruction of the intangible cultural heritage, in particular owing to a lack of resources for safeguarding such heritage."

In spite of the compromises palpable in its qualifications, this passage paints an ominous picture of deterioration, disappearance, and destruction. These threats loom large in all of UNESCO's work in the past decades through which the concept of intangible cultural heritage has been brought into being. As a rule of thumb, one can expect one or more references to globalization and its damaging effects in any document, debate, or presentation on intangible heritage within UNESCO.

This sense of danger shadows the notion of intangible heritage in UNESCO discourse. Actually, the menace of globalization is so consistently associated with intangible heritage that it seems intrinsic to the concept. In this, the concept brings with it connotations of urgency always associated with folklore and popular tradition, but it adds a distinctly global twist. Indeed, intangible heritage appears forever to be on the verge of destruction.

Looming threats provide grounds for intervention. As ministers of culture from UNESCO member states declared at the close of a top-level meeting in Istanbul in 2002, "the extreme vulnerability of the intangible heritage . . . requires that governments take resolute action" (UNESCO 2002).

I have argued elsewhere that heritage is best seen as an active intervention through which things, sites, practices, and expressions are incorporated into administrative structures that lend them legitimacy and value (Hafstein 2004a). Whether it is decreed by authorities or claimed by subaltern groups, heritage is a representation in terms of hegemony. Heritage converts the residual and alternative into the archaic, in Raymond Williams's sense of those terms (1977: 122). "Intangible cultural heritage" should, I suggest, be understood as a tool of intervention. As such, it transforms the practices it designates. It transforms the ways communities relate to their practices. Ultimately, intangible heritage transforms the communities themselves. That is the angle I will pursue in the balance of this chapter: that is, intangible heritage as an instrument of reform.

Culture and Governmentality

In June 2003, as a member of the Icelandic delegation to UNESCO, I observed the third session of the Intergovernmental Meeting of Experts that drafted the Intangible Heritage Convention.[2] In what follows, I draw on disputes in this meeting, as well as interviews and archival sources. I juxtapose these with theories of heritage and governmentality to argue that the structuring of community and orchestration of differences are central goals of the convention.

It is of course important to remember that although select traditional practices and expressions are canonized people continue to rework residual representations and create emergent ones in ways "that have little to do with the canonized repertories and sometimes even serve to subvert them" (Klein 2001: 69). In that sense, as folklorist Barbro Klein points out, "folklore lives through a flow of creative reshapings in daily life at the same time as it is utilized for a host of political and related purposes" (69). Nevertheless, the broadened scope of heritage, extending now into the realm of the intangible and the popular, redefines such marginal practices (marginal to the dominant culture, that is) as objects of cultural policy and administration. While this broadened scope may be more democratic, such "aesthetics of marginalization" (Kirshenblatt-Gimblett 1988: 149) also remap the territory of government, extending it further still into the habitus and habitat of populations.

The history of UNESCO's work in this field in the 1970s and 1980s has been documented elsewhere (e.g., Blake 2001; Bortolotto 2008; Hafstein 2004a; Sherkin 2001). In the 1990s, these endeavors shifted away from an archival paradigm of European pedigree. Documentation and research moved down the agenda, while intergenerational transmission became the new priority—the attempt to actually ensure continuity of the traditions targeted. Japanese and Korean programs on "living national treasures" and laws for the protection of "intangible heritage" (on the books since 1950 in Japan and 1962 in the Republic of Korea) provided new blueprints for UNESCO's activities in this field (Hafstein 2004a; Bortolotto 2008). From this paradigm shift emerged the so-called Living Human Treasures program in 1993, and the Proclamation of Masterpieces of the Oral and Intangible Heritage of Humanity adopted in 1997 (Nas 2002), and it culminated in the entry into force of the Convention for the Safeguarding of the Intangible Cultural Heritage in 2006 (Bortolotto 2008; Hafstein 2009).

The paradigm shift of the 1990s is significant. Instead of preserving textual or audiovisual recordings of performances, UNESCO's declared objective is now to preserve the enabling conditions of performances—the social fabric and the necessary habitat—and to provide incentives for transmission from one generation to the next. Making sure that people keep singing their songs tomorrow is very different from archiving the songs they sing today.

Beyond the general imperative to safeguard intangible heritage—for which there is unanimous support among UNESCO member states, though exactly what it entails is up for debate—there is no uniformity of purpose regarding the effects of intangible heritage policy on the populations that it addresses. The convention is flexible enough to allow for a diversity of objectives, as indeed it had to be in order to be adopted by UNESCO's General Conference and widely ratified by national legislatures.

The insinuation of government into vernacular practices—practices that were previously only of incidental interest to administrators—gives rise to greater regulation of public life. What intangible heritage interventions do, in effect, is to create instruments to act on populations; not so much to directly shape their conduct from above as to influence people to reform their conduct of their own accord. In this, heritage parallels previous uses of art and aesthetics in liberal governance. Historically, they have served as instruments to involve individuals as active agents in the processes of their own transformation and self-regulation (T. Bennett 2000: 1415). Likewise, intangible heritage provides government with a means to intervene in the regulation of social life while also keeping a distance from it.

My argument here is indebted to a body of work published since the early 1990s that constitutes a field of inquiry emerging around the concept of "governmentality." Taking its cue from Michel Foucault's essay "On Governmentality" from 1978 (Foucault 1991), this work concerns the rationalities and arts of governing by means of what Foucault describes as "the conduct of conduct." Such "government at a distance" (Rose 1999: 49) is characteristic of liberal political formations that emerged in the eighteenth and nineteenth centuries. In contrast to other forms of rule, liberalism seeks not to crush the capacity for action of its subjects, but rather to recognize that capacity and act on it (3–4). The conduct of conduct takes place at thousands of scattered points and requires a profusion of techniques and programs for connecting agendas in political centers to those dispersed sites where operations of power connect with the population and its customs, beliefs, health, hygiene, security, and prosperity (18).

Foucault refers to this proliferation of programs and techniques as the governmentalization of the state. It encourages an equal proliferation of independent authorities and experts (demographers, sociologists, folklorists, anthropologists, doctors, psychologists, managers, social workers, and so on) and of fields of knowledge and expertise relating to the population. It also depends upon ways of aligning political aims and the strategies of experts, and upon establishing lines of communication between the calculations of authorities and the aspirations of free citizens (Rose 1999: 49).

The perspectives of governmentality theory were brought to anthropology and cultural studies in the 1990s and have proven particularly fruitful in the critical analysis of cultural policy. Indeed, many techniques for the conduct of conduct belong to what we usually refer to as "culture." With the benefit of governmentality theory, Tony Bennett has argued that we are equipped to move beyond the two culture concepts—the aesthetic and the anthropological—to a third understanding of culture as a specific set of instruments for acting on the social with particular ends in view. In this view, culture as a concept and category is a historical formation that has emerged alongside governmental forms of rule. It constitutes a complex of relations between what were previously considered unrelated practices, forging from these a new effective reality (T. Bennett 2003: 58). In much the same way as "society" and "the economy" have come to be seen as historical formations emerging out of governmental forms of rule that take the population as their object, Bennett shows how "culture, too, can be approached as consisting of a range of particular forms of expertise arising out of distinctive regimes of truth that assume a range of practical and technical forms through the variety of programs for regulating 'the conduct of conduct'" (56).

It is customary to account for the prevalence of the "anthropological" sense of culture as a whole way of life over earlier formulations of culture as "the best that has been thought and known in the world" (Arnold 1998 [1869]: 8) in terms of a democratic extension of the culture concept. However, when culture is understood historically as a set of instruments for acting on the social, Bennett argues that "this development presents itself in a different light: that is, as a result of the incorporation of ways of life within the orbit of government and, thereby, the production of a working interface between culture and the social" (2003: 59). Folklore may be understood in the same fashion, as a subset or parallel set of instruments for acting on the habitus and habitat of particular segments of the population: the peasants, the *Volk*, the "people," the subaltern, or, conversely, "any group of people whatsoever who share at least one common factor" around which a sense of identity can be organized (Dundes 1965: 2; cf. Dundes 1980).

Heritage and Community

To label a practice or a site as heritage is not so much a description as an intervention. In fact, heritage reorders relations between persons and things, and among persons themselves, objectifying and recontextualizing them with reference to other sites and practices designated as heritage. Heritage assembles previously unrelated buildings, rituals, paintings, and songs, and it constitutes these as something to be safeguarded, that is, acted on through programs, schemes, and strategies carried out and evaluated by experts whose operations connect the calculations of authorities with the desires and ambitions of citizens.

In an interview with the *World Heritage Newsletter*, Joseph King of the International Centre for the Study of the Preservation and the Restoration of Cultural Property (ICCROM) argues that the "conservation of heritage can be a very important aspect" of development on the African continent. Even in "those places facing more serious problems," he continues, "conservation of cultural heritage can play a part (even if small) in improving the situation" ("Africa 2009: Interview with Joseph King" 2001). Together with Jukka Jokilehto, chief of ICCROM's architectural conservation program, King explains this in greater detail in their jointly authored "Reflections on the Current State of Understanding" of authenticity and conservation in the African context. Here, they clarify that it may not always "be possible to insist on continuing traditional habitat as a 'frozen entity'" for "it may sometimes be taken as arrogance to insist on conservation of traditional ways of life if the population does not appreciate this." The question then arises, they go on, "of how to control and guide such modifications in life patterns?" In response, they urge that "the present community should be given every opportunity to appreciate and respect what is being inherited from previous generations." "This is a learning process," they explain, "which may require incentives and examples, and which is especially founded in a close collaboration between the population and authorities." The goal, they conclude, is to "identify ways to generate a cultural process that desires such heritage, and therefore takes care of its safeguarding" (Jokilehto and King 2001: 38).

These directions are a fine example of how heritage-making and safeguarding serve as instruments for acting on the social field, to "control and guide modifications in life patterns" and to "generate a cultural process." They also underline that heritage is a transformative process. It transforms the relationship of people with their practices and, as a consequence, their relationship with each other (mediated through those practices). It does so by appealing to their civic duty and moral responsibility for maintaining a particular alignment between the past and the present, in which strong emotions and identities are invested. In this sense, heritage is a technology for acting on the social, giving rise to changed behavior.

The alignment of the past with the present is central in generating a cultural process "that desires such heritage." As Barbara Kirshenblatt-Gimblett has noted, "the possession of heritage—as opposed to the way of life that heritage safeguards—is an instrument of modernization and mark of modernity" (Kirshenblatt-Gimblett 2006b:183). By cordoning off certain places and practices as sites of continuity with a cultural tradition or a historical past, everything else is in effect severed from that tradition and history. Inheriting marks the passing away of the social relations that heritage objectifies; it signals a radical disjuncture between the past and the present. Hence, to possess heritage is to be modern; it is a modern way of relating to the past. This past, as it is given material form in heritage sites and performed in intangible heritage, is inevitably a product of the present that appoints, organizes, and represents it (Bendix 2009; Berliner 2010; Björgvinsdóttir 2010; Klein 2006; Rastrick 2007; L. Smith 2006; T. Thompson 2006; Tornatore 2011.

Historically, heritage played a significant role in the creation of modern nation-states. As heritage held in common, monuments, landscapes, and folklore were invested with national symbolism, focusing the political imagination on particular representations of the national community (Anttonen 2005; Anderson 1991; Abrahams 1993; Bendix and Hafstein 2009; Klein 2006; Mathisen 2009; Ó Giolláin 2000; Hálfdánarson 2001; Löfgren 1989; T. Thompson 2006). The appointment of cultural and natural treasures conveyed a sense of common responsibility for their transmission to a collective future rooted in a particular territory. This common responsibility gave rise to a series of national institutions, including parks, archives, and a variety of museums. In turn, these new institutions required their own dedicated personnel and their own forms of expertise; they were constructed according to a transnationally diffused matrix and appointed with the task of reforming citizens, instructing them, and instilling a consciousness of their responsibility and allegiance to the national community (T. Bennett 1995, 2001).

Taken over from probate law, the concept of heritage (or patrimony) points to one of the metaphors for the nation: that of the family. Projecting onto the state intergenerational relations, obligations, and succession in the family, the republican nation-state carried over to the cultural sphere a dynastic model that it did away with in other areas of government. At the same time as it evokes an earlier model of the body politic, however, the notion of national patrimony democratizes what previously belonged to elites alone (cf. Bendix 2000, 2009; Bendix and Hafstein 2009). The idea of a common cultural heritage transfers "the goods and rights of princes and prelates, magnates and merchants" (Lowenthal 1998: 60) to the public at large; it throws open the doors of the Louvre to the throng in the streets outside (Poulot 1997). Extending the scope of heritage to vernacular, popular culture makes this inclusive and encompassing heritage a matter of public, national concern—and interpellates, in that same act, a national public.

Heritage continues of course to be an important instrument for representing the nation, rallying citizens around a common identity and sense of belonging. The uses of folklore for this purpose have been documented in a wide range of contexts (see, e.g., Anttonen 2005; Dundes 1985; Herzfeld 1982; Hobsbawm and Ranger 1983; Ó Giolláin 2000). Frequently, this has been achieved by glossing over difference, demanding allegiance to a uniform national culture and history through selective oblivion and at the expense of alternative fealties.

It is increasingly difficult, however, to imagine such national monocultures, what with the multiplication of diasporic and cross-border communities, as well as the resurgence of a variety of indigenous groups and local communities. Under these circumstances, many governments have come to acknowledge and even promote "communities" as cultural and administrative units. Although such communities represent a slippery slope for the project of the nation-state, a new form of governmental rationality is emerging that focuses on "the organization of self-regulating and self-managing communities that are, in some respects, disconnected from the larger wholes of nationally defined societies or, in the case of diasporic communities, cut across them" (T. Bennett 2000: 1421).

According to sociologist Nikolas Rose, governing through community is part of an important turn in liberal government. It represents a shift in focus away from the individual in society toward communities as mediating entities to which individuals owe allegiance and through which they reform and manage themselves. This turn responds, in part, to new forms of identity politics emerging out of civil and human rights movements, in addition to diasporic migrations and the newfound vocality of indigenous groups. However, it is also closely related to processes of economic and cultural globalization, and to the generalization of neoliberal policies through trade agreements and aid programs enforced by bodies like the International Monetary Fund, the World Bank, and the World Trade Organization.

Indeed, such processes and policies make it possible to speak of an emergent global governmentality or a governmentalization of international relations, in which states play a diminishing role, but transnational organizations, corporations, coalitions, and diasporic networks steadily assume greater responsibilities. This delegation of responsibility to the citizenry is an essential aspect of the neoliberal political project, integrating individuals into their own government and giving them responsibility for conducting themselves individually and each other in communities. This move also characterizes "third way" politics in various guises; from Great Britain to Taiwan, third way politicians have identified community as a "third space" between the state and the individual that proposes itself as a solution to the problems of excessive state interference in the lives of citizens but also to the anomie and insecurity associated with excessive individualism.

At various levels of government, from local to international, we observe this new emphasis on communities as an innovative way to make sense of collective existence, but also to make it calculable and administrable. Over the last twenty-five to fifty years (beginning at different times in different places), but especially in the last decade, "a whole array of little devices and techniques have been invented to make communities real" (Rose 1999: 189). Within a fairly short period, there has been a phenomenal upsurge of new sorts of expertise through which "community"—which began as a language of resistance—has been transformed "into an expert discourse and a professional vocation" (175). As Rose points out, "community is now something to be programmed by Community Development Programmes, developed by Community Development Officers, policed by Community Police, guarded by Community Safety Programmes and rendered knowable by sociologists pursuing 'community studies.'"

We can add to this list the many institutions and programs of community heritage: community museums, community archives, community heritage festivals, community heritage registers, community heritage centers, community heritage commissions, and community heritage grants. And there is a parallel profusion of experts and professionals, like community curators, community heritage commissioners, community historians, community folklorists, community exhibition designers, and community heritage development officers. This trend is not limited to the public sector, for the past two decades have witnessed a great variety of public-private partnerships in this area with a concomitant mushrooming of interdisciplinary consulting firms, such as Community Heritage Partners in Pennsylvania, who help "property owners, local governments, and community organizations develop realistic solutions to preserve and renew their architectural heritage, strengthen their community character, and enhance their quality of life," and are not content merely to provide technical assistance in preservation but also "develop strategies for community participation and private initiatives to build awareness and change attitudes" (Community Heritage Partners n.d.).

Every claim of community refers to something that already exists and to which we owe allegiance. Yet our allegiance to these communities is something we need to be made aware of and requires "the work of educators, campaigns, activists, [and] manipulators of symbols, narratives and identifications" (Rose 1999: 177). Despite or indeed because of its central role in the conception of governing, as Tony Bennett remarks, "community has constantly to be rescued from its imminent disappearance or, because the perceived need for community often precedes its existence, to be organized into being" (2000: 1422–23).

In much the same way, then, as a common heritage is invoked to forge national community, it is also central to the constitution of local, indigenous, and diasporic communities. The communalization of heritage and cultural policy helps to form and to reform population groups and thereby to orchestrate differences in the state. In other words, it is a strategy for coping with difference. From this perspective, intangible heritage emerges as an instrument in the production of a strong (but not exclusive) sense of belonging for community members. Population groups subjectify themselves as "communities" and objectify their practices and expressions as "intangible heritage." Government can then act on the social field through communities and by means of, among other things, intangible heritage policies.

This parallels recent developments in environmental conservation, where there is now widespread preoccupation with community, and programs proliferate that devolve to communities the responsibility for putting environmental policy into practice. Political scientist Arun Agrawal coined the term "environmentality" to describe this governmental rationality in which communities are interpellated as "environmental subjects" (Agrawal 2005). Populations learn to conceive of their habitat as "the environment" and to appreciate the need for its conservation, and—through an infusion of expertise and in cooperation with state, nongovernmental, and intergovernmental organizations—are charged with administering themselves and their environmental practices (e.g., Agrawal and Gibson 2001; Li 2001; McDermott 2001).

Whose Heritage?

Issues of communities, their proper place in an international convention, and their relations to states and intergovernmental organizations were intensely debated in the meeting of experts that drafted the Convention for the Safeguarding of the Intangible Cultural Heritage. Member states differ, of course, in whether and to what extent they govern through community, and relations between official and minority cultures are differently structured in different states. Indeed, the question of communities was one of the most contentious issues at the meeting's third session in June 2003 at UNESCO headquarters at Place Fontenoy in Paris. The delegate from Hungary, more than anyone else, spoke out in favor of community rights in the convention and for maximal requirements for consultation with practicing communities and nongovernmental organizations (NGOs). He took every opportunity to do so, and opportunity presented itself in connection with a number of different articles drafted and approved at this session, in particular with respect to various provisions on safeguarding at the national level (arts. 11–15 in the final text). He was far from isolated in his position, however; among others, the representatives of Vanuatu, Papua New Guinea, Zimbabwe, Peru, and Finland expressed similar points of view.

This issue had been debated at previous meetings and it resurfaced immediately on the first day of the June session. The preliminary draft convention distributed to delegations stated (in article 4) that "each State Party recognizes the duty of safeguarding its intangible cultural heritage." As soon as the floor was opened, the Hungarian delegate raised his sign and made the observation that "There is a difference between speaking of 'its' intangible cultural heritage and intangible cultural heritage 'present in its territory.' It is *not* the state's intangible cultural heritage. It is not created by the state but by communities and groups. This is a point of principle!"

The point here concerns different ways of imagining community and locating culture, and the Hungarian principle holds that these are not isomorphic with the state, though the state has duties toward communities within its borders. In response, the South African delegate warned that "many issues will arise from the phrase 'present in its territory'" and asked that the term "its" be retained.

He was followed by the delegate from Papua New Guinea, who objected to the homogeneity presumed by the notion of a state's heritage: "We don't talk about 'our national heritage,' but about different cultures in our territories. We are against the notion of national cultural heritage. We therefore support using the phrase 'present in its territory.'"

Several other delegations expressed their preference for one or the other of these formulations, before a Chilean delegate intervened with the preposterous suggestion to use both: "to safeguard *its* intangible cultural heritage *present in its territory*." Perhaps this proposal is best understood as an example of deliberate misreading—not an uncommon tool of diplomacy—for it clearly retains the idea of the state's own heritage and makes the qualifier "present in its territory" more or less superfluous (or else refigures it from an inclusive to a restrictive sense).

This debate over a possessive pronoun is typical of the often convoluted process of transnational consensus building in UN organizations. I have observed the exact same tortuous process in the World Intellectual Property Organization in Geneva. Moreover, anthropologist Sally Engle Merry describes similar debates in the UN's Commission on the Status of Women in New York, and as she notes, "Although the wording debates seemed trivial, they revealed political differences in subtle ways" (Merry 2006: 40). Negotiating terminology—debating the use of pronouns—is the UN way to circumvent irreconcilable differences in order to reach consensus in a roundabout way. It is easy to agree with Merry that one is deeply impressed observing "people from countries all over the world trying to put together some words that every one of them could live with, despite their differences" and actually coming up with a binding agreement (47).

Predictably, the most vocal critics of the emphasis on consultation with communities were states in which conspicuous ethnic and cultural minorities present a serious challenge to the state's monopoly on the moral resources of community: states like Russia, Turkey, India, and Spain. Although their specific concerns remained unspoken, it was evident that these states were reluctant to take on international commitments in a convention that could conceivably be used as an instrument of separatism, sedition, or minority rights struggles by Chechens and Ingush in the Caucasus, Kurds in Kurdistan, Assamese and Khasis in Northeast India, or Catalans in Catalonia and Basques in Euskadi, to name but a few examples.

In response to a UNESCO questionnaire in the year 2000 (on the application of its 1989 Recommendation for the Safeguarding of Folklore and Traditional Culture), Spain's UNESCO commission stressed that Spanish legislation "does not allow for any conceptual confusion between the terms 'traditional communities' and 'cultural minorities' "; cultural minorities receive no special protection under Spanish law, whereas it makes provisions for fostering and promoting the practices of traditional communities (Blake 2001: 43). A revealing example of the political uses of taxonomy, this sort of legal sensitivity undergirds the opposition to international obligations to protect the cultural heritage of all communities in the state's territory and to actively involve communities in policy decisions and safeguarding.

Conversely, in some cases equally palpable circumstances account for an emphasis on consultation with communities and their role in the convention. By way of illustration, the most outspoken champion for community rights, Hungary, has its own ax to grind. Hungary lost two world wars, and the resulting changes to the map of Europe left ethnic Hungarians dispersed among nine of its neighboring states: Romania, Slovakia, Serbia, Ukraine, Russia, Austria, Croatia, the Czech Republic, and Slovenia (in descending order of importance). It goes without saying that the position of these Hungarian minorities is of great concern to Hungarian authorities. Thus one and a half million people of Hungarian descent constitute one-third of the population of Transylvania, a province of the Austro-Hungarian Empire that reverted to Romania at the end of World War I. For most of the twentieth century, Romanian authorities saw them as an unruly minority and attempted to assimilate them by means of their so-called Romanianization policy (involving, e.g., forcible relocation, job reassignments, and school mergers). Disputes over this minority are at the root of protracted hostilities between the governments of Hungary and Romania.

In a spirit of compromise, article 5 in the preliminary draft convention distributed to participants at the June session stipulated that "each State Party shall endeavour insofar as possible, in a manner which enriches cultural diversity in the context of national life as a whole," to implement a number of safeguarding measures at the national level (UNESCO 2003: App. 2, 3). Not only does this tortuous phrase twice remove the obligation of *shall* (with *endeavour* and *insofar as possible*); it also stipulates that the manner in which that obligation is to be fulfilled shall conform to a unity-in-diversity vision of the state. This stipulation was ultimately dropped, but not without a good deal of debate. As the meeting's chairman, Mohammed Bedjaoui (who went on to become Algeria's minister of foreign affairs in 2005), explained on the first day of the session, "The ambassador of India, who I see is not present today, was very insistent at previous meetings and fought to use the phrase 'in a manner which enriches cultural diversity in the context of national life as a whole.' India is of course a very multicultural country and there are lots of things to balance there."

To be sure, there are many manners of safeguarding, transmitting, revitalizing, and promoting traditional practices and expressions that do not situate them within "the context of national life as whole." To name but one example from the northeastern states of India—a cauldron of contending ethnic communities with a number of insurgency movements against the rule of the New Delhi government—folklorist Desmond Kharmawphlang recounts in *Indian Folklife* (newsletter of the National Folklore Support Centre in India) how a colleague of his was abducted from his home by rebels and taken to a clandestine training camp operated by a Khasi insurgency group. "They asked him to stay there for two weeks," Kharmawphlang relates, "to talk about folklore of the Khasis in order to inspire some sort of unity among the cadres" (Kharmawphlang et al. 2004: 19).

Conversely, folklore training also serves in a great number of instances to promote allegiance to national unity and to inspire its forces. By way of illustration, the Lithuanian Law on the Principles of State Protection of Ethnic Culture from 1999 provides (in article 9, paragraph 3) that the "Ministry of National Defense along with the Ministry of Education and Science shall include ethnic culture in training of military personnel and patriotic education programmes" (WIPO Lex 2010).[3] Such state protection of ethnic culture, with its military aspect and patriotic pedagogy, is not insignificant in a small state with sizable Polish, Russian, and Belarusian minorities, where ethnic Lithuanians only account for about 56 percent of the population of Vilnius County, which includes the capital Vilnius (but 83 percent of the entire population) (Department of Statistics to the Government of the Republic of Lithuania 2005).

Back in the meeting room at Place Fontenoy, Bedjaoui urged the meeting to keep the phrase "in a manner which enriches cultural diversity in the context of national life as a whole," and not to "take advantage of India's absence to delete it in one fell swoop." Korea and France, however, suggested dropping the phrase for the sake of a shorter and clearer text, for, as the French delegate said, "this is a legal document and generations of young lawyers will interpret it." He hastened to add, "no one will suspect France of not favoring cultural diversity," but "the whole convention is about cultural diversity; why say it in one article rather than another?" The Chilean delegate agreed and suggested that a note on cultural diversity be put in the preamble to the convention. The delegation of Honduras, however, said it supported the article as it stood and in particular the phrase in question. Moreover, the Turkish delegate insisted, "we should retain the phrase we are discussing" because "it promotes tolerance within the community towards the intangible cultural heritage of other communities and groups" (and "we should also show some respect to India even though they are absent").

Some raised questions regarding the relevance of "national life as a whole" to the duties undertaken by states in the article, and there was clearly a measure of discomfort surrounding this phrase among some delegations. Reacting to this, the delegate from the Dominican Republic frankly suggested that the committee stop skirting the issues with vague phraseology and just come out and use the term "nation-state," since that was clearly what was meant by "the national life as a whole." "Ah, non," chairman Bedjaoui was quick to rebut, "the 'nation-state' is an explosive term!" "If we say 'nation-state,'" he went on, "the political scientists will gut us!"

In the final text of the convention, states that become parties to it take on the (conditioned) obligation to "endeavour to ensure the widest possible participation of communities, groups, and, where appropriate, individuals that create, maintain and transmit such heritage" in the framework of their safeguarding activities at the national level "and to involve them actively in its management" (article 15).

Sovereignty, Territory, Community

This debate may seem, at first glance, far afield from the topic of intangible heritage. In spite of appearances, however, it speaks directly to the sort of intervention constituted by that heritage and its safeguarding—the manner in which it is instrumental in acting on the social. Neither the degree and modalities of community involvement in this intervention nor the conditions imposed on expression are extraneous to the manner in which traditional practices of cultural communities are selected, promoted, and protected as intangible cultural heritage. These are crucial factors affecting how heritage is used to imagine community, to structure allegiance, to channel or suppress dissent, and to orchestrate differences so as to organize either homogeneity or cultural diversity within political unity. The debates and negotiations in UNESCO's drafting committee thus afford important insights into the international politics of heritage and how these correlate with national politics, global governance, and human rights.

A recurring issue in global governance is the tension between national sovereignty and the mandate of international organizations. Sovereignty is constantly asserted and "rescued" from subordination to supranational authority, even as intergovernmental organizations depend for their legitimacy on the sovereign powers of their constituent governments. This relationship is negotiated anew in the creation of nearly every international instrument.

The Convention for the Safeguarding of the Intangible Cultural Heritage is no exception. During the debates on community involvement and on mechanisms for civil society representation in the convention's execution (e.g., through NGO consultations), the Colombian delegate reminded the drafting committee that "this is a convention between states and they are responsible for it," and the Zambian delegate warned that "the committee may be infringing on national sovereignty." Although their objections did not meet with approval, concerns about potential infringements of sovereignty were still rife in the committee.

German diplomats emerged during the June meeting as ardent defenders of national sovereignty against supranational incursions. They received strong support especially from their colleagues from Turkey, Austria, Japan, Grenada, and the Czech Republic.[4] There was, for example, a lengthy debate at the meeting concerning the power to place particular items of intangible heritage on the heritage lists created through the convention; should the convention's executive committee be able to do so of its own accord or should the initiative in all instances come from the state party involved? The Italians spoke out in favor of the former position: "We favor a solution which allows the committee to place intangible cultural heritage on a list at its own initiative. Therefore, we favor deleting the phrase 'at the request of the state party concerned.' Italy believes the intangible cultural heritage is the heritage of humanity."

The Hungarian delegate concurred and likewise emphasized that "we are concerned here with the general heritage of humanity." Responding to this perceived threat to national sovereignty in the name of humanity at large, Germany stressed that it was crucial that the committee not be given powers to act without the consent of the state party involved: "Do we want to invite states parties to ratify a convention which might entail as a consequence that political pressure will be applied to them because of intangible cultural heritage in their territory? . . . This is dangerous."

Germany was not alone in smelling danger. The Chinese delegate took the floor next and stressed that China agreed with Germany: "It is very important to China to keep the phrase 'upon the request of the state party concerned' " (consider Tibetan traditions and you'll know why). And the Indian delegate insisted on the retention of this condition, cautioning that its deletion "would be very dangerous" (consider the Khasi insurgents who kidnapped a folklorist to inspire the cadres).

Germany and its allies in the protection of national sovereignty won the day. The final text makes listing of heritage contingent on its proposal by the states parties concerned. The principle of territorial sovereignty cited by the German delegate, though its invocation is a leitmotif in the negotiation of most international instruments, is particularly notable for the consideration of heritage and can help to shed light on what is new in this convention.

The World Heritage Convention from 1972 defined heritage in spatial terms, as monuments, groups of buildings, and sites, and as natural reserves and parks. In contrast to the more recent "environmentality" model of conservation, the convention's conception of "natural heritage" has been criticized for being all too spatial in its lack of attention to human populations that live in areas designated as parks and reserves, or whose subsistence depends on them, alienating these populations from their administration (Munjeri 2001: 19; Pressouyre 2001: 152). World heritage is thus by definition expressed as territory; territory that can be delimited, measured, and mapped (Pressouyre 2001: 57).

This spatialization of heritage is recognizable in innumerable heritage maps and geographies that belong all at once to statecraft, the tourism industry, and global governance. In *Imagined Communities*, historian Benedict Anderson remarks that maps were used to classify and create spatial reality in the colonies, marking out territory through abstract delimitations in an effort to put space under surveillance. Old sacred sites were incorporated into the map of the colony, lending time depth to newly created territorial unity; in this way, the mappers would drape themselves in ancient prestige and, Anderson notes, "if this had disappeared, as it often had, the state would attempt to revive it" (Anderson 1991: 181–82).

Heritage has thus long been central to the conception of territory: it aligns present claims of territorial sovereignty with past authority; it lends itself to easily recognizable representations of the territory and its unity; and it infuses such claims and representations with prestige and legitimacy. Conversely, territory is a defining characteristic of heritage. In fact, it is so central that it is fair to say that in certain respects heritage is territory. It is other things besides, but whatever else it may be, *heritage is territory*.

Of course that applies primarily to the cultural and natural heritage of the World Heritage Convention. A distinction needs to be drawn between monuments, groups of buildings, and sites, on the one hand, and the emergent category of the intangible cultural heritage on the other. Intangible heritage shifts away from territorial definition. The relationship of intangible heritage to populations is not mediated through land or territory. Instead, intangible heritage objectifies the practices and expressions of human communities. It is defined ethnographically rather than topographically. Intangible heritage emerges out of an intervention in community practices, and this intervention defines and delimits the community. If then tangible heritage is territory in some sense, then by the same token it stands to reason that *intangible heritage is community*.

Safeguarding Community

The safeguarding of intangible cultural heritage represents a subtle innovation in governmental rationality, disciplining populations through a conversion of their customs, practices, and expressions into heritage (the threatened nature of which makes it morally imperative to intervene). Ultimately, this shift makes community itself subject to conservation in the face of its purportedly steady decline in the modern world. Community is thus the most fundamental intangible heritage that UNESCO's 2003 convention sets out to safeguard. In this sense, it is an important objective of the convention to build communities with which their members identify, even if many states are careful to circumscribe the terms of such empowerment. This desire to empower communities is apparent in the convention's definition of intangible heritage: "The 'intangible cultural heritage' means the practices, representations, expressions, knowledge, skills—as well as the instruments, objects, artefacts and cultural spaces associated therewith—that communities, groups and, in some cases, individuals recognize as part of their cultural heritage" (article 2, paragraph 1).

This is perhaps better described as an indefinition; the relative clause that follows the second dash defers the power to define intangible cultural heritage to the communities themselves (and groups and, in some cases, individuals). In this way, the convention "endeavors to ensure" that the community is involved in any safeguarding measures or that such measures are at the very least not conducted without the community's approval—it delegates responsibility to communities as collective subjects (Blake 2009; Bortolotto 2009).

The convention's circular formula—that "intangible cultural heritage" means the practices that communities recognize as part of their cultural heritage—begs the question of what the term "community" denotes. In fact, it requires the definition of the communities with which state actors are supposed to consult and cooperate. In order to involve communities in safeguarding it is necessary first to delimit them, to define membership in them, and to designate a mechanism for consultation or cooperation (a "competent authority").

Part of the political attraction of communities lies in their apparent naturalness (Noyes 2003). Nevertheless, despite appearances and like nations before them, communities need to be made up. Boundaries and distinctions have to be put into place. Communities have to be visualized, surveyed, and mobilized. Intangible cultural heritage does just that: it converts cultural practices into resources for administering populations. In this way, empowerment depends on subjection. This is the classical paradox of subjectification for, as Foucault argues, subject formation takes place in the element of power (in the double sense of the French *pouvoir*: the noun "power" and the verb "to be able to"). The moment at which we attain status as subjects (the subjects of our thoughts, words, and deeds, and subjects in our relations with ourselves and others) is also the moment of subjection in which we become subject to a set of rules, norms of behavior, and to definitions, boundaries, and exclusions already imposed on the discourse in which we assume a subject position.

Thus the communities to which UNESCO's concept of intangible heritage refers itself are all positioned squarely as collective subjects within states and subject to states. Indeed, their empowerment cements their administrative bonds to central government, even as it loosens their cultural bonds. By defining community, providing it with outside expertise, and conferring official prestige on its marginalized practices and expressions, this process demonstrates how residual and interstitial cultural representations—craftsmanship, oral traditions, rituals, performing arts—are incorporated into the hegemonic order of representation.

Orchestrating Difference

In a comment on UNESCO's Proclamation of Masterpieces of the Oral and Intangible Heritage of Humanity (a predecessor to the convention and its lists), Henri J. M. Claessen expresses misgivings about the induced survival of moribund cultural practices: "Governments will pay people to dance dances the use of which no one sees any longer, to sing incomprehensible songs that have long since lost their meaning, to perform mystery plays in which no one now believes" (Claessen 2002). Claessen goes on to ask: "Why do this? Why spend a lot of money and work to make a list of such endangered masterpieces?" Why indeed?

One answer might be that in many cases practicing communities would very much like to see their traditions represented on such a list, which confers honor on them and draws attention, not least from local and national authorities. If these communities find it meaningful, if they see the use in it, and they believe it is worthwhile, then their desire to safeguard certain practices provides a partial answer to Claessen's question, "why do this?" I have argued here that the desire to safeguard and strengthen communities is another partial answer. The third piece in this puzzle is the will to safeguard and promote cultural diversity. These three answers are entirely consistent; they address the question at micro, medium, and macro levels, respectively (the same question has often been asked of those who advocate revitalizing endangered languages and is answered in Dorian 1987).

The Istanbul Declaration, issued by UNESCO ministers of culture in 2002, emphasizes that "The multiple expressions of intangible cultural heritage constitute some of the fundamental sources of the cultural identity of the peoples and communities" and maintains that they are "an essential factor in the preservation of cultural diversity" (Istanbul Declaration—Final Communiqué). In the past few years, this reciprocity between cultural identity and cultural diversity has been the backbone of UNESCO's rationale for its activities in the field of intangible heritage and in particular for the creation of the 2003 convention. In fact, the Istanbul Roundtable was held under the banner "The Intangible Heritage: A Mirror of Cultural Diversity."

There is more than one way to understand diversity, however, and more than one way to give it policy expression. There is hardly a state in Western Europe or the Americas that does not pay at least lip service to such diversity and that has not implemented a policy at the national level to promote cultural diversity, though those policies vary considerably in their scope and objectives (T. Bennett 2001). A great number of states elsewhere in the world have likewise put in place policies of cultural diversity, which also conceive in different ways of the sort of diversity desirable and the ways in which it is to be maintained and managed. Such policies rely on a range of practices and techniques to govern subject formation in the new multiple field of identity and allegiance. Organizing communities as spaces of emotional relationships and of strong, but not exclusive, identifications is a subset of these practices. Government through community and the orchestration of difference should be seen as aspects of one enterprise.

Differences between communities are arranged, celebrated, and often overstressed and exoticized in media structured according to a global grammar of festival and exhibition. Usually, these integrate the communities into some program or other of unity in diversity. Through such heritage politics, differences are orchestrated as cultural diversity, as groups within the state are given a voice but also given a score to sing in harmony. These politics play out in a remarkably uniform fashion across the globe, as Arjun Appadurai explains: "Typically, contemporary nation-states do this by exercising taxonomic control over difference, by creating various kinds of international spectacle to domesticate difference, and by seducing small groups with the fantasy of self-display on some sort of global or cosmopolitan stage" (1996: 39).

The Convention for the Safeguarding of the Intangible Cultural Heritage sets just such a cosmopolitan stage. Its lists are designed to highlight and promote, to bring attention to select local practices and expressions, as well as to rally resources to their safeguarding. Although they are modeled on the World Heritage List, these lists differ in that the heritage inscribed on them is embodied by living persons in practicing communities and has no existence apart from these communities. In effect, UNESCO's intangible heritage lists showcase communities in a manner that owes as much to the global grammar of multicultural festivals as it does to the World Heritage List. Organizing aesthetic markers of difference in lists, brochures, documentaries, web pages, and spectacles, UNESCO's intangible heritage initiatives display the diversity of cultures and coordinate it under the sign of humanity—as unity in diversity.

Homogeny and Hegemony (or, Danishness Transposed)

Koïchiro Matsuura, UNESCO director general (1999–2009), missed no opportunity to stress the importance of the intangible heritage for the promotion of cultural diversity worldwide. In an address in Copenhagen in June 2004, Matsuura posed the question "why has the protection of intangible cultural heritage become a matter of urgency in recent years?" (UNESCO 2004). Responding to his own query, he continued:

> The answer, I believe, comes in large part from a growing recognition that accelerating globalization is placing enormous new pressures upon cultural diversity. These pressures have given rise to fears of greater cultural homogenization and associated threats to the world's cultural diversity, especially in its local, indigenous and living forms. These fears, which are widely shared, have stimulated the demand that something must be done before it is too late. The Convention is a vital part of this process of urgently addressing the cultural challenges of globalization. (2004: 2)

Fear of the global homogenization of culture can put a peculiar spin on international policymaking under the aegis of UNESCO. Matsuura himself illustrated this peculiarity with his subsequent remarks in the Copenhagen address:

> This very meeting is part of a process of national self-reflection in Denmark on the question of intangible cultural heritage. Such reflection can be both stimulating and unsettling. It may provoke some hard questions. For example, what is at the core of Danish identity and

> culture? What is it that you do not want to lose at any cost? . . . Can this distinctive feature be defined and labeled? Do you want to preserve it? Can you imagine Denmark and "Danishness" without it? These are the kinds of questions, transposed to all the countries of the world, that are shaping the agenda of intangible cultural heritage. (3)

Leaving aside, for present purposes, the problematic notion of culture as essential expressions of difference, it is primarily the national inflection of this notion that troubles me here. I find it disconcerting that a process of "national self-reflection," designed to define "Danishness" and label "the core of Danish identity and culture," should stand, in the director general's opinion, at the center of "the agenda of intangible cultural heritage." Although it is meant to respond to perceived threats to the world's cultural diversity and to mitigate fears of homogenization, such a process—"transposed to all the countries of the world"—would inevitably defeat its purpose.

In an interview at UNESCO headquarters in Paris, a member of the UNESCO secretariat expressed views similar to those of the director general. When I queried him as to why he considered it imperative to safeguard intangible heritage, he asserted that this heritage was necessary to maintain cultural diversity in the world because "that's what makes Colombia different from Bolivia, and so on!" (personal communication, November 25, 2003). In an important article on the politics of heritage, Regina Bendix has remarked on this elastic capacity of heritage "to hide the complexities of history and politics" (2000: 38). Indeed, as my interlocutor's remarks make evident, intangible heritage can serve to highlight certain differences while occluding others—say, in the case of Colombia and Bolivia, the differences between militia and electoral politics, which surely distinguish Colombia from Bolivia as effectively as their respective popular traditions (which, after all, are closely related).

To be fair, I should add that later in the same interview, my informant acknowledged that intangible heritage "also problematizes national identity, especially in cross-border communities" (personal communication, November 25, 2003). This observation gestures toward what should be obvious: a world where cultural difference is expressed as a collection of coexisting nationalnesses—"Danishness," "Japaneseness," "Indianness," "Zambianness," "Colombianness," and so on—is less diverse, not more diverse, than the one we currently inhabit. International policy that imagines such a world as its objective, if it were to have any effect, might be more perilous to global cultural diversity than the "cultural challenges of globalization" that occasion it.

There is good reason to be skeptical. As Appadurai has remarked, fears of homogenization can be "exploited by nation-states in relation to their own minorities, by posing global commoditization (or capitalism, or some other such external enemy) as more real than the threat of its own hegemonic strategies" (1996: 32). For an illustration, one need merely recall UNESCO's etiological account of how it came to concern itself with folklore: the Bolivian minister's alarm in the face of the "process of commercially oriented transculturation destructive of the traditional cultures," and the simultaneous suppression of indigenous identities and appropriation of indigenous culture by the Bolivian state.

A UNESCO-sanctioned imperative for cultural diversity that foregrounds international diversity and backgrounds cultural differences within states can and no doubt will be used to justify the suppression of minorities. The director general's peculiar spin on cultural policy is perhaps best understood, therefore, as co-optation of human rights discourse on diversity. Distributing difference between states rather than within them, it legitimizes the eradication of difference in the name of defining, labeling, and, ultimately, bringing into being an orderly collection of internally consistent national identities and cultures.

The director general is not wrong in his conviction that intangible cultural heritage and the convention for its safeguarding can be useful instruments for addressing "the cultural challenges of globalization." He is right, but for the wrong reasons. Their importance is not that they get at the core of national identity or that they help to label distinctive features of national character. What is significant is the way in which the concept and the convention enable a reimagination of heritage and encourage the relocation of culture in communities. Intangible heritage, as defined and instrumentalized in the 2003 convention, enfranchises and invests capacities in practicing communities; it contributes to their organization as partially self-regulating administrative entities.

The model of communalization, as analyzed by Nikolas Rose, is undoubtedly most applicable in states characterized by advanced liberalism—whether in its neoliberal, social-democratic, or "third way" inflections. It is important to note, however, that this model does not apply equally or consistently to all liberal states even in the "developed world." Rather than conceive of communalization as a single model of government, it is probably better to admit of a range of different degrees, modes, and methods of governing through community. This is even more important with reference to "developing" countries, for globalization and its concomitant liberalization do not produce the same results everywhere. There are certainly many liberalisms, and citizens are integrated into their government to various degrees. In countries where nine out of ten persons do not have access to a telephone (or electricity, or roads, or a secure source of drinking water) and where relatively little effort is made to invest powers in the citizenry, the modes of government instituted will not look quite like the governmentality model (cf. Grossberg, Miller, and Packer 2003: 34).

Voicing Community

If the communalization of government delegates a number of the tasks of social governance to the community level, it maintains all the while a loose affiliation of all communities in the sovereign territory with each other and with the state; this loose affiliation is organized around the common citizenship of the individual members of different communities, rather than around their cultural ties. Likewise, the subjectification of communities in UNESCO's Intangible Heritage Convention neither excludes nor supersedes the nationalization of the social body, nor is it antithetical to its globalization. On the contrary, as evidenced by discussions in the meeting of experts that drafted this instrument, communities are one point of reference in a dynamic triangulation between community, state, and international authority. Each of the three is increasingly understood as a constitutive element of the other two, albeit in a hesitant, incomplete, and differentially realized process of governmentalization of the global sphere. This process multiplies collective subjectifications, adding to the national subjects of intergovernmental organizations a plethora of communal subjects, organized around a variety of common identities and heritages, but also adds the emerging collective subject of humanity.

It remains to be underlined here that the emergence of community and of humanity as legal and ethical subjects, and of the construction of heritage as their objects, does not necessarily herald the dawn of a postnational era. States remain central actors in international relations and they are ascribed crucial responsibilities in UNESCO's Intangible Heritage Convention.

The intangible cultural heritage, as conceived of by UNESCO, is appointed, assembled, and interpreted in part by or in consultation with practicing communities, whose identities are intertwined in its representation. To the extent that community members are integrated into and made responsible for the work of representation, intangible heritage enfranchises and gives voice to communities. In so doing, however, an attempt is made to fix particular sets of relations and authority as relatively stable units—communities—that can speak with one voice.

Inevitably, such attempts instigate jockeying for power at ground level (see, e.g., Berliner 2010; Bortolotto 2009; Kuutma 2009; Lowthorp 2007; Noyes 2006; Tauschek 2009; Tornatore 2011). In a discerning analysis of some early consequences of the nomination of the Patum festival in Berga, Catalonia, for UNESCO's Proclamation of Masterpieces, folklorist Dorothy Noyes gives an unnerving account of how attempts to fix the community can play out locally. A popular street festival and collective performance with a long history, the Patum has always been a vehicle of intense contestation among Berguedans, but it has also fostered a delicate sort of social equilibrium through its multivocality and indirection. Moreover, the festival has helped incorporate new inhabitants into full membership in Berga's social life, and its importance in this regard has grown in the last few decades with new waves of immigration into the city (Noyes 2006).

As Noyes, explains, "in the early 1990s, a certain group of festival participants well-connected in City Hall created a foundation, a Patronat for the protection of the Patum: a festival with thousands of passionate adherents that is in no conceivable danger of dying or losing its formal integrity" (Noyes 2006: 38). This foundation controls some of the material elements of the festival—instruments, effigies, costumes—but its board is not directly elected, there is no explicit structure of rotation in office, and it includes members of some groups of festival participants but not of others who have different views. And yet outsiders, if they look no further, have no reason to doubt that the Patronat represents the community. In practice, UNESCO and the Catalan Department of Culture both seem to regard it as the "competent authority" for administering the Patum festival (38).

Berguedans are divided about this state of affairs. While some contest the Patronat's authority, others have instead opted to withdraw their labor and retreat from participation. In a town of roughly 15,000 inhabitants, where the effort of all is needed to maintain local vitality, "some of the most talented actors have surrendered control to the bureaucrats" (Noyes 2006: 39). The exit and exclusion that have accompanied the festival's institutionalization carry consequences that are important for the organization of community and the administration of the social field in Berga, as Dorothy Noyes demonstrates:

> The members of the Patronat stem from the "respectable" wing of Patum opinion, and in many incidents over the years this wing has attempted to control participation with a view to controlling the Patum's potential for social change. There are indications that this control . . . is part of the Patronat's agenda. For example, recently a system of "points" was created for designating the festival administrators, an honorific office accorded every year to four newly married couples. Among other things, points are given for having been born in Berga and having been married in church. In a city with a large immigrant population and in which the working class is historically anti-clerical, these are highly divisive criteria. (Noyes 2006: 40)

It is evident, then, that the language of intangible heritage—its programs of preservation, protection, documentation, research, promotion, education, and revitalization, and its specialist knowledge and expertise—offers tools and techniques that communities can use to organize themselves as spaces of identification, to conduct the conduct of their members, and to find their voice in the polyphony of contemporary, pluralistic societies. The danger is that in finding their voice, these communities, in cooperation with administrators and experts, will suppress their own multivocality; that they will amplify one voice and drown out dissent. To the extent that this is the case, the convention safeguards not only cultural heritage but also a political heritage of subjection. In principle, UNESCO's slogan of "unity in diversity" represents harmony and understanding. In practice, it runs the risk of enforcing conformity within the diverse communities it designates.

Chapter 2

Heritage, Legacy, Zombie: How to Bury the Undead Past

Dorothy Noyes

> If we connect up with the law, we'll be connected to this man, this body, for the rest of our lives. We've got to get rid of him.
>
> —James Dickey, *Deliverance*, 1970

> Das Widerstehn, der Eigensinn
> Verkümmern herrlichsten Gewinn,
> Daß man, zu tiefer, grimmiger Pein,
> Ermüden muß, gerecht zu sein.
>
> Recalcitrance and wilfulness
> Can mar the most superb success,
> Til to our painful, deep disgust
> We tire of trying to be just.
>
> —Goethe, *Faust* Part II, Act V

The protagonists of James Dickey's novel are saved from the consequences of a murder by the construction of a dam. Modern development projects create their own state of exception by making no exceptions. Connections formed by history are sundered by the flood of present necessity. Particularities are forcibly submerged. It is nothing new: in Goethe's Ur-narrative of development, Faust regretfully leaves his pastoral hosts Baucis and Philemon to be dealt with by henchmen so that his dike building can proceed unimpeded, just as earlier he abandoned Gretchen, singing at her spinning wheel.[1] Nor has anything changed in that larger portion of the world we still call "developing." New dams along the Yangtze, Mekong, Tigris, and Euphrates Rivers continue to displace millions of people and submerge millennia of human history, with artifacts rescued here and there to serve as "heritage" (Goldman 2005; Morvaridi 2004; Shoup 2006).

In the nineteenth century, Gretchen's song was recognized to have the same instrumental value as Gretchen's spinning. Both the expressive and the productive labor of the common people were conscripted in the construction of the nation-state. The former was christened folklore.

But Gretchen's body posed a problem; the will attached to it still more. If the modern subject Faust is to preserve his freedom of action, he must be allowed to break his connection with her. Thus she is seduced and goaded into acts of petty violence that disrupt not Faust's plans but her own community, and these enable her to be condemned to death. Now her song becomes not an adjunct to labor but an uncanny trace of her personhood, issuing from the prison to remind Faust of his own violence against her. "Fliege fort!" she sings. The song flies away, but she cannot.

Folklore is both resource and reminder, both incorporated into and excluded from modernizing projects. Neither arrangement is an easy one. Emergent in the intimacy of making and performing at close range, folklore can never be wholly cleansed of the trace of the subaltern body, with its possibility of independent action. This is the undertone of the nineteenth-century conception of folklore as cultural survival, for while E. B. Tylor and others emphasized the anomaly and absurdity of survivals in a changed lifeworld, the very word asserts vitality and persistence. Early modern and nineteenth-century scholars, who often and not coincidentally were clergymen, state officials, or colonial administrators, were typically concerned not just to document but to eradicate superstition and other purported survivals of premodern social forms. Some survivals threatened efficiency; some of them posed outright political threats—and here we can think of a long history of suppression of worker and indigenous social organization.

Discredited by twentieth-century ethnographic and historical scholarship, survivalist explanations have themselves survived to be revived in the post-Cold War political realm. "Age-old hatreds," "medieval attitudes," "cultural tradition," and so on are routinely applied to the myriad local impediments that once again rise up to challenge the renewed expansionist ambitions of capital or disrupt the reconfiguration of the international community. Survivalist theory as a discursive resource anticipates and molds the range of policy devices that seek to contain, manage, or eradicate threats to processes defined in their turn as progress.

In this chapter, drawing on examples from Afghanistan, Northern Ireland, and Appalachia, I explore some of the successor concepts to the nineteenth-century notion of survival, "heritage" being both the most fully developed and the privileged choice within a broader matrix shaping the ways in which local disruptions can be named and addressed under neoliberal conditions. I use the word "local" well aware of its ambiguous status as the constructed contrary of the equally constructed "global." Of course I do not mean to construct the local as a bounded, homogeneous small-scale community or the global as a massive engineered apparatus of predation. Rather, I intend "local" to refer to a cluster or node situated in a complex network. But in contrast to some recent deconstructions of the concept, I continue to privilege those nodes tied to actual places. The characterization of place as no longer relevant to a flat world of global flows has been notably disproved in Afghanistan, where we have learned that it's still location, location, location—to say nothing of terrain.

The label of heritage marks local practices as temporally anomalous and their practitioners as nonmodern, as has frequently been observed. Just as important is that the transfer (or we might, in information-technology terms, call it the migration) of heritage from "first life" to "second life" (Kirshenblatt-Gimblett 1998a) reduces the typically holistic entailments of vernacular practice to the domain of culture, narrowly defined. Politics, economics, society, religion, education, technology, and other dimensions are cut away. Incidentally or not, this cuts network ties to the larger world, reducing all relationships to that between cultural performers and extracultural spectators. This is part of the violence worked by categorization (Kapchan, Introduction). It seems that culture waxes as lifeworlds wane. Case study after case study reports that the hoped-for payoffs in economic prosperity and political recognition rarely follow on a major local investment in cultural heritage (Hemme, Tauschek, and Bendix 2007; Noyes 2006; this volume). The rising discourse of cultural rights accompanies a larger discourse on human rights, to be sure, but both may seem rather—dare I say—intangible to those on the ground. When not dancing for tourists, most of humanity is busy coping with the erosion of customary rights in a context of advancing propertization, of bargaining rights in a context of union busting and international trade agreements, and of citizenship rights in a context of labor migration and special enterprise zones.

In some cases an inverse correlation between cultural rights and human rights can be directly traced. This is most dramatic in such matters as female genital cutting and other gendering practices (cf. Das 1999), but even such apparently benign acts of cultural protection as the creation of a World Heritage Site can carry unexpected consequences. In Lijiang, Yunnan Province, China, members of the Naxi ethnic minority are subject to fines for not wearing traditional costume in the UNESCO-protected Old Town during the tourist season. Old Town businesses, required to have at least one costumed employee, often employ only Han workers who thus wear Naxi dress as well.[2] Even in democratic Estonia, young women in the protected Kihnu Cultural Space have felt pressured to remain on the island practicing subsistence agriculture and labor-intensive traditional handicraft rather than go off to university; Kihnu cultural activists have difficulty persuading government officials to let them pursue more flexible and self-directed strategies of "safeguarding" (Kuutma 2007: 188–89). Rent-seeking states may use culture as an excuse to impede even the core neoliberal right to individual economic enterprise, as when Ghanaian craftsmen and musicians are obliged to purchase a license to practice what has become protected national culture ("Expert Criticises Copyright Bill" 2005). Far from being empowered, local actors often pay for protection.

The right to be cultural easily slips into the obligation to be cultural. Just as the legal personhood of corporations takes ever-greater precedence over the less weighty personhood of individuals in the rich world,[3] so the growing legal personality of cultures tends to accompany the depersonalization of individuals in the poor one. This flattening of the ground that puts large actors on the same footing as small ones, a basic feature of neoliberal governance, also informs this period's extension of the definition of heritage from the treasures of elite Western creation to the wider universe of non-Western, indigenous, and vernacular creation, the latter defined as intangible and, significantly, as "living." Many key actors in the initiative to create the Intangible Cultural Heritage convention and most of those charged with implementing it are of course sincerely concerned to confer dignity on people hitherto denied it and to facilitate agency through inclusion. Viewed another way, inclusion is incorporation in a regime of governance. And in practice this regime equates the embodied living traditions of the poor with the dead detached things of the rich.

Heritage has become both euphemism and policy in relation to troublesome minorities, collapsed industries, dying languages, and other societal liabilities: local situations that look from above like impediments to efficiency and, on the ground, like the aftermath of structural violence. But recalcitrant realities sometimes resist containment in culture. The situation may simply be too complex to stabilize; the practices may not be suitable for celebratory display to tourists; the actors may refuse to play along, having scripts of their own in mind—and their economic needs, political rights, and capacity for making trouble must be taken into account. It is not always possible to get rid of the body.

Heritage or Legacy?

In the world of "fast-capitalism," where the pace keeps accelerating and the expectation of return grows ever out of proportion to the proposed investment (Holmes 2000), the immediate past poses a greater threat than the age-old. Temporal anomalies are constructed at ever closer range. This affects the domain of business as much as that of culture, for business often has an interest in getting rid of inconvenient bodies. Thus, just as expressive labor is detached from the body and fetishized as culture, so productive labor is today detached from the body and fetishized as skill set (Urciuoli 2008). Where the skills in question are not "transferable," that is, cannot travel freely in the marketplace across industries and localities because their practice depends on a material, social, and infrastructural context, they are judged to be "outdated." The possessors of such skills, if they lose their jobs, are categorized under U.S. labor statutes as "dislocated workers"—paradoxically, for it is usually the job that moves away from them rather than vice versa. If they must for some reason be retained, they are marked with a euphemism now rapidly expanding in scope: "legacy."

In long-standing American academic usage, candidates whose family connections procure them preferential admission to a fraternity or private college are referred to as "legacies."[4] Despite the positive aspect for the institution, which hopes to receive literal legacies from these students, the term has a pejorative cast, for in many cases they would not have been admitted on their own merits.

It is the pejorative implication of being stuck with something, rather than the hope of benefit from its presence, that carries over to the context of business information systems, in which the use of "legacy" as an adjective applied to computer hardware, software, or applications is documented by the Oxford English Dictionary as of 1989. Tasked with the creation of smooth workflows and data flows, information technology specialists face the challenge of integrating myriad local systems developed ad hoc to automate various business processes: order entry, shipping and receiving, invoicing, and so forth. These processes were originally integrated manually by employees—data entry clerks and the like. From the 1980s on, with the cult of the MBA consultant, the acceleration of new technologies, and the focus on stock price as an indicator of value, competitive pressures increased to reduce cycle time by eliminating the manual lag. Later, with the mantra of the "real-time enterprise," corporate IT departments were charged to integrate automated processes into an agile System of Systems.

This was more easily said than done. Typically an organization does not have the resources to upgrade all of its computer systems and migrate all of its data simultaneously, nor can it halt operations in order to do this all at once. The larger the organization, the greater the number of particular and redundant systems accumulated over time. So integration proceeds over the course of years, meeting considerable resistance from individual units and employees who see their existence as well as their routine threatened. The IT staff thus have the ongoing responsibility of jiggering communicability between new pieces of software and old pieces of software, maintaining archaic databases for which support is no longer being provided, and so forth. By 1993, the association in management thinking between efficiency and the reduction of workforce had brought an extension in usage: employees with outdated skill sets were referred to as "legacy people."[5] Today the term is being generalized: at my university, for example, we recently reviewed "legacy courses" and "legacy majors" to see which could be dropped and which reintegrated into consolidating programs. More consequentially, there was much discussion in the 2008 banking crisis of "legacy assets" that could not simply be disowned but had somehow to be managed and recuperated.

What does all of this have to do with heritage? Well, there is first of all a symmetry and contraposition between the terms. Both of them seem to be conceptual derivatives of the old notion of cultural survival, splitting its implications between them. Both identify certain continuities of practice or existence as problematic in the present. Both facilitate the broader ideological move defined by Johannes Fabian as the denial of coevalness—the assertion that the Other does not coexist with us in shared historical time, but belongs to the past and therefore, in ethical terms, need not be encountered face to face (1983).

But heritage conceptualizes the persistence as isolable from the larger lifeworld, something that can be preserved in an enclave and indeed requires an enclosure to protect it. Contact with the present is assumed to denature heritage or to threaten its very existence. In practice, of course, this conceptualization legitimates and enables the actual process of creating an isolate. Heritage cuts a practice or an environment or a community loose from its moorings in the world and fixes it in a dedicated frame deemed capable of containing it: an official holiday, a museum, a nature reserve, a tribal reservation. The concentrated practice or resource is frozen and reduced in meaning to an icon of identity. Still more important, the aspects of the lifeworld that it once helped to integrate wither and die when their roots are cut—a result that is sometimes desired (Noyes 2006).

Legacy, on the other hand, recognizes the practice as a necessary part of a larger whole. Under current conditions it cannot be isolated or expelled, and now the shoe is on the other foot: it is not the system that threatens the practice but the practice that threatens the system. So containment is not possible. Accommodations must be made, and in extreme cases a strategy must be found for reclassifying, repurposing, or otherwise recycling the difficult survival.

Afghanistan

An extreme case, if ever there was one, is posed for the U.S. government and NATO allies by contemporary Afghanistan. It is in this context of international intervention that an explicit relationship between the two terms "heritage" and "legacy" seems likely someday to take shape. As the projects of war and development merge (Duffield 2007), local practices become resources for appropriation as well as impediments to be managed.

The concept of legacy has already migrated from organizational systems into international engagements. On December 31, 2007, journalist Steve Inskeep interviewed William B. Wood, the Bush administration's ambassador to Afghanistan, on National Public Radio's *Morning Edition*. Known to wags in Kabul's diplomatic community as "Ambassador Narc" (Margaret Mills, personal communication), Wood came from a previous posting in Colombia, where he had dedicated himself, with mixed success, to the reduction of cocaine production.[6] To the debate over rapidly increasing opium production in the Afghan countryside, Wood brought his prior enthusiasm for aerial crop eradication. But neither the Afghans nor other NATO allies, notably the British, favored large-scale aerial spraying that would poison Afghan fields, destroy the country's single export crop, and alienate hearts and minds still further. Said Wood, "In purely technical terms, aerial spraying is by far the most efficient method. There's also a political environment. There's also a social environment. There's also a drug environment. And we are going to do the best job we can against drugs using all of the tools that we think are appropriate for the Afghan environment."

A tense interview unfolded without explicit discussion of another problematic form of intervention from the air. After recurrent incidents of heavy civilian casualties resulting from NATO airstrikes, this mode of targeting Taliban fighters had become a still greater point of contention between the U.S. command, NATO allies, and the Afghan government (Gall and Sanger 2007). Thus the ambassador's reluctant recognition of the "political environment," amid continual reiterations of the urgency of the drug problem and the value of spraying, betrayed nostalgia for the straightforward efficiency of aerial interventions in a moment when the paradigm had, however ambiguously, shifted. It was no longer possible to think of either poppies or Taliban fighters as anomalous excrescences upon the territory, to be surgically eradicated without implications for the general population. As the new counterinsurgency strategy laid out in U.S. Army/Marine Corps *Field Manual 3-24* had articulated most clearly, interaction on the ground rather than intervention from the air would have to become the new key to U.S. engagements abroad (2006). But it wasn't going well. Pushed by Inskeep as to whether the Karzai government was in genuine control of the provinces, Wood acknowledged that in some districts there might be "political pushback" to a given initiative from local officials, just as often happened in the United States. Asked whether the analogy to, say, California having a separate policy on stem cell research was truly appropriate, Wood conceded, "This is not yet a strong government. There are problems of corruption, as President Karzai himself has said. There are some legacy warlords and others who interfere with institutional government here."

Inskeep did not comment on the extraordinary temporal juxtaposition of the latest management jargon with the exotic archaism by which U.S.

authorities designate Afghan paramilitary leaders and other nonstate actors.[7] Indeed, we have become habituated to such hybridities. But the whole bent of the interview challenged the implied manageability of the problem in Wood's description of it as the need to make the new political order interface with legacy systems. Completely on the defensive by the end, Wood abandoned this technocratic idiom and took refuge in a far more sweeping declaration of otherness. "I think that we often feel we understand the country we're in more than we really do. Afghanistan is forcefully, determinedly its own country with its own culture and its own background. It is poor even by African standards. Many parts of the country are tribal, and it is a foreign country, and living in an environment where security constraints limit your access, limit your freedom of movement, does make the job harder."[8] What the U.S. military had begun to term the "human terrain" (McFate and Jackson 2005) of Afghanistan was as difficult to navigate as the geographic: neither offered an integrated system permitting easy communicability between points.

Here the invocation of Afghanistan's "own culture" signals the larger framework in which neoliberal actors conceptualize contemporary conflicts. When not contained as heritage, culture becomes a problem. Understood since the nineteenth century as the natural foundation and legitimation of the nation-state (Handler 1988),[9] with the post-1945 breakup of empires culture has also taken on the relativist baggage of the postwar culture concept popularized and simplified from Mead and Benedict. This double endorsement, nationalist and postcolonial, has helped to naturalize culture and to foster its reification as "human terrain" in the counterinsurgency strategy. While the idiom of cultural diversity was instituted in such normative texts as the Universal Declaration of Human Rights and the Convention on Cultural Diversity to promote the dignity of non-Western, indigenous, and minority peoples, it is often invoked in more directly self-interested ways. Subaltern actors may use it to claim rights. Dominant actors may use it to signal incommensurability and incommunicability; in some cases, to disclaim responsibility for ongoing interaction. Wood's usage seems to fall in this category, for by the end of his tour in autumn 2008, he had retreated from the interactional paradigm altogether: "Afghanistan is the most foreign country in the world. . . . It's a ferociously foreign country" (May 2009).

In December 2007 it was still possible to envision a happy outcome from Ambassador Wood's perspective. A stabilized Afghanistan, purged of its poppy fields, could provide a romantic backdrop for historical epic films[10]—which indeed furnished the image most Americans had of it before the Soviet invasion—and, better yet, for adventure tourism. We would be treated to tales of imperial adventures from Alexander to Kipling; of ancient feuds between haughty tribal leaders. Their swords, if not their severed heads, would be mounted on the walls of our hotel lobbies, and their picturesque garb would be worn by our tour guides.

Some indicators of this development could already be traced. Exile-run websites such as Afghanistan Online (http://www.afghan-web.com), dating from at least early 2006, offered a wide range of historical, cultural, and geographic information on the country, with pages on nature, scenery, the National Museum of Kabul, and so on. The online shop sold cookbooks and clothing; there was a chatroom; the site's advertisers came largely from the international tourist industry, and the site's front page read "Afghanistan: The Friendliest Country in the World, Possibly the Universe." The site was designed to foster a vision of Afghanistan as a normal country and clearly anticipated tourism as key to economic development. Potential demand on the consumer side was also evident, notably in Western fascination with Hamid Karzai's wardrobe. When the creative director of Gucci declared Karzai "the world's most chic man" in 2002, the BBC followed up with a photo gallery and commentary implying that fashion could model a new style of political accommodation between the local and the global. Karzai, "marrying classic tailoring with ethnic fashions . . . [might] breathe new life into the way leaders dress around the world" ("Afghanistan's 'Mr. Chic'" 2002).[11] Elements of Afghan traditional male costume could be bought on many websites, particularly the emblematic headgear: the wool cloth *pakol* with the rolled brim, badge of the mujahideen, and the *karakul*, the elegant lambskin cap worn by Karzai to show allegiance to northern minorities and balance his Pashtun *shalwar* (Christia and Chantziara 2009).[12] You could follow your favorite warlords, read their heroic deeds of war and rhetoric, examine their weapons, and buy coasters featuring their portraits on the website Warlords of Afghanistan.com, created in 2005. In short, the manly, feudal trappings of Afghan leadership were already becoming incorporated into American celebrity, hobby, and consumer culture when Wood was interviewed. In the best case scenario, instead of legacy warlords making trouble Afghanistan could soon have heritage warlords making money.

Northern Ireland

A second case from a different conflict suggests that my imputation of this particular fantasy to the Bush administration is not utterly implausible. I turn now to Belfast in June 2006. Officials of the conservative Protestant Orange Order had been meeting all through that spring for the first time with the government of the Republic of Ireland, the Catholic primate in Northern Ireland, and the nationalist Social Democratic and Labour Party of Northern Ireland, in order to consider how both this unionist organization and its notoriously provocative Twelfth of July parades might continue to exist in the era of reconciliation.

Commemorating the 1690 Battle of the Boyne in which English Protestant control over Ireland was decisively established, the Twelfth of July parades and the bonfires on the eve had long stirred sectarian tensions. With the Twelfth a government holiday, the parades were celebrated throughout the North. The flood of lodge banners and the shrill flute bands with their huge Lambeg drums passed along much-disputed routes, claimed as traditional but often passing through Catholic neighborhoods. The parades were received as visual, sonoral, and territorial aggression by most Catholics, and in some cases were meant as such. From the outbreak of the Troubles in 1970, the parades saw repeated sectarian skirmishing, with violent disturbances in the mid-1990s leading to the banning of the parade from nationalist areas in 1998. Still after the Good Friday Agreement, tensions were sustained by the combination of old habits and heavy drinking, and in 2005 loyalist paramilitary violence had broken out after one local parade, while Catholics attacked police after another.

Thus in the era of reconciliation the Orange Order was obliged to confront its own reputation as a body of legacy thugs. In June 2006 the secretary of the order's Grand Lodge, Drew Nelson, announced a solution: a "rebranding" of the marching season as Orangefest, a celebration of the heritage of one of the United Kingdom's ethnic minorities. "I would like to see the Twelfth of July become a tourist attraction. It's one of the most colourful spectacles. . . . Only the Notting Hill carnival can beat it in the British Isles. Notting Hill has overcome its problems of drugs, [policing, and] deaths. We can overcome our problems" (Bowcott 2006).

To substantiate its good faith, the Grand Lodge moved toward developing a code of conduct for the parade and even conceded that some form of regulation from the government would be helpful, recognizing at last the authority of the Parades Commission created in 1998. The Order accepted containment as a condition of survival. The pain was sweetened by government concessions: for the first time since 1970, the British Army was not deployed on the streets of Belfast to keep order during the parade ("Soldiers in Barracks for Twelfth" 2006). And the Grand Lodge obtained a grant of £104,000 from Northern Ireland's Ministry of Social Development to hire a "development officer" to manage the conversion to Orangefest ("British Govt Slammed" 2006).

The transformation of the parades from tangible threat to intangible heritage moved slowly, however, not least because the other side had some reason to doubt the Order's ability to contain the parades. One official of the Social Democratic and Labour Party responded, "We would like to see a carnival atmosphere too, but it's difficult when one community has victims from past paramilitary attacks." Sinn Féin was likewise not encouraged by the creation of "bigotfest" (Bowcott 2006; "Hansen's 'Orangefest'" 2006). Nor were all moderate Irish Protestants. Henry McDonald, Ireland editor of the *Observer*, observed that his middle-class neighbors in Belfast, including many families of an actively unionist background, were choosing the marching season as a time to go on vacation and avoid confrontation altogether: in his view, "the Orange Order was marching into history" and the parade ritual had already become meaningless (2006).[13] A more worried Reverend Brian Kennaway, a disaffected former official of the Order, argued in the *Irish Times* that the current culturalist move was inventing an exclusionary tradition for the Order that narrowed its base and denied the authentic cultural, religious, and regional pluralism found in the history of the organization (2006). Women activists from unionist families expressed skepticism that the rebranding would change the heavy parade drinking, which they described as an almost inevitable incitement to violence both sectarian and domestic (Community Arts Forum 2007). The parade could hardly be inclusive of Catholics and immigrants when it was not even inclusive of Protestant women, one observed.

The *London Independent* documented the second production of the Twelfth of July as festival in 2007. A tourist brochure referred to the event as a "kaleidoscope of culture and colour" and a "family-friendly pageant," although it suggested avoiding the bonfires that would take place the night before.[14] Once an exclusionary claiming of public space, the parade now offered itself to the gaze of the other. "We want the whole community to gain from this festival," said Drew Nelson. "We went to Notting Hill Carnival, to learn from that." The *Independent* identified a profit motive supporting the peaceful turn: a block of two-bedroom flats in a newly renovated industrial building along the Ormeau Road, frequent scene of parade conflicts in the past, had recently sold out within hours at £360,000 per unit ("Orange Order Marches On" 2007).

A new resonance thus emerges in the ongoing parallel to Notting Hill (the parade was by now routinely described as "Britain's second-largest carnival, after London's Notting Hill Carnival"). Home to supermodels and Conservative Party leader David Cameron, Notting Hill is known today as one of London's most expensive enclaves after two hundred years as a slum, heavily populated since 1948 by immigrants from the West Indies. But in London as in Belfast, gentrification in fact resolved nothing: the stigmatized population was pushed away but continues to push back. The Notting Hill Carnival, begun in the late 1950s as an act of self-assertion by Trinidadian migrants in response to white violence, has burgeoned in the face of continual tension with both the police and the borough authorities. One side alleges repression, the other violence and disorder. The strategy of accommodation, as later in Northern Ireland, has been "rebranding": a public relations campaign to transform the image of the event in order to generate wealth from it, nominally by clarifying its unique appeal to consumers and in fact by changing its key.[15] The carnival is now represented by its organizers and explicitly recognized by media and local authorities not as a black political event[16] but as a multicultural celebration. As is typical, this has involved much disciplining of the public spaces and a migration of the performances most important to insiders to the less visible peripheries of the event. The carnival bills itself now as the largest street festival in Europe, drawing artists and performers from around the world and hundreds of thousands of nonblack Londoners in search of a good party on the August Bank Holiday. Media coverage of the event is found not in the political news or the social news but is divided rather between the leisure section and the police report.

For the Orange Order to claim a parallel to the Notting Hill Carnival thus spoke to more than just the hope for economic revival through gentrification. "We're celebrating our survival," said Drew Nelson. "As a community that has been constantly under attack for 400 years, so we have" ("Orange Order Marches On" 2007). Good faith can be questioned when a normative parade celebrating Protestant identity and allegiance to the United Kingdom is compared to the inversive carnival of a community enslaved and then colonized by that same power. Still more curious is that the Ulstermen should choose to mark themselves and become cultural, claiming kinship with a subaltern population rather than, as historically, standing on their dignity as representatives of the mainstream. As is traditional in the masking practices of Western community-based protest, they may find the disguise of an imperfectly assimilated other to be the safest way of signaling to the state—and contemplating for themselves—their continuing inassimilable existence. More simply, they may just have found that the assumption of otherness is the price of voice for actors too unimportant to gain a hearing by Habermasian means.

The adoption of a culturalist idiom by a once-dominant social group may be seen as a defensive move, and that is surely the case here. But with the present emphasis on cultural rights in international arenas, culture can also be invoked to draw a line in the sand. Said Lord Laird, a unionist peer and parade organizer, "This is a day which celebrates our culture—we are proud of our Ulster-Scots and Orange background. We want people to come out and join us, and people who don't know what we are about to come and understand who we are" ("Thousands March" 2006). No longer a commemoration of a historical event open to reinterpretation, the Twelfth had become a celebration of irreducible identity. It demanded the presence of others to recognize and accept Orange difference as an essence not subject to challenge. Thus by converting history into identity, the heritage process reduces both the meaning and the flexibility of events.

Going cultural has also allowed Ulster Protestants to garner resources. Since the initial £104,000 to hire a development officer, the Orange Order and the new organizations generated around Orangefest have established themselves among the entities vying for and routinely receiving grants from the overlapping political, cultural, and economic development institutions whose missions they can viably claim to support. In 2008, a company set up by Orange Order lodges along the border received €250,000 from, of all places, the Republic of Ireland Ministry of Community, Rural, and Gaeltacht Affairs ("Ó Cuív Grants €250,000" 2008). In Belfast, the local business community, eager for any activity to counter the current crisis, has embraced Orangefest, now enhanced by street performers, children's activities, and staged concerts. In 2009 the downtown shops opened on the Twelfth for the first time since the beginning of the Troubles. The Belfast City Centre Management partnership company obtained a grant of £23,000 from the European Union's Peace III Fund for street cleaning and other services for the occasion ("Orangefest Aims to Bridge the Gap" 2009).

Orangefest is the most publicly visible feature of a larger heritage turn that began in the 1990s (Kockel 2007; Wilson and Stapleton 2007). In 1992 the

Ulster-Scots Language Society was founded, arguing that the local version of Lowlands Scots now constituted a separate "West Germanic language" deserving protection under European Union provisions.[17] To be sure, the linguistic status, number of speakers, and very existence of Ulster Scots are hotly contested, with less than scholarly criteria on both sides of the argument.[18] Ulster Scots was mentioned in the 1998 Good Friday Agreement as part of the "cultural wealth" of Northern Ireland, and when the UK ratified the European Charter on Regional and Minority Languages, organizers received a Ministry of Culture grant to develop an Ulster-Scots Academy.[19]An Ulster-Scots Heritage Council was created in 1995 with unionist politician Nelson McCausland as its first director; he became minister for culture, arts, and leisure for the Northern Irish Government in July 2009, and for social development in 2011. In short, going cultural has achieved in the Ulster Protestant case what it achieves in many local contexts: creating administrative positions that may become sinecures or political platforms for individuals, as well as providing access to grant monies and legitimation from outside institutions. Heritage institutions help small-group elites to maintain or improve their position in a new political climate (Noyes 2006).

Because the right to culture cannot be challenged in current neoliberal international frameworks, culture can provide cover for inadmissible political projects (Noyes 2009). Although the militaristic tone of the Orange Order parades is monitored and controlled, in more private "Ulster Scots" milieus it is cultivated in a vigorous culture of commemoration and reenactment, not only of the Battle of the Boyne itself, but of the 1688 Siege of Derry, the 1789 Battle of Saintfield, which set off the Irish Rebellion, and more circuitously the prominence of the Royal Ulster Rifles in the First World War. In learning about their heritage, young boys may handle rifles, dress up in uniform, and play at military formations; photographs of this socialization commonly adorn Ulster-Scots publications.[20] The military exploits are naturally Ulster heritage, and need not imply any sinister present agenda. But they are indisputably prominent in Ulster-Scots Heritage activities, more so, for example, than linen and shipbuilding, and more so than any activities of women. Thus outsiders and former enemies might well find this emphasis disquieting, perhaps all the more so now that the military commemorations are increasingly relegated to in-group settings.

In the meantime, although the objects of violence shift, the disaffection of unemployed Protestant youth in Belfast has not been resolved by the celebration of heritage or the commercial success of Orangefest. In 2008, the festival organizers mentioned as proof of their success that Polish and Romanian immigrants had been seen in the crowd. In July 2009, an Irish blogger noted that their return was unlikely.[21] In June, a racist mob chanting slogans from the UK-wide neo-Nazi group Combat 18 assaulted the South Belfast homes of Roma immigrants in a week of violence, breaking windows with stones and setting houses on fire. Twenty families fled to a nearby church for protection, and at least a hundred Romanian nationals immediately left the country. On July 10, a letter signed "Combat 18" was delivered to Islamic, Polish, and Indian community centers in Belfast. Decorated with skulls and loyalist slogans, it read "Get out of our Queen's country before our bonfire night and parade day. . . . Other than your building will be blown up [*sic*]" (McKittrick 2009). The inclusive Orangefest is, then, a work in progress.

Have the Orangemen lost power by admitting their marginality and going cultural? Although the subaltern actor seems doomed to perform by the very fact of marking, to have his or her message eternally inflected by the fixed mask of identity through which it is spoken, the power dynamic is less straightforward than it might appear. The local is not simply subordinate, either culturally or politically. The popularity of the Notting Hill Carnival, indeed, and of the vast number of European "summer carnivals" modeled on it, is but one indicator of the power of so-called premodern performance genres upon postmodern subjects, what I have elsewhere referred to as the cultural warming of the northern hemisphere (Noyes 2007). This cultural influence, prone though it is to commodification and appropriation by global capital, is nonetheless arguably a conduit of political and economic influence, increasing the global weight of states like Brazil. Many kinds of political actors in Europe and North America, feeling a deadening of the old structures of authority, now seek to appropriate the vitality of the cultural.

More obviously, the heritage riots of the Orange Order and still more the legacy warlords of Afghanistan remind us that the local node has power to hold the entire system hostage. The U.S. military, the arm of a superpower that not long ago fancied itself a hegemon, has acknowledged that the greater the asymmetry, the greater the strategic advantage of the apparently weak party. According to *Field Manual 3-24*, "Insurgents succeed by sowing chaos and disorder anywhere; the government fails unless it maintains a degree of order everywhere" (U.S. Army/Marine Corps 2006: 4). In their different fashions, cultural containment as heritage and sociopolitical incorporation as legacy are both strategies for buying off local actors who can neither be controlled nor eliminated.

Appalachia

I first gave a talk about the conceptual relationship between legacies and heritage in March 2009, while the Obama administration was struggling to construct a bank bailout plan. In that climate, my audience immediately observed that I had missed a third term: zombie. Jason Baird Jackson and Merrill Kaplan formulated the typology between them. Heritage is what you freeze cryogenically at the point of death; legacy is what you keep on life support because you can't afford to kill it off; and zombie is the thing that you try to kill but can't: it keeps coming back to life and attacking you, like the so-called zombie banks that were devouring capital as we spoke.[22]

Less straightforward and more inadvertent than applying the legacy label or creating a heritage industry, zombification is a third possible treatment of the kind of people we once called the folk. It is not a buying-off but a refusal to engage the problematic population. It is apparent in American pop-cultural representations of rural areas, and notably of Appalachia. A heavily forested mountain region, difficult of access, with a pervasive but historically elusive Native American presence displaced by mostly Scots-Irish settlers in the eighteenth century, Appalachia was not easily incorporated into the United States' evolving machinery of governance. On the contrary, it exemplifies James C. Scott's account of why the state can't climb hills (2009). Land could not be readily surveyed and parceled, straight roads could not be built, populations could not be concentrated in urban areas, illegal liquor production (or, today, marijuana crops and crystal meth labs) could not be monitored, and schools, police forces, and mainstream churches could not reach much of the population with any regularity. Appalachia has long been the site of tax resistance and some war resistance, a place of refuge for criminals and deserters. At the same time, since the nineteenth century it has been imagined as the true reservoir of American folk identity, inhabited by the descendants of those who fought the Revolution, mountaineers who are still self-reliant, beholden to nobody, ethnically pure, and practicing their age-old traditions (Batteau 1990; Hufford 2006; Whisnant 2008). Appalachia is one of certain culturally marked regions in America, imagined as deviant not through creolization, like Louisiana, or border conflict, like Texas, but precisely by being at the heart of the old white settler nation, closed in on itself, incestuous. Appalachia is deep America: it is folk.

The image of Appalachia as isolated and untouched by modernity is belied by its centrality since the nineteenth century as a site of resource extraction: timber cutting, coal mining, and hydroelectric dam-building. State and industry have wrought continual violence on the region's landscape and its people, whose struggles for equitable labor conditions have repeatedly been met with repression unbecoming a democracy, served out by company-paid private security firms and the U.S. Army itself (Eller 1982, 2008; Portelli 1991). The Appalachian landscape has been transformed by the Tennessee Valley Authority's submerging of whole territories under water, by long-burning coal fires in the deep mines, later by strip mining that contaminated watersheds, and most recently by mountaintop removal (Davis 2000). This technique for efficient extraction with a minimal labor force involves the construction of huge machines in situ that blow and scrape the top off a mountain to reach massive seams of coal easily, dumping the residue in the adjacent valley.

Public alarm about the environmental implications of mountaintop removal and vigorous local activism face powerful counterweights. The coal companies themselves, with generations of lobbying experience, have a comfortable relationship with legislators and judges in the mountain states. Ever-mounting demand for energy in a context of anxiety about foreign oil and nuclear power means that coal-burning power plants are likely to remain the primary feeder of the American power grid and the major source of carbon emissions for years to come. The political concern with energy independence tends to distract attention from the problems of coal, and perhaps a changing imaginary of energy, abetted by coal company rhetorics, makes it still easier for Appalachia's problems to disappear.[23]

Energy companies represent themselves to the public as providing a frictionless flow of clean energy that sustains the power grid, itself, like the Internet, an image of a flexible self-adjusting, all-encompassing network. The companies have names like "Constellation Energy": their advertisements show stars twinkling in clear skies, or light zapping through networks, at once pristine and postmodern (Tucker 2009). And indeed we no longer think of the globalized U.S. economy as bound to localities, mechanical processes, smoke, and dirt. The smokestack is an image of an industrial past, which we can still imagine as contemporary in China, but not in our own "postindustrial" economy with its outsourced manufacturing. Instead, the grid has become the synecdoche of the new world order: Manuel Castells has gone so far as to say that it is not power but connectedness that primarily determines well-being in the network society (1997). But it is precisely the online world of infinite communicability and the associated consumer electronics, never turned off or unplugged, that demands the construction of more and more coal-burning power plants (Mouawad and Galbraith 2009; Bouissac 2009).

Both rural and industrial, its jobs and some of its people departed, Appalachia is a space off the grid, easily forgotten. The companies represent it as empty land that will be made habitable and amenable to development through mountaintop removal's creation of flat space. Thus far, those flat spaces have seen the development of one coal company golf course and a couple of prisons (Tucker 2009).

Yet Appalachia is not empty despite ongoing outmigration, and this creates problems. Some problems are visible only to inhabitants. Although the forest on the mountaintops is not incorporated land, it is an important resource for local people. As Mary Hufford has shown, the forest serves as a symbolic commons, containing old cemeteries, hunting grounds, place names, and sites of legend (2000). It is still more important as an economic commons in a context of scarce options. Appalachia is the major source for the Chinese market in wild ginseng, which garnered $450 per pound as of 2002; in 1994 the United States exported 178,111 pounds of wild ginseng (Hufford 2002: 101). Appalachians have always foraged for their own subsistence, and with the vogue for local foods forest plants such as ramps, morels, and berries have become a meaningful source of extra income. Illegal uses of the commons, such as scavenging for Native American artifacts to sell or cultivating marijuana, have for a few people replaced older income supplements such as fur trapping and moonshining. Central to local economies and economies of meaning, to say nothing of a larger environmental balance, the forest is not valued in the calculus of mountaintop removal. Because of its economic value, wild ginseng can be harvested only with a permit, with severe penalties applying to individual violators. But the plant's habitat can be legally destroyed by mountaintop removal (117). On the other hand, death wins more legal respect than life: the presence of a cemetery and proof that it is regularly visited has in at least one case delayed the construction of a slurry reservoir (116).

The immediate human consequences of coal extraction receive some attention from investigative journalists and from civil society within and beyond the region. A 2009 series of articles in the *New York Times* cited routine, unprosecuted violations of the Clean Water Act by coal companies and coal-burning power plants, exacerbated rather than improved by the spread of residue-accumulating scrubbing technologies. The consequences include not only long-term, hard-to-substantiate increases in cancer and other diseases, but widespread incidences of skin burns and damaged tooth enamel immediately associable with the use of the public water supply in areas such as Prenter, West Virginia ("Toxic Waters" 2009). Some churches have assumed an activist role as their parishioners find their water supplies contaminated or cut off by mountaintop removal, intensifying a growing environmentalist movement among American evangelicals ("Is God Green?" 2006). Advocacy groups such as Ohio Citizen Action conduct "good neighbor campaigns" relying on community pressure rather than the slow machinery of law and regulation to influence the practices of companies, but their successes to date have come from industries other than coal.

Catastrophes, with their immediate impact, spectacularity, and, not least, expensive consequences might be supposed more newsworthy than the slow damage inflicted by most coal pollution. Nonetheless, perhaps few Americans outside the region are aware of the spill of coal ash over Kingston, Tennessee, in December 2008. This was the largest industrial accident in U.S. history prior to the April 2010 BP Gulf of Mexico oil spill, and an environmental accident more than thirty times the size of the Exxon Valdes oil spill. Carcinogenic fly ash from a containment pond at the Kingston Fossil Plant, eventually measured at 1.1 billion gallons, spilled over three hundred acres of land and into the Emory River, a tributary of the Tennessee River, which provides the drinking water for millions of people downstream.[24] The most timely coverage in a major U.S. newspaper appeared in the *New York Times* the following day, with photographs of a quasi-lunar landscape, but not on the front page, appearing on page A17 in the national news (Dewan 2008a). Most news media barely noticed it in the following weeks, although the *Times* and the Associated Press have covered major developments in the aftermath.[25] The affected land being largely owned by the Tennessee Valley Authority, there were no immediate human injuries. Twenty-two residences were immediately evacuated, and area children started coughing once the sludge dried back into fine ash; other effects will, as always, be more ambiguous and slower to reveal themselves (Dewan 2008a; Copeland 2009). The TVA's immediate response was felt by many locals to have been inadequately candid: it did not warn people to avoid direct contact with the ash until one week later and issued analyses of water samples judged drinkable that were in fact collected upstream from the spill (Dewan 2008b). The means of redress are characteristic. An estimated $1 billion will be spent on cleanup, focused on protection of the Tennessee River. Efforts at remedial regulation to secure sites elsewhere are stalled. Site cleanup has involved the negotiation of the removal of the ash to a site in Perry County, Alabama (impoverished and 70 percent black), where local residents are anxious in their turn about the safety of the proposed landfill but have been promised thirty jobs and a hosting fee that increases the county's existing annual budget by 40 percent (Dewan 2009). Compensation paid to displaced families in Kingston provided for their resettlement elsewhere rather than for the cleanup of their properties ("TVA Buys 71 Properties" 2009). In addition, Roane County leaders are seeking $40 million in compensation from TVA to help the community to repair its image and economy, based on real estate for retirees ("Tennessee County Wants Millions" 2009). Displacement and image repair take precedence over regulation and land repair. None of this is exciting significant national attention.[26]

Consigned still deeper in the past of the American imaginary now that the heroic age of industrialization and unionization is over, Appalachia has come to embody what economists call externalities (Hufford 2004). We might just call it spillover: the unintended consequences of pollution and destruction that are not considered in the design of industrial production processes or calculated into their costs. They are also external because we on the grid rarely talk about them. But while damaged land and human suffering have long been effaced in national narratives of progress, it is not so with Appalachian culture, which in the form of music has become both self-reproducing and phantasmagoric, like Gretchen's song from the prison. The haunting voice of Ralph Stanley singing "O Death" forever announces the disappearance of the body that emitted it, while ever spreading its own social reach. Bluegrass music focused and stylized Appalachians' own idealization of their past as their world changed around them or they were forced to leave it (Cantwell 2003). Country music today performs the same service for a larger Anglophone world of displaced or marginalized rural people, embodying nostalgias from Australia to Newfoundland. The music moves independently of the land and increasingly of its inhabitants, too fluid even to be pinned down to a list of intangibles connected to place. To be sure, Appalachia also has a conventional heritage industry and heritage institutions, evolved from the folklorism of social work in the region in an earlier age. But these have increasingly been appropriated by local people and turned to local agendas (Whisnant 2008). Conversely, the larger American public is uneasy about Appalachia in ways that are not amenable to its containment as heritage, while structural embarrassments do not conduce to Appalachia's mobilization as legacy. Damaged environmentally and economically beyond easy repair, still infrastructurally deficient in ways unimaginable to suburban Americans, effaced from public view as far as possible, the region nonetheless contains rights-bearing American citizens. This contradiction is registered as uncanny.

When Kentucky sculptor Willard Tucker suggested to me that the hillbilly was being fused with the zombie in current popular imaginings, I did a Google search. "Zombie" plus "hillbilly" raised almost four million hits in April 2009. Although many of these referred to an industrial rock album called *Hellbilly Deluxe* by a musician named Rob Zombie—itself a telling title—the pervasiveness of the image was nonetheless apparent. It occurred frequently in the neighborhood of Halloween costumes and haunted houses. A homesick student volunteering in Burkina Faso posted photos of his October 31 hillbilly zombie getup on Flickr; an Ohio man enjoys a lively virtual life as a "Hillbilly Zombie Hunter."[27] Most extensively, the mad hillbilly, inbred and illiterate, has indeed migrated from American legendry and jokelore to the world of horror movies, both serious and burlesque.

The template for the current story is a mainstream Hollywood film, John Boorman's 1972 *Deliverance*, taken from the 1970 novel by James Dickey. It deals with four men from suburban Atlanta who go on a canoeing trip in northern Georgia to ride "the last wild, untamed, unpolluted, unfucked-up river in the South" before it is submerged beneath a new dam.[28] The men are received with suspicion as probable emissaries from the power company. They themselves have strong stereotypes of the mountain people as moonshiners damaged by generations of incest, and their preconceptions of chaos come true when they are assaulted in the wilderness by a pair of hillbillies with shotguns. The rape of the landscape is repaid by the rape of one of the visiting canoers. Confronted by the natives, the wildness of the river, and their own weaknesses, the men's commitment to civilization dissolves, and after multiple murders, the survivors escape, hoping to leave the evidence behind them as the gorge is inundated by the dammed waters.

A succession of B-grade horror films reproduces the plotline, continuing into the present with such do-it-yourself titles as *Hillbilly Zombies from Hell.*[29] Some of the most influential, like *The Texas Chainsaw Massacre* (1974) and *The Hills Have Eyes* (1977) are set in rural regions elsewhere, but by the turn of the millennium they were concentrating in Appalachia.[30] In every case the chronotope is a deviation off the road of modernity into the backward space of the hills (cf. Stewart 1996). A car accident or a camping trip brings normal middle-class suburbanites into contact with animalistic, often cannibal hillbillies, driving pickup trucks, wearing overalls, carrying old shotguns or perhaps Indian bows and arrows, moving easily through the wild nature that obstructs the vision of the visitors. But like *Deliverance* itself, each film carries an opening reminder that the hills are not genuinely isolated from modernity: it is modernity that has transformed them. The first intimation of a shift between worlds often takes place at a gas station, the liminal place that perhaps reminds us that the need to harness energy maintains a link between civilization and wilderness. Moreover, the films typically begin with an overt reference to environmental transformation.[31] The hydroelectric dam of *Deliverance* is echoed in films of less artistic ambition. In *The Hills Have Eyes* there is an abandoned Defense Department testing site; the 2003 *Wrong Turn* (Summit Pictures) has a chemical spill; less directly, in *Cabin Fever* (Black Sky Entertainment, 2002) the water carries a skin-eating disease. In the extreme spoof *Redneck Zombies* (Troma Entertainment 1987) radioactive waste is used to spike moonshine. Although the main characters speak of the natives as primitive and backward, these clues in the films make clear that the hills do not predate but postdate civilization, that the violence suffered by the metropolitan characters is an inevitable return, a mimetic acting out of harm done (Shaw 2005).

Hillbilly horror in this respect can be seen as a variant of the postwar "toxic avenger" narrative that starts with the mutant dragon Godzilla: movies about monsters of hybrid autochthony, the local muck animated into menacing but inchoate form by the residues of environmental contaminants. Although it is burlesque horror film that memorably names the genre, the linkage between hybrid monsters and industrial failure exists in oral tradition as well. For Appalachia itself we can cite the 1966–67 Mothman reports from West Virginia, sighted repeatedly in the vicinity of an abandoned dynamite factory and a suspension bridge that collapsed a few months after the sightings, killing forty-six people (Tucker, personal communication; and the invaluable *Wikipedia*).

But the peculiar horror of the hillbilly zombie comes from the humanity of the monster. The famous "dueling banjos" scene in *Deliverance* tests the possibility of community between the visitors and the natives, ultimately refused by both sides. Notable in the momentary musical communitas is the pattern of interrogatives. Waiting at the gas station, the outsider Drew offers a chord on his guitar, waiting to see whether a boy with a banjo on the porch of a nearby house will pick it up. The boy is albino and appears to have Down's syndrome. ("Talk about genetic deficiencies," murmurs another of the visitors.) Encouraged by the response, he tries another chord, a harmonic pattern, a melodic line, another line. The boy first tentatively repeats, then varies the phrases, later takes the melodic lead, and finally leaves the visitor behind altogether. The visitors clap along awkwardly; one of the men from the gas station begins fluently to dance. The scene encapsulates the mimetic relationship of the entire film, but, an inverted mise en abyme, it models positive rather than negative reciprocity. Music alone can make a bridge across the river. One of the phrases tested is the first line of "Yankee Doodle." Through his guitar, Drew is asking the child, "Are you, too, American?"

American, yes. Assimilated, no, and unwilling to be made invisible. This is the message of the cultural style associated with postindustrial and postmigration Appalachia, known as "white trash." From a stigmatizing label imposed from outside, the term has been appropriated as a badge of subcultural identity and interfused with American patriotism. At the same time, its resonance has changed somewhat. Scholars have commonly understood the label to mark the anomaly of white poverty in a society that naturalizes social class as racial hierarchy (Hartigan 1997). But increasingly, perhaps, the emphasis falls on trash rather than whiteness, signaling the transformation of the industrial working class to a residue of modernity, people for whom society has no current use.[32] This marginality becomes a site of performative freedom, allowing acting out of a kind unavailable to those of us with a stake in the system. White trash culture performs matter out of place: junked cars on front lawns, bodies bursting out of clothing, shouting in public places, twanged notes that veer out of tune (Cantwell 2009). It lends itself to burlesque (Penley 1997). It has become the preferred idiom of recreational transgression for working-class white people.[33] A broader conservative populist culture celebrates drinking, guns, junkyards, wild behavior, pickup trucks, country music, racism and xenophobia, nonstandard English, and patriotism combined with antitax, antigovernment rhetoric. The point of this behavior is less its traditional character than its conspicuous flouting of middle-class norms in the present, but these actors also have reason to associate cultural change with the rise of a postindustrial capitalism that has hurt them.

The outrageousness lends itself also to serious protest, as when gentrification is fought by the self-trashing of a community (Morris 1998), and in the carnivalesque elements of mountaintop removal activism (Hufford 2004). Larry Gibson, the Kayford Mountain activist who has defied death threats and lawsuits in refusing to surrender his property for mountaintop removal, now lives on a single hilltop surrounded by 12,000 acres of scraped earth. In his campaign against removal, he wears overalls and a straw hat every day, speaks the dialect. He is a zombie: his cause should be history, yet he refuses to go away. Horrific, burlesque, or both, the hillbilly image today stands for a return of the repressed. At the end of Boorman's film, the protagonists leave the river and the dead bodies behind, trusting the lake made by the new dam to cover up all evidence of their misadventure. But the narrator, now apparently safe back in his suburban home, dreams of the dead hand of the murdered hillbilly rising out of the lake to point an accusatory finger.[34]

From Framing Anomalies to Universal Marking?

I have described three very different levels of discursive practice: the rhetorical spinning of a tactical accommodation in Afghanistan, a rebranding campaign with a complex institutional apparatus in Northern Ireland, and a diffuse social imaginary that has emerged in relation to Appalachia. Aware of the mismatches between these cases, I want nonetheless to suggest that there exists a broad semantic field in which problematic survivals or local threats can be addressed from a position of power. There are different ways in which coevalness can be denied. Each predication of pastness, euphemistic or dysphemistic, entails a different policy option for managing the problem (Fernandez 1986); see Table 1.

Each example highlights an asymmetry: powerful actors go unmarked, while the subaltern are marked by their presumed alterity. Each framing nonetheless recognizes the agency of the marked actors. The legacy warlords are acknowledged as too powerful to be eliminated or assimilated by force. The zombie fantasy implicitly concedes the persistent existence and citizenship rights of the people of Appalachia, and Appalachians themselves may exaggerate their perceptible distinctiveness as an assertion of presence. The heritage strategy, as practiced in Northern Ireland and elsewhere, is effective in buying off local elites and containing potential excesses for the time being, but by reifying differential identities it also reinforces essentialisms and may incubate subsequent extremisms.

Nor are these three terms the only alternatives. A more complete paradigm can be constructed along two axes: whether a practice and its practitioners are construed as of the past or present, and whether they are incorporated into or kept at a distance from mainstream institutions (see Figure 1) Needless to say, I am constructing ideal types and am speaking of representations, not realities.

Table 1. Conceptualizing Threats as Survivals

Project	*Threat*	*System threatened*	*Strategy*	*Discursive relegation to past; euphemism or dysphemism*
NATO Afghan mission	Diversity of population and local strongmen; →failed state and regional instability	International system, Western hegemony, Afghan state	Eradication preferred, but impossible; *incorporation* through buying off and encouraging relations	*Legacy* warlords [vs. externalization of "the terrorists"]
Northern Irish reconciliation; Belfast reconstruction and development	Orange Order parades	NI political order; UK economy	*Containment, reduction, disguise*; *incorporation* through buying off and allowing cultural enclave	OrangeFest as *heritage*
Mining and damming Appalachia for energy resources	Local protesters; environmental disaster	Energy supply→"the grid"	*Externalization* as means to eradication	*Empty* land, but irruptions of the effaced population as degenerate or *zombie* hillbillies

The most fully institutionalized of the concepts is "heritage." Heritage creates an enclave. Heritage is framed and sacred: to be looked at, not touched by outsiders. It has the right to be but not the right to do. Although it generates economic activity around its edges, heritage itself is conceived as inert and defiled by change. When heritage is celebrated to the neglect of present engagements, it becomes like Snow White in the glass case, a death in life arousing a kind of necrophilia, which, needless to say, does not reproduce the community.

"Legacy" falls squarely in the middle of the diagram: it has to be made to work but is marked as a problem. "Zombie" is represented as external to the system but invasive of it, damaging to it.

But there are other ways of framing the anomaly, with generally more positive implications. "Fusion" and the broader framework of "world culture"

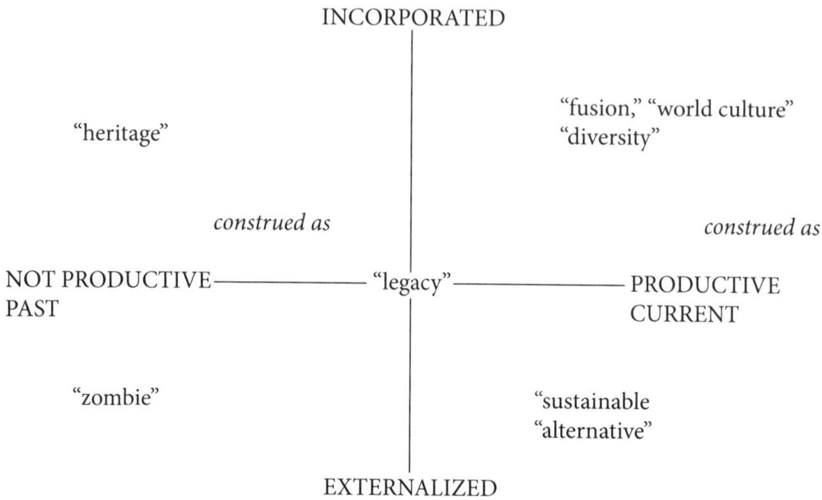

Figure 1. Labeling anomalies: a broader view.

allow traditions to live and interact in the present, with all of the trade-offs entailed. If heritage is pure, fusion is impure. Heritage is enclosed; fusion is networked. Heritage is immobile; fusion takes commodity form and circulates. “Diversity,” attached to persons more than to practices, is a euphemism according positive value to difference. Like heritage, it attaches difference to social identity and so restricts it from circulation, but unlike heritage and like legacy, it purports to integrate difference into social and political institutions.

In the final quadrant of the figure we find terms such as “alternative” and “sustainable,” applied to practices more often than to persons. For confirmation that they fall into a common paradigm with terms like “heritage,” I can point to the implicit understanding of my own tribe, the sort of scholars and culture workers who belong to the American Folklore Society and in safe settings refer to themselves as folklorists. One such practitioner, Rory Turner, took the lead in creating a master’s program at Goucher College in Maryland. It is essentially a program in what insiders call “public folklore,” but this labeling was not judged viable, and they deliberated for some time between “Heritage Studies” and “Cultural Sustainability,” ultimately opting for the latter as better capturing the usefulness of vernacular performances and practices. “Sustainable,” in contrast to “alternative,” implies the desirability of eventual incorporation into the mainstream, but for the time being this quadrant serves as a reservoir of possibilities to be explored for that moment when, as Lewis says in *Deliverance*, "machines are gonna fail."

In all this frenzy to label and categorize, what disappears by definition is what Michael Thompson calls "rubbish" (1979). By this he means not trash—the visible pollutant or transgression—but the overlooked, the forgotten. If the mainstream is, in linguistic terms, unmarked, rubbish is the unremarked. Appalachia would be rubbish, were there not people in the region who decline to be overlooked as well as a growing ecological consciousness among people outside the region that has enlarged the modernist conception of the system to something more holistic.

By its nature the process of seeing, categorizing, and ascribing value is not fully accessible to the consciousness of actors, so my observations are accordingly limited. It strikes me nonetheless that in the post-1968 era both the zone of the unmarked and that of the unremarked have been shrinking in relation to an ever-expanding politics of marking (endogenously claimed as a politics of recognition). One side of this history is well known. The universalisms of democratic citizenship and later of more global frameworks such as human rights were called to account for their practical exclusions, their construction of an unmarked subject that is in fact shaped by modern Western masculine bourgeois assumptions. The early civil rights movements of colonized peoples, African Americans, Northern Irish Catholics, women, and other categories attempted to claim unmarked citizenship for their members, to demonstrate that they too were rational individual actors bearing rights and capable of exercising them responsibly. When formal acceptance of such arguments failed to overcome real social exclusions, social movements turned toward identity, embracing the marked status they could not escape.

In the process, the movements succeeded not in unmarking themselves but in marking the hitherto unmarked. Actors who had imagined themselves as mainstream, average American citizens, were revealed in the course of civil rights struggles as carriers of irrational prejudices, social identities, and so on: they were not interchangeable individual units after all, but themselves located in particulars. The system was not straightforwardly enlarged to become more inclusive, as expected, but reconfigured as it incorporated new actors on terms of difference rather than uniformity. In some cases there was a defensive response from within: black power inspired white power, feminism provoked the men's movement, one fundamentalism or nationalism brought forth its mimetic rival.

Modernity did not wither away. In the absence of violent upheaval the machinery of powerful institutions does not dissolve. Rather, politicians, bureaucrats, and social entrepreneurs fighting for job security as well as corporations needing to create new market niches in a consumer economy encouraged the multiplication of identity labels and markings,[35] as did ordinary people attempting to find their footing in a world where old ways of belonging had lost credibility. The nation-state, once the mechanism of exclusion and the locus of legitimate difference, now became the guarantor of multiculturalism. Deep in our conceptual habits, the nation also furnished the model for smaller and cross-cutting identities, which reproduced many of its essentialisms, not least the necessity of having a culture (Handler 1988). Thus signs of difference proliferated without transforming underlying structures or power relations, and insofar as the signs became enshrined in institutions they trapped a growing number of actors into ever narrower identity jails.

But these rearguard actions on the part of global, national, and provincial elites attempting to maintain their positions in an existing order are countered by the forward motion of more confident or more desperate actors at all levels of power. The revelation of markedness in a world of mobile humans, commodities, and technologies taught some actors not that identities were fixed but that they were performative, to be assumed and thrown off as needed. The mark is an act as well as a fact. If some actors have an investment in the structured community with its center, periphery, and boundaries, others celebrate the flexible network, or have no choice but to construct it. Disruptive as he is to the powers above him, the warlord nonetheless has his own power base to conserve. But the zombie has to go out and find food.

The real legacy system is what the 1960s called "*the* system." And the real legacy discourse is that of modernity, the operating fiction that (1) the system exists; that (2) it would be transparent, knowable, and predictable were it not for local disruptions; and that (3) good management can either incorporate or eradicate these disruptions. Would anyone still make these assertions of the international financial system? Are they tenable of the international political system, with the U.S. rueful admission of our vulnerability to the "unknown unknowns"? Complexity theory would tell us that increasingly, the system *is* the disruptions, the events. Thus those of us concerned with cultural practices should not be too quick to conclude—optimistically or pessimistically—that incorporation into the inventory means real containment or that the ICH regime is the end of history. On the contrary, the world is being remade from each of those little local nodes. However many bodies we bury, the intangibles of performance and practice will continue to elude our grasp.

Chapter 3

The Right to Remain Cultural: Is Culture a Right in the Neoliberal Caribbean?

Philip W. Scher

> Stamped on that image is the old colonial grimace of the laughing nigger, steelbandsman, carnival masker, calypsonian and limbo dancer . . . trapped in the State's concept of the folk form . . . the symbol of a carefree, accommodating culture, an adjunct to tourism, since the state is impatient with anything it cannot trade.
>
> —Derek Walcott, "What the Twilight Says"

> No one shall have a cultural identity imposed or be assimilated into a cultural community against one's will.
>
> —Fribourg Declaration

This chapter attempts to forge a link between theories of the commodification of culture, national identity, neoliberal political economy, and Michel Foucault's concept of *biopolitics*, as a way of thinking through the idea of cultural rights as human rights. I am examining here state-sanctioned instances of national heritage, both tangible and intangible, in the Caribbean to suggest that culture in these small, postcolonial societies is increasingly seen as a valuable commodity. Furthermore, it is seen as a resource on which the state can draw not only to develop the economy but also to reinforce the state's claims to sovereignty. Through such strategies as nation branding and cultural and heritage tourism Caribbean governments encourage local populations to consider their actions and behaviors, both public and private (a distinction that is increasingly blurred), as self-consciously cultural. In addition such cultural behaviors, appropriately maintained and perpetuated, are seen as vital for the prosperity and strength of the nation as a whole. In this way culture ceases being simply a right for people and becomes an adjunct to the aspirations of the state as it promotes its cultural brand globally. There are of course, many sites of tension, resistance, and unpredictability where simple co-optation is just not possible. In other words, this is by no means a fait accompli on the part of the structures of governance. Indeed, as we shall see, because of the relatively diffuse nature of such mechanisms of power the ability to control actions and behaviors is somewhat limited. What concerns me here is not the complete efficacy of state cultural policies but their nature and design. These reveal a great deal about the position that small states find themselves in with regard to how to think about culture as a resource and how to manage it effectively.

It is important, early on, to establish that what I mean by state-sanctioned public performances or instances of heritage includes a general definition of what the state means by "heritage" (and how such ideas circulate globally), the idea of the heritage itself enacted or on display in a space theoretically accessible to all, and the notion that what is being performed is of the public; created by them or their forebears and performed for them. I stress this early on, because I would like to distinguish my exploration of cultural policy here from that work that deals with culture that is not, in the first instance, conceived of as "folklore" or "heritage," but perhaps considered part of the contemporary arts.

This is an important distinction, even if only very roughly made at this point, not because it distinguishes kinds of art or culture in any important generic way, but because it distinguishes attitudes about such arts in ways that illuminate not only general conceptions of these kinds of art but, more important, state conceptions of government's role in public life. That is, in many cases the role of the government in supporting, censoring, or critiquing art is decried when that art is thought to originate from private individuals acting in their capacity as free citizens. However, the notion of government support or intervention tends to be considered quite differently when the arts in question are understood to be part of a collective or national patrimony, created not by known individuals, but by the "people."[1] This distinction, like so many in the world of heritage and cultural rights, must be made with the understanding that it is not a clear one. There are many examples, for instance, of indigenous artists using aspects of "intangible heritage" in their production of art forms that circulate in the contemporary art market. The status of the artists as indigenous, the content as partly "collective," and the medium as modern or perhaps even strictly "Western," should give pause to anyone devoted to neat categories.

My essay intervenes in this debate at precisely the point where the state has decided, in addition to helping define, preserve, and protect national culture, to utilize it as an explicit part of its economic development policy. This version of the general idea of the commodification of cultural forms is a kind of governmentality (L. Smith 2007; Hafstein 2004a) that has become, in the contemporary climate of neoliberal globalization, truly imperative for, specifically, Caribbean nation-states. That is, with dwindling options for the generation of revenue, national cultural heritage is seen as a way to diversify primarily the tourism economy. It is a new product to sell. The novel opportunities presented by the development of heritage tourism industries in the Caribbean encompass both tangible and intangible worlds (and yes, again these cannot be neatly separated). But whether heritage tourism development has focused on intangible cultural forms such as carnival in Trinidad or Maroon villages in Jamaica, natural heritage such as national parks in Grenada or Dominica, or built/tangible heritage such as Haiti's Citadel, the old cities and plazas of the Dominican Republic, Cuba, Curaçao, or Bermuda, or serial forms of heritage that encompass it all such as the sugar industry in Barbados, it has become bound up with a nationalist ideology whose agenda has now been reconfigured by the growing hegemony of the economic order of globalization. That is, the state, increasingly limited under neoliberal regimes, finds what appears to be its proper role in the stewardship of the tangible heritage and expressive cultural activities of its citizens.

Thus the state's role in marshaling nationalist sentiment extends beyond the definition and presentation of national cultural heritage in the service of fostering local loyalties. For the state, redefining itself under a new political economic ideology, "selling" culture, acts as a strategy for diversifying the economy *and* reinforcing its claims as a legitimate political presence. There is in this, of course, the persistent tension between the tenets of neoliberalism and the definition of the state in that whereas the former is generally viewed as striving to limit the powers of the state, the state may find in the commodification of national culture the only way to preserve its sovereignty and centrality in the governance of a given population. Ironically, the state often seeks private sector assistance in the form of marketing executives and advertising agencies in developing its national cultural product for sale: generally called "nation branding" (see Aronczyk 2008). What makes this relationship more complex is that because expressive culture has to do with performances, there is always the threat of changing meanings, innovations, creative appropriations, or utter disinterest on the part of performers and audiences. This makes state management of a consistent, iterable, and controlled cultural product extremely difficult.

In the case of the Caribbean, a region shaped by and ultimately dependent upon the larger nation-states of Europe and North America and now such transnational organizations as the World Trade Organization, World Bank, International Monetary Fund, and UNESCO, culture is increasingly seen as a major source for the generation of revenue especially as other economic options fail. Although export-led strategies (the newest area of hope for economic strategists in the region) tend not to focus on tourism, nation-branding strategists do focus on tourism as one element of the consumption of products with a national brand identity. This has a variety of consequences for Caribbean people and the performance of their national identities. Indeed, under nation-branding initiatives and tourism expansion projects more and more of the daily behaviors of Caribbean people come under scrutiny *as* national identity and in this way a greater share of daily life is evaluated as "culture" and governed accordingly. In this way, I see the intervention of the state as a part of the "biopoliticization" of culture.

Biopolitics

The concept of biopolitics I use here comes from the work of Michel Foucault. His formulation of "biopower" and the biopolitical comes from his later work.[2] In earlier writings Foucault had spent a great deal of energy theorizing the "disciplinary society." That is that society "in which social command is constructed through a diffuse network of *dispositifs* or apparatuses that produce and regulate customs, habits, and productive practices" (Hardt and Negri 2000: 23). The society of biopower, or the society of control as opposed to the society of command, emerges slowly through industrialism and blossoms in the era of postindustrialist capital production, in the era most commonly referred to as "postmodern" but which we might more fruitfully label as the age of neoliberalism in this context.

Under this new regime of production, control becomes increasingly democratic, "immanent to the social field, distributed throughout the brains and bodies of citizens" (Hardt and Negri 2000: 23). No longer reliant on institutions such as the asylum, the prison, the hospital, and the school, power is now exercised through technologies such as information networks and communication systems as well as through the monitoring of bodies through policies related to health and health care, nutrition, sexual practices, and so on. Michael Hardt and Antonio Negri point out that multinational corporations largely supersede the authority of nation-states by putting them at the disposal of flows of goods, services, technologies, and people. Yet inasmuch as the nation-state has adapted to the pressures of neoliberalism, it has increasingly thought of itself as a kind of corporate entity or at least a body that should adopt some of the practices of corporations. In this sense the nation-state becomes an instrument of the logic of neoliberalism. And whereas I agree with some of this position, the Caribbean provides ample evidence that Hardt and Negri's characterization of the direction of neoliberalism requires some modification (Ong 2007; Ferguson 2007). Specifically, their assertion that with neoliberal globalization there is/will be a "decline of the nation-state" and a "withering of civil society" accompanied by a freeing of people from the "biopolitical technologies of national citizenship" ignores the contingency of national culture being the marketed commodity and the state emerging as the vendor.

Thus, I am making an argument for the expansion of what Michel Foucault meant by biopower: "forms of power exercised over persons specifically in so far as they are thought of as living beings: a politics concerned with subjects as members of a population, in which issues of individual sexual and reproductive conduct interconnect with issues of national policy and power" (Gordon 1991: 4–5). Here, of course, I am moving the notion beyond reproduction and sexuality, health and safety, to include forms of censure and sanction related to cultural performances. But the key issue is the relationship between conduct and national policy and power. For Michel Foucault, who developed the theory of biopower through a series of lectures in the mid-1970s, "biopolitics deals with the population, with the population as political problem, as a problem that is at once scientific and political, as a biological problem and as power's problem" (Foucault 2003: 245). Foucault does not explicitly refer to cultural practices or performance in these lectures. Indeed, Foucault cautions that what he is talking about is not a disciplinary technology enacted by the state on individuals or individual bodies as such. It is not the same kind of disciplinary technology that he discusses in other works such as *Discipline and Punish* (1977), in which the sovereign marks individual bodies with the legible exercise of power, and in which individual bodies are straightened, aligned, regimented, and/or otherwise made orderly. Biopower speaks at a more abstracted level of populations, of statistics dealing with such issues as birth rates, mortality, disease and sees these phenomena as directly within the scope of power.

My reading of Foucault, however, sees implicit in this discussion a link between analyzing and managing populations as an aspect of sovereignty that is, ultimately, charged with preserving the productivity of the constituency. He writes with regard to the phenomena of illness: "These were illnesses that were difficult to eradicate and that were not regarded as epidemics that caused more frequent deaths, but as permanent factors which—and this was how they were dealt with—sapped the population's strength, shortened the working week, wasted energy, and cost money, both because they led to a fall in production and because treating them was expensive" (Foucault 2003: 244). In other words, new technologies of power, those he calls biopolitical, signal a shift from sovereign power inscribing its will on individual bodies to discipline them to managing populations in order to control or at least predict mass phenomena especially as it is linked to their economic and political effects.

Yet in this distinction, one still finds something missing. Namely, that there is something between technologies of discipline and technologies of biopower, or perhaps more accurately, there are overlaps between these technologies of power, that they work in concert and that they work at different levels. In terms of the institutions surrounding the formation and perpetuation of the tourism industry in the Caribbean, the imbrication of nationalist and economic spheres in the region yields new strategies on the part of local institutions and the state. Nationalism is directly related to a specific industry, overlays that industry in the sense that since it is culture being sold and since it is local/national culture being sold, the degree to which, as a citizen, one contributes to the health of that industry is the degree to which one contributes to the health of national culture. And as participation in the "commodified nationalism" of the region increases, the scrutiny of those national behaviors increases by powerful institutions through biopolitical technologies.

I want to address, then, the idea of culture as a *right*, in the context of culture as a commodity. Additionally, I want to raise a question about the idea of culture as a right under circumstances where culture, increasingly defined along fairly narrow lines, becomes not simply a "right" but a kind of economic requirement. As culture becomes something regional governments and their related agencies in the Caribbean are interested in marketing and selling, it is analogized with other export commodities such as oil, natural gas, or sugar cane. In likening expressive culture to other exportable material goods state agencies speak of gaining market share, acquiring brand name recognition, and finding a niche in the global market of culture and tourism. And just as it would be considered an act of sabotage or perhaps treason to destroy such natural resources, it is similarly conceived as unpatriotic not to do one's cultural duty.

Yet the act of name branding nations and their cultural forms in the interest of securing a comparative advantage in the region has consequences for thinking of culture as an individual or even a collective right. The commercial role culture plays and the way in which it must play it remove culture as a community choice in terms of both whether or not individuals care to engage with it and how it is defined in the first place. Additionally, the criteria for who does and does not "belong" to certain groups and therefore who does and does not have the "right" to identify with, participate in, or even profit from a given culture is still a dangerously open question.

Theoretically culture as a right would allow for community cultures to survive, flourish, or disappear as the case may be, inasmuch as certain cultural forms and practices continue to be relevant to the population in question. But the global circumstances that create the contexts in which cultural activities exist are rarely in the hands of the culture bearers themselves. In some instances, such as in the Caribbean, at least in the rhetoric of state agencies, culture literally cannot afford to be lost or changed. And this impetus does always or even often emerge from within the group but from without in two (linked) ways: the first economic and the second perceptual. Before continuing on to a detailed analysis of these two issues, some background on cultural rights as human rights is necessary.

Culture as a Human Right: Some Background and Problems

In elucidating the origins of the idea of cultural rights as human rights one is immediately struck by the obvious conundrum, how is a group identity a part of the inalienable rights of individual humans? If we understand the historical and constructed nature of culture can we still ascribe it an almost genetic permanence and immutability? For we seem to need to ascribe to culture that notion of concreteness if we are to make it a part of the other rights we normally confer on people in the sense that we must be able to identify something or some things to which people have some kind of right. Or do we? In article 3 of the Universal Declaration of Human Rights we already run into a "cultural" problem. The article claims that "everyone has the right to life, liberty and security of person." Life and security of person, for all intents and purposes, may be rather generally and unproblematically seen as transcendent in the sense that they relate to the physical body of the individual (although even this is hardly unproblematic). But the issue of liberty, to me, seems highly charged and can be almost immediately contested on cultural grounds. What is meant by liberty? For whom? Who defines such a thing? How are individuals seen as exercising liberty? But the issue of culture as a human right becomes explicit if rather tangential in article 27, in which it is stated that "everyone has the right to freely participate in the cultural life of the community." Here the idea of culture as a right is actually better framed as the idea that the right itself is manifested as a choice to participate in something called "the cultural life of the community." The content of that cultural life, what it actually looks like, is composed of, is of course, left open. How can it not be? The "cultural life" of any community is theoretically diverse and in the continual process of change. But at the same time, any cultural life, at any given moment, must have some kind of substance that can be described or experienced. Otherwise what can someone choose to participate in? If we look at the wording of the Fribourg Declaration on Cultural Rights, article 2 we find the following definitions:

> a. The term "culture" covers those values, beliefs, convictions, languages, knowledge and the arts, traditions, institutions and ways of life through which a person or a group expresses their humanity and the meaning they give to their existence and to their development;
> b. The expression "cultural identity" is understood as the sum of all cultural references through which a person, alone or in community with others, defines or constitutes oneself, communicates and wishes to be recognized in one's dignity;
> c. "Cultural community" denotes a group of persons who share references that constitute a common cultural identity they intend to preserve and develop.

One can see fairly clearly the immediate problem at least regarding the idea of choice or intent. If culture and a cultural community are considered to be the ways one "constitutes oneself" (or better yet, the way in which one is constituted) then there is no individual consciousness outside of culture that can do the choosing. Culture is not a right or a choice; it is simply a fact. But that idea would, of course, eliminate the idea of agency from culture. We can and do think of culture in objectifying ways. Indeed it is this ability that allows for the commodification of culture as a set of things. Reconciling the definition of culture as that which is constitutive (a worldview kind of definition) with the definition of culture as a catalog of things a community "intend(s) to preserve and develop" seems to me to be a crucial first step in understanding culture as a right.

Finally a problem: the universal quality of individual human rights is meant to take precedence over cultural rights. It is of course entirely possible that the list of human rights is itself a list of cultural ideas the elevation of which functions to ascribe to them a status "beyond" culture. What is left is a definition of culture that hardly threatens deep and truly different notions of personhood, identity, morality, and so on but merely views culture as that which is safely different (Wilk 1995). As I proceed in this essay I understand that the definition of culture most generally used by the state is that which sees culture as a collection of goods and activities. This is the concept most easily converted to economic considerations. It is also the definition that facilitates the idea of culture not as a right but as a duty or requirement. In establishing this idea, however, it is important to be mindful of the very different nature of the goods and resources under discussion, for these are goods and resources that have another dimension to them: they are crucial in the self-imagining that takes place in the process of cultural identity formation. The problematic set forth here involves the appropriation for economic purposes of elements crucial to the public presentation of cultural selves. It is in that sense that these cultural elements become biopolitical, and, perhaps by extension, we could see them as part of a biopolitical economy.

The Economic Problem: Nation Branding and the Case of Jamaica

The development of cultural and heritage tourism in the Caribbean comes as a result of distinct historical and economic pressures. Most recently the shaping of local economic strategies has been by agents of neoliberalism, such as the World Bank, IMF, Inter-American Development Bank, WTO, and others. The influence of such powers as the United States and European nations is not, of course, new to the region. The Caribbean, as we know it, was created almost entirely by such "global" economic powers. What is somewhat newer is the elimination of whole economic sectors by the dismantling of colonial or postcolonial era protections and guarantees that has resulted, overall yet unevenly, in a massive tourism sector. Based originally on the foreign enjoyment of the natural attributes of the islands, Caribbean tourism and the landscapes promoted to foreigners through travel advertisements very quickly became enmeshed with representations of the people themselves who inhabited the islands (K. Thompson 2007).

In Caribbean tourism, as far as many North American consumers are concerned, there was little to differentiate one island from the next or, more recently, one all-inclusive resort from the next. In the parlance of the tourism industry this is the danger of substitutability. Transcending this "substitutability" by supplying comparative advantages has become a primary strategy in gaining market share. In that sense, seizing on that which differentiates one place from the next has meant commodifiying cultural forms, such as carnival in Trinidad and Tobago or "scratch music" in Saint Croix. This strategy is not only imperative; it leads to specific interventions into expressive culture in order to secure viability into the future. Such interventions range from institutional oversight and protection of cultural forms to exploring legal protections (Scher 2002).

That being said, some amount of substitutability is clearly desired. That is, in terms of Caribbean clichés that European and American consumers will readily recognize, a certain stability is required especially in such areas as climate and landscape, vernacular architecture, music and festival, and so on. I can recall a Trinidadian friend explaining to a visitor during carnival that Trinidad is not "typically Caribbean" in terms of appearance. For that, he said, one must travel to Tobago, which has the classic appearance of a Caribbean island with its white sand and turquoise waters.

This brings up a continuing tension in marketing between that which all recognize as being fundamentally Caribbean and that which differentiates one place from the next in such a way as to make it a specifically desirable destination. Striking that balance is not easy, especially when another dimension of neoliberalism is the opening up of markets to an influx of foreign businesses that threaten to homogenize the local.

The concept of "nation branding" is designed to solve some of these problems. "Nation branding" as an idea and practice has been pursued by such diverse countries as Taiwan, Jamaica, Poland, New Zealand, and Botswana. Briefly defined, "nation branding" involves "engaging the profit-based marketing techniques of private enterprise to create and communicate a particular version of national identity"(Aronczyk 2008: 42).

With regard to Jamaica, nation branding has been a key strategy for economic development, and national culture figures prominently in its implementation. Indeed, by its very definition, nation branding trades on the creative output of the people. Jamaica's Ministry of Industry, Investment and Commerce, through its agency Jamaica Trade and Invest (JTI), has pursued nation branding aggressively. In a recent speech given at the "Target Growth Competitiveness Committee's Minister's Forum" on 'Competitiveness in Manufacturing,' at the Hilton Kingston Hotel, JTI president Robert Gregory said that "leveraging Jamaica's culture into high-value, globally competitive niche products and services for economic well-being and sustained prosperity, represents the next economic frontier for the 'creative economy.'" He further stated "that over the last 20 years, Jamaica has been transformed from a primary agricultural producer, to a predominantly services-based provider. Mr. Gregory contended that the only way the country's goods and services could achieve the competitive edge, is through the nation's culture, 'which makes us different from the rest of the world'" (JIS 2008).

Compare this, for instance, to Trinidad's National Carnival Commission's statement regarding its attempts to protect and preserve the traditional characters of carnival:

> The characters in Trinidad's traditional Carnival are the repositories of very important features which distinguish Carnival Trinidad and Tobago style from other Carnivals. They add to the uniqueness of the national festivals which, with calypso, pan and above all else, the spirit, create a differentiation of the product as Trinidad and Tobago Carnival claims a niche in the world economic market. (Cupid 1994: 3)

Or yet again, from the Barbados National Initiative for Service Excellence (NISE):

> The national vision for Barbados is to be a fully developed society that is prosperous, socially just and globally competitive by the year 2025.

> The national strategic plan embodies the theme "Global Excellence, Barbadian Traditions," which conveys the message of a Barbados that is a successful and globally competitive society, fully integrated into the world economy, but at the same time capable of preserving and strengthening its own identity, enterprise, national sovereignty, and traditions. (NISE 2010)

Strongly evident in this kind of rhetoric is the idea that culture is the key to economic success because it creates clear product differentiation. In its conception, nation branding makes a strong case for the preservation of the nation-state as the legitimate political entity because it has the ability to define, safeguard, and promote that which is key in creating economic health and competitiveness: culture.

I have argued above that the state's penchant for historical and heritage preservation is something new within—or, perhaps we might say, in the enduring aftershocks of—neoliberalism and would further suggest that participation in national cultural activities reduces at least part of one's performances to a kind of "playing in the brand."[3] This is so, especially in peripheral economies like the Caribbean, where the liberalization of trade has impinged upon many countries' protected access to markets and ability to compete. Neoliberalism, in general terms, reduces economies in the Caribbean to niche markets that are defined by locality (whether geographical or cultural) and encourages the production of goods that cannot interfere with larger economic interests as defined by the major economic players in the region, such as the United States and the United Kingdom (Klak 1998).[4]

A primary point of tension here—one might even say paradox—emerges between the desire to protect/preserve and a resulting stagnation. State preservation strategies often cannot reconcile the dynamic changes that expressive forms undergo to keep them relevant to the population at large (and therefore potentially popular) with the volatility that such change implies. In other words, expressive culture is made of performances, the physical regulation of such performances becomes imperative first to objectification and then to the commodification process, thus, theoretically, radical changes in cultural forms deter their objectification and control by state agencies. By their very definition these kinds of management tactics seek to limit change in performances. Furthermore, in heavily touristed sites, such as the Caribbean, cultural performances are not restricted to those obvious forms of expressive culture, such as music, dance, costume, and so on, but extend, ultimately, to potentially public behaviors of all kinds such as fishing, selling in a market, driving a taxi, dancing in a public place, and so on.

This has led governments to pursue strategies of internal management of public behavior seen as potentially detrimental to the effective sale of the cultural product. Indeed, the justification for the implementation of such strategies as the National Initiative for Service Excellence is not just to create good customer service, it is to try to conform actual interactions between Barbadians and tourists to what tourists expect of the Barbadian national character.[5] In the early 1990s a series of public service announcements (PSAs) were broadcast with the thematic tagline "Tourism: It's Our Business." These PSA short interstitials generally showed a street scene of some kind in which tourists were looking for help. The narrator would then encourage viewers to help foreigners if they found themselves in similar situations. After the vignette there would be a return to a narrator who would mention something about the Barbadian national character and then intone the tagline "Tourism, it's our business, let's play our part."

A similar program was implemented by Jamaica. Anne P. Crick shows how, due to certain key initiatives on the part of the Jamaica Tourist Board, the people of Jamaica and their behaviors "were as much on show as were the island's natural attributes" (2002: 167). The result has been a series of public campaigns and internally focused initiatives driven by the state tourism board to ensure that the image and idea of a Jamaican national personality is borne out in the actual attitudes of real Jamaicans in their interactions with foreign visitors. Part of this strategy, of course, is to convince Jamaicans that the state's idea of what a national personality is conforms to how Jamaicans see themselves and thus becomes embodied in day-to-day encounters. Thus an off day, a bad mood, a negative attitude is contextualized as an aberration, a glitch, as essentially untrue, because "real Jamaicans," as defined by the state, are "happy."

Indeed, Crick has investigated strategies of this nature in several Caribbean countries, including Saint Lucia, Jamaica, and the Bahamas. As she says, "tourism internal marketing is usually directed at creating an acceptance of tourism. . . . The goal is to influence the attitudes that the host population holds towards tourists and to ultimately influence the way that they interact with tourists" (Crick 2003: 161–62). She concludes, "The three countries examined have built their tourism promotions on, among other factors, the warmth and friendliness of their people. Their internal marketing strategies are therefore focused on trying to make sure that when tourists come to the country they do in fact experience this warmth and friendliness" (165).

However, this is not simply a service improvement initiative. Indeed, it cannot be that alone, tied as service is to the economic fate of the society. If one examines more closely the rhetoric of the vision statement something else emerges:

> Our mission is to promote and facilitate the achievement of sustainable excellence within organisations and to assist individuals in developing excellence as an ethic. Our goals are: To create a national culture of Service Excellence, to help Barbados become known worldwide for Service Excellence, to motivate and provide the tools for all Barbadians to become involved in the achievement of Service Excellence. (NISE 2010)

Global competitiveness is dependent on the service industry (tourism), which is dependent on the performance of its employees, who are held up to a global standard of excellence. Yet the vision statement is also quite clear in stating that not only will Barbados keep its identity, it will be strengthened by this global integration. I would go farther to say that Barbados, in the interest of global competitiveness, *needs* to preserve its traditions in the framework of what is commercially viable, as that is precisely what the market is based on. And with that in mind, the government's role is to safeguard this new form of nationalism. It does so through reformist interventions. David Scott describes this process in Jamaica in these terms: "Liberal freedom depends upon constructing a relation between government and governed that obliges individuals to become the 'subjects of their lives,' obliges them to exercise a responsible self-conduct, and this in turn depends precisely upon the 'character' that an improving reform seeks to bring into being . . . in which power seeks to operate through the shaping of conduct" (2001: 447).[6] In other words, "Let's play our part."

The Perception Problem, or the Problem of "No-Culture" Shock

In the mid-1990s I stood waiting with a group of masqueraders on the bright, hot streets of Port-of-Spain. We were all costumed similarly as members of

Peter Minshall's masquerade (mas') band The Odyssey. Indeed, we formed part of a special section of masqueraders portraying the black ships of Odysseus. The band as a whole was quite large and made up of many sections, each one depicting an aspect of that heroic Greek's epic journey back to Ithaca from the battlefields of Troy. Throughout there were sly references to Trinidad, such as a section aptly named "The Land of Calypso." Our section also carried dual references. We were dressed in black, and on our backs were golden wire armatures that held aloft beautiful, graceful biremes, decorated in golden braid and translucent black cloth, and featuring enormous sails emblazoned with the classic "eye." We were clothed in sailor's attire, not the outfit of Greek sailors, but that of the Trinidadian "fancy sailor," a well-known costume whose popularity crested in the 1950s and early 1960s. The traditional fancy sailor's outfit is generally white, with black usually reserved for another form of sailor character, the stoker.

We were waiting, as a group, for the signal to send us marching across one of the judging venues in town where crowds gather to see the masqueraders and some of the judges sit to assess the mas' bands. As we stood there, a French journalist and her photographer approached us to take pictures. Politely she asked if some of us could step aside. The photographer wanted to photograph just the Trinidadian masqueraders. Being a foreigner and not thinking too much about the request, I stepped aside. The French journalists then began to ask others in the group, whom I knew to be Trinidadian, to step aside: a Chinese Trinidadian, a very light-skinned female Trinidadian, and an Indo-Trinidadian among others. When the photographer was finished, the journalist interviewed two of the remaining masqueraders about their experiences, what carnival meant to them, and other fairly usual questions.

As we passed down the streets sometime later I listened carefully as two of our group who had been asked to step aside laughingly discussed the incident. The journalists, they said, had asked to photograph and interview the Trinidadians in the group, but obviously they did not ask for passports or birth certificates. They simply assumed that being Trinidadian meant being black. Of those who were excluded only a few were in fact actual foreigners. Operating on a preconceived notion of Caribbeanness and without an understanding of Trinidad's quite multi-ethnic history and heritage, the French journalists blithely reproduced a vision of the Caribbean held by many outside the region. I asked one of the men who had been interviewed if he was aware of what had happened; laughing, he told me "of course!" Ironically, as I amassed images of carnival for my own research, an interesting pattern became clear: the local Trinidadian press often featured images of white foreigners (especially women) dancing in costume in the streets (an anecdotal measure, if you will, of the success of carnival's global popularity), while the foreign press almost never showed tourists. An interesting ballet of mutual symbolic annihilation seemed to be at work, with each press corps working hard to cater to the (unwritten) expectations of its audiences. Of the 273 images of carnival collected from both foreign and local newspapers in the years 1994 to 1998, Trinidadian and Caribbean media sources were far likelier to show whites (often, but not always foreigners). Of the 124 images surveyed from foreign news sources, 13 explicitly depicted tourists, 11 had incidental whites/foreigners, and the rest were, presumably, locals of predominantly African descent. There is, of course, far greater nuance to these images than, I believe, the photographers were, of themselves, aware. Most of the images were of young women and many of these were lighter-skinned as compared to images of men and older people who were almost always of darker complexion. There were no images of "white" men. But the overall impression one gets in even a cursory examination of these images is that the global construction of locality works to imagine a Caribbean space that conforms to a fairly narrow set of criteria. The local imperative, with regard to images, is not concerned with selling an image to outsiders, but rather in convincing locals that carnival attracts outsiders. The appeal of Trinidadian culture, the message implies, is not only something to be proud of, it's good for business too.

Overall, the emphasis on the production of local goods, services, and even attitudes encompasses the world of what has come to be thought of as culture. This would include local exotic produce, spices, and foodstuffs such as pepper sauces, local beers and other spirits, as well as items of clothing such as T-shirts and hats emblazoned with place names or local businesses, crafts, works of art (especially "folk art"; see Scher 1999). It would also include exotic bodies for sale. Prostitution, yes, but also manual labor whose productivity is conceived of through local stereotypes, and expressive forms of "culture" that are manifested through local accents and voices, dances, musical styles, verbal arts, and so on (Klak and Myers 1998). Finally, cultural production requires a certain kind of cultural space; that is, the maintenance of certain key spaces as identifiable places in which certain activities and forms are properly ("authentically") situated. Globalization and neoliberalism do not necessarily encourage the disappearance of localness. In fact, the brisk trade in difference extends as much to places as to performances.[7] Neoliberalism produces not cultural imperialism writ small (conquest at the level of content), but a kind of multiculturalism, which is, as Richard Wilk has said, cultural imperialism writ large; hegemony as a structuring force wherein difference is expected but shaped according to recognizable criteria (Wilk 1995). Within this structuring force, in fact, there must be identifiable differences or else one runs the risk of having consumers experience what I call "no-culture" shock, or the disorienting feeling of having traveled in search of novelty only to be confronted with sameness. The active maintenance, then, of an appropriately "culture-full" population situated in a recognizably appropriate landscape is a key component to the branding of nations. Appropriate attitudes and culturally specific behaviors in recognizable locations are the lifeblood of the traditional or heritage-based cultural economy.

Returning to Trinidad, there has long been middle-class involvement with carnival marked by what we might call a "reform-through-competition" strategy. That is, the image of a carnival that would reflect the true nature of Trinidadian national ideals is something that middle-class reformers within the country have been working on for a long time. The results of this strategy are frequently cultural forms produced under the auspices of state-controlled competitions or showcases that are self-consciously performed in the service of displaying identity.

In the early years of carnival competitions the intent was to reform what were considered vulgar practices within carnival. However, even in these cases, issues of national identity and national culture could play a part. As independence approached in the early 1960s, carnival competitions and carnival itself were pitched as examples of national culture, while the character of reform activity shifted toward a concern with national identity and national reputation. Differently put, the attention on carnival stressed the development of a purely local, yet virtuous, content. National culture building always contains within it a sense of a moral imperative. As Trinidadian writer Willie Chen remarked in a newspaper editorial concerning the state of carnival music: "I say bring back the golden art of yesteryear tunes. . . . They are pleasurable exercises of art and discipline in the control of mind and body movements. Only animals jump, uncontrollably which leads to lewdness and vulgarity" (*Trinidad Express*, February 19, 1994).

The true culture of the nation, which resides in the past and must be recovered, is not only aesthetically superior but morally superior as well, as evidenced by the controlled, not dangerously unpredictable behaviors of the people. The revitalization process proposed by the state and middle class has an imbricated set of goals, which include rescue or recovery, moral improvement, international standing, and profit making. Further examples from Trinidad and Jamaica shed light on the sanction mode that the state (and, if successful, the general population) moves into when certain activities negatively impact the national image. These strategies generally revolve around the issue of "vulgarity."

"Wining" and Biopower

Wining, the erotically charged dance that is practiced throughout carnival in Trinidad, as well as other carnivals, such as Jamaica's and the Crop Over in Barbados, is perhaps the most visible target of the state's biopolitical activities. Briefly, wining is a dance form in which dancers gyrate against each other, mostly pelvis pressed against backside. The dancer in front is usually bent at the waist slightly or even significantly, giving the movement a distinctly sexual quality. The dance is not limited to male/female interaction (two women may frequently do it together) nor is it limited to two people. In its most extreme forms the participants may crawl on the ground, raise their legs in the air, and climb on top of each other.

Yet to say that it is only or purely the state that objects to wining is to limit our understanding of what I understand Foucault to have meant by biopower and the biopolitical. The nature of this form of power, it seems to me, is in its diffuse application and its ability to create subjects within self-limiting paradigms, the parameters of which appear as debates within society. But the debates are coercive, in the sense that neither side is a choice. This idea is indebted to the general concept that the social construction of identity is linked inextricably to power.

But what is of importance is the notion that such debates are conceived of in consistent ways. Namely, the debates in carnival about wining are constructed always as if the fate of the culture rested upon their outcome. That is, culture in Trinidad is perpetually seen in a state of emergency. Whether it is the general feeling that others are profiting from Trinidadian culture financially (as in the threat of the loss of steel drum patents, for instance) or simply that Trinidad is not getting the recognition it deserves (which is often, ultimately, framed in economic terms as the loss of a niche market), "the culture" exists as a topic for debate inasmuch as it is always seen in jeopardy. So the question is, how does an emergency debate such as this get formulated? Who, exactly, is panicked by the threat of culture loss or dilution? Who, to put it baldly, cares? The assumption is that everyone should care, and that, not a solution to the debate, is of key importance.

Wining is continually scrutinized for its lewdness and lasciviousness and yet implicitly celebrated as a "national dance" by its association with carnival. Daniel Miller (1991) is perhaps the only anthropologist to have addressed the issue of "wining" in carnival. Miller notes the controversy that often surrounds the dance and speaks of the seemingly constant outcry against lewd behavior from year to year in carnival. He rightly points out that such admonitions in carnival, which usually come from the elites, are not new. But historically the outcry that issued from such corners of society as the church, the colonial administration, or the white elites was not geared toward a fear of the impact such behaviors would have on the economic health of the society. Nowadays wining's lewdness and vulgarity are frequently cited as inappropriate, given the fact that families may be watching and, furthermore, that it might send the wrong message to foreigners watching about the kind of people Trinidadians are. At the same time, wining is frequently featured in carnival magazines, news stories, film clips, and so on to demonstrate the allure of the festival. Campaigns against lewdness and vulgarity are not restricted to Trinidad carnival. Dancehall music in Jamaica has faced similar programs. Indeed, in 2009 a ban on dancehall lyrics made headlines in Jamaica.

These various techniques of governance are not simply about the disciplining of bodies under the scrutiny of the state as a form of punishment, a show of force, or a subjugation of unruly physicality. It is not exclusively about a disciplining of the body even if it plays out in a discussion about overly erotic bodies, or vulgar bodies. In keeping with the expanded notion of biopower defined earlier, this is about productivity, and as such it is about people living their lives in a right way, the rightness of which is tied to that productivity. It also is also about realizing, through an amalgamation of performances, a finished product called "carnival in Trinidad," or "the cultural experience" in Jamaica, or simply the "experience" of Barbados writ large. Each one of these activities is charged with representing the national culture in some way and is an integral part of an enormous industry. Local citizens, whether they mean to be or not, are part of that larger picture, and the way in which they perform has consequences. The citizen/subject is encouraged that right behaviors are in their own self-interest because that interest is shared with the nation. "Tourism is *our* business," the slogan says. But the project of the nation has slipped away from what it was. Nationalist rhetoric continues to bank on the power of images of collective struggle and universal gain, but it is now a different kind of "technique of government" mobilized in the service of an economic relationship that has tied the fate of the nation to the health of the private sector. And this has reshaped the role of the state. The new role that national identity plays in the service of tourism is largely a result of the global forces of a new economic agenda that has expanded an industry that relies heavily on the consumption of culture.

Conclusion

State agencies responsible for national cultural forms are involved with identification research, development, promotion, authentication, and evaluation. The construction of tradition usually leads to its incorporation into a whole structure of evaluations, authentications, critiques, judgments, awards for authenticity, and so on. Copyright laws provide for and, indeed, encourage the authentication of expressive cultural forms by "recognized authorities" in the fields of anthropology, archaeology, and folklore (L. Smith 2007). David Scott (1991) has critiqued such authentication projects exactly because any such attempt is bound to immobilize cultural change into "tradition." As evidenced above, the rhetoric that accompanies state-generated or organized projects such as these makes it clear that national cultural performances are conceived of as "assets," "resources," "goods," and so on in the state-economic imaginary.

Yet the marketing and selling of cultural forms is also intended to do work that the sale of other products cannot do, and that is to bring attention specifically to the nation itself and, by extension, to its ruling government. Furthermore, selling culture combines what in other industries are distinct spheres of activity: advertising and production. That is, in tourism, even in the case of selling the natural environment, the activities represented in promotional campaigns are both what is being sold and what is doing the selling. Cultural forms such as carnival and each of the multiple acts of performance within it, then, would constitute what Benjamin Lee and Edward LiPuma call performatives: "a self-reflexive use of reference that, in creating a representation of an ongoing act, also enacts it" (2002: 195). In the case of festival events, such as the carnival in Trinidad, the state capitalizes on the existence of thousands of individual performances, masquerades, dances, and so on, and unifies them under the general rubric "Trinidadian culture" on display. There is a certain amount of complicity in this on the part of the dancers, for instance, in front of the television cameras of the local and foreign press, but, for the most part, the very public nature of an event such as carnival yields hours of "free advertising" for the state.

At the center of this vision of national culture is a complex of highly visible, recognizable cultural products that, in keeping with a sort of economic/state philosophy, can be controlled, coordinated, marketed, in short, easily manipulated for presentation on a global scale. However, in this case study I have not focused primarily on the construction of nationalist culture, per se, but on what we might call a viable nationalism, a nationalism that works for the state as it exists at a particular historical moment. As Ernesto Laclau points out, a nationalist identity promoted by a ruling or dominant group must "show its ability to become a realistic alternative for the organization and management of the community" (1994: 16). Thus what counts as national heritage in the contemporary Caribbean is often what may convey to the consumer an appropriate vision of the region. This form of heritage ties the rhetoric of nationalism to the rhetoric of marketing because such conflation serves the limited authority of the contemporary Caribbean state.[8] Furthermore, changing visions of national culture respond to the changing tastes and expectations of consumers. Indeed, one nation may have several national cultures that can be exploited in a variety of ways. That is, the national character of a population may be made to accommodate a variety of desires expressed by visitors, while at the same time cultural or ethnic diversity within a state may pose serious problems in terms of the presentation of national culture.

In other words, in producing an objectified national culture the state must successfully present itself as the logical and natural administrator of that culture—not as its originator, but as its champion. Indeed, often it must avoid at all costs the idea that the content of nationalist culture originates with itself. But it is one thing to demonstrate how a given state *reifies* cultural forms and organizes them in relation to other state policies and quite another to maintain that it *commodifies* them. And it is still another thing to argue that state-sponsored commodification is itself a necessary strategy in relation to a global neoliberal economic climate. But to what degree does this impinge on seeing such cultural forms as rights?

In the introduction to their 2007 publication *Cultural Heritage and Human Rights*, Helaine Silverman and D. Fairchild Ruggles detail some of the ways in which the misuse or appropriation of heritage has resulted in egregious human rights violations in twentieth-century history (10–11). They further point to examples of the ways in which the appropriation of traditional knowledge through, for example, biopiracy, may enrich large multinational corporations at the expense of the local communities whose expertise in the use of local flora and fauna was exploited in the first place. Generally the common denominator in the exploitation or misappropriation of heritage, whether by accident or intent, is the lack of control over the heritage in question by its purported beneficiaries.

Although the great hope of such acts as the UNESCO World Heritage list and the Convention for the Safeguarding of the Intangible Cultural Heritage has been restoring control and stewardship of heritage to the communities to which it belongs, they have garnered their share of criticism for, among other things, a penchant to reify culture and failure to define who exactly should "own" heritage (Olwig 1999; Scher 2002; Barkan 2007). Furthermore, there is, of course, the irony of combating the ill effects of globalization, imperialism, and colonialism through large-scale, Western-based global organizations such as UNESCO and the World Intellectual Property Organization. Indeed, the latter is of particular interest, since the safeguarding of heritage has been increasingly sought (although not always successfully) through legal protections and the extension of copyright laws over cultural heritage. Most of this work has focused on ways in which communities seeking increasing control over heritage might make recourse to legal protections. Even beyond the difficulties of creating and enforcing such legislation over intangible cultural heritage, a persistent problem in the "protection" of culture is defining what is to be protected and discovering the appropriate stewards for its management.

As Lisa Breglia has pointed out in her study of Mexican archaeological sites, a simple recourse to indigenous claims to rights over heritage spaces is rarely the result of the mandate to restore control to such groups. In fact, as she says, "patrimony claims are instead situated in complex relation to (1) state policy regarding ownership and custodianship of cultural materials, (2) issues of jurisdiction and access within archaeological zones, and (3) the ongoing efforts of U.S. and Mexican interest groups to develop archaeological sites and to promote scientific knowledge of ancient Maya civilization as well as international cultural tourism" (Breglia 2006: 8). Certainly there seem to be cases where conflicts related to the uses of heritage are more minimal (Brumann 2009), and even in the Caribbean, despite much rhetoric and occasional action from state and state agencies, cultural heritage changes and develops over time.

There is, however, a crucial distinction in the instances I have examined. This distinction stems from the overwhelming role that tourism plays in many Caribbean nations and the conviction that what the Caribbean has to offer in terms of cultural heritage products must play an increasing role in tourism as a whole. Thus, although tourism accounts for as much as 16 percent of the total GDP of the region (and much higher for certain states), the Caribbean is also losing market share and consistently fails to integrate tourism with other aspects of the economy. This means that, although the numbers are still strong and growing, there is increasing pressure to diversify the types of tourism available. This pressure is augmented by the fact that what many people come to see (the sun, sand, and sea attractions) are common to many of the islands (Daye, Chambers, and Roberts 2008). Internal competition between countries requires, as I have mentioned above, increasing the comparative advantage of each place through the elevation of its unique cultural and heritage features. Thus, although in the abstract culture is a right, in the Caribbean, in reality, given its place in the economy, culture increasingly emerges as a requirement.

PART II

The Ironies of Heritage

Chapter 4

Cultural Heritage, Human Rights, and Reform Ideologies: The Case of Swedish Folklife Research

Barbro Klein

In Sweden today, politicians, museum employees, members of local tourism boards, academics, and many others tend to use big words when they speak about the protection of cultural heritage: a moral good, a democracy issue of great importance to civil society, a human right. Heritage issues are deeply entangled with hopes to improve integration in a country that during the last few decades has received great numbers of refugees and other immigrants in proportion to its population of nine million. Indeed, today's expanding heritage project can be seen as a reform ideology for our time.

On the following pages, I sketch some of the background to the current concerns with heritage protection and human rights. I do this by examining the contemporary heritage project in Sweden in relationship to the history of folklife research (or ethnology) in the country. Of course, the concerns addressed here are not limited to Sweden; they can be found also elsewhere, albeit in different configurations. Two aspects are of particular interest. One is reform ideology and reform politics. In a way, one could speak about the entire history of Swedish folklife research as a series of engagements in social and moral reforms. Tony Bennett's *Culture: A Reformer's Science* is basic in this context (T. Bennett 1998: 87–106).

It could be said that whenever the field has been truly successful, it has been preoccupied with reforms, sometimes in ways that have not been immediately apparent, neither to the scholars themselves nor to the public at large. A second aspect in focus is that folklife research can be said to have been more clearly implicated in the production of cultural heritage than many other academic undertakings. A main reason for this is that the discipline grew out of the folklife museums or cultural historical museums and their efforts to collect, preserve, and present the culture and arts of the peasant folk (cf. Kirshenblatt-Gimblett 2007). The field developed because these museums needed researchers to classify and study their growing collections. Sweden was one of the first countries in which this happened on a large scale. Therefore, its folklife research is an interesting case in the study of heritage issues.

Creating a National Cultural Repertoire: 1870–1910

Efforts to preserve the arts of the simple folk were begun in Sweden as early as the 1600s. At this time, the country had imperial ambitions and heroic songs and ballads were eagerly collected. A hundred years later, parish ministers and other dignitaries authored massive inventories of local cultures, as was also the case in other European countries. However, I will forgo these early efforts and begin with the years 1870–1910. All over Europe, this was a period of immense social and cultural transformations: agricultural restructuring, population increase, urbanization, industrialization, crop failures, emigration, workers' movements, temperance movements, struggles to achieve universal suffrage, new communication technologies—and the founding of scholarly disciplines and cultural establishments, such as museums. One could say that having culture was "one of the main duties of a modern state" (Beckman 1998: 17, my translation), and the cultural achievements of nations were repeatedly compared in international congresses and world's fairs.

Artur Hazelius (1833–1901) was internationally the best known of several learned and enthusiastic museum founders and scholars in Sweden at the time. In 1873, he founded the Scandinavian-Ethnographic Collection, which, in 1880 was renamed the Nordic Museum (Nordiska museet), and, in 1891 he established its open-air pendant, Skansen. While, at first, it was not clear what kinds of materials were to be emphasized in the Nordic Museum, it was eventually decided that the museum was to concentrate on the cultural history of Sweden. All groups, social classes, and geographical regions were to be represented: the nobility, the urban bourgeoisie, tradespeople, the Sámi, and the peasantry, landed or not. (The growing numbers of urban/industrial workers were not yet considered possibilities.) Yet, in actuality, Hazelius gave priority to peasant (*allmoge*) culture, and Skansen was organized as a miniature of rural Sweden, containing its natural and cultural varieties: animals, houses, people, and industry typical of most of the provinces from north to south.

Yet, Hazelius and other intellectuals did not aim to erase cultural differences when they made peasant culture a part of the urban public sphere. On the contrary, they were eager to select and celebrate the best and the most original of local and regional traditions. Hazelius thought that, if he could open the eyes of all Swedes (particularly the urban middle classes) to the beautiful diversity in the country, their feelings for the fatherland would be awakened and maintained. To teach all Swedes to "know themselves" was the great reformatory task of his museums, and he pronounced the various spiritual and material traditions of the peasantry as the base on which the future cultural repertoires and moral standards of the nation were to rest. He and his collaborators assured Swedes that they aimed to preserve provincial customs and dialects at the same time as they wished to create a sense of cultural wholeness. Maintaining difference was simultaneously an act of unification. As time went on, these efforts to produce unity out of diverse rural traditions became the basis for the development of a special Swedish cultural repertoire with a distinct "feeling tone" or "structure of feeling" (R. Williams 1984: 64–88), that is, a national cultural repertoire easily recognized by all insiders (Frykman and Löfgren 1986). Thus, this early repertoire became linked to aesthetic standards, to gestures, movements, fragrances, dialects, and often to deep feelings. However, the word for heritage, *kulturarv*, was rarely used, although it had been coined as early as the 1880s (Klein 2006). And it was not to be used—at least not in a marked sense—for most of the 1900s. And most certainly the idea of human rights was never mentioned in connection with the efforts of the folklife museums.

But peasant creations could not be exhibited in their pristine condition. It was important to select the very best of them, clean them up, and arrange them in an appealing fashion. And even more transformations took place as artists, crafts enthusiasts, composers, economic reformers, literary luminaries, and others joined Hazelius in the massive efforts to collect, exhibit, preserve, study, promote, or sell the most aesthetically pleasing of the costumes, tools, furniture, and other arts of the country folk. In other words, neither Hazelius nor the artists and reformers thought that documentation and preservation were their only goals. Rather, all of them created something new on the basis of peasant culture, something that was regarded contemporary in spirit and would appeal to middle-class viewers, readers, or buyers. Nor did reformers such as Lilli Zickerman, the forceful founder of the Swedish home-craft movement (*hemslöjdsrörelsen*), romanticize the peasants; rather, the rural folk had to be taught to recover some of their forgotten skills so their wares could appeal to a choosy bourgeoisie (Klein 2000b, 2013). The folk had to be rescued from moral decay in order to become citizens of a modern nation that promised a richer and cleaner life.[1] The efforts of Hazelius and others can be seen as components in a reform project aiming to unite disparate regions of the country and prepare people to become citizens of a modern state (cf. Eriksen 1993).

In many ways we can say that there was, around 1900, a "tight integration" (Kirshenblatt-Gimblett 2007: 5–6) between knowledge formation, collection, museums, the creation of a national repertoire of cultural forms, and social reform work. But as time went on, also other needs became urgent. The Nordic Museum and Skansen needed qualified researchers to study all the artifacts and texts that had been brought together: houses, costumes, and tools, as well as textualized and archived ballads, legends, sayings, and fairy tales. To this end, a new academic discipline was founded in 1909: Nordic and Comparative Folklife Research (Nordisk och jämförande folklivsforskning). Eventually, this discipline became a cooperative concern involving the Nordic Museum and Stockholm University.[2]

Consolidating the Cultural Repertoire: 1930s–1950s

In 1934, Sigurd Erixon, who had long been employed at the Nordic Museum, was invited to hold the professorship of Folklife Research. It was now and for two or three decades to come that this discipline, together with the Nordic Museum and Skansen, established itself as a true force in the national and international academic, cultural, and political landscape. It was during this, the great Erixonian, era that the documentation efforts initiated by Hazelius assumed gigantic proportions. It was now that Erixon, with the help of a host of researchers, published seminal, and sometimes magnificent, books on material culture, in particular books on traditional housing types (for example, Erixon 1947).

At an early date, Erixon realized that the fervor to document and exhibit had to go hand in hand with interpretive scholarship. He and his colleagues read voraciously. They studied German *Volkskunde* and *Völkerkunde*, British social anthropology and North American cultural anthropology. Particularly, the new discipline of sociology made a strong impression on Erixon. At this time, sociology's main concern was social planning, an activity in which he and several other academics were deeply involved during the 1930s and after World War II. As planners these academics took part in a monumental effort to create the Swedish welfare state, or a *folkhem* ("folk home").[3] Thus, during this period, the shaping of a "folk" discipline went hand in hand with the shaping of a twentieth-century "folk home." As Bo G. Nilsson (2004) observes, the period from 1930 to 1970 constituted the true Swedish "folk" era, not only in terms of government politics, but also insofar that Sigurd Erixon placed the discipline of folklife research in the service of state social planning. Erixon was a member of various planning committees, and, for a while, he collaborated with Alva Myrdal, who along with her husband, the internationally eminent economist Gunnar Myrdal, was one of the architects of the Swedish welfare state.

As a member of planning committees Erixon argued that folklife research offers "the kind of information in support of the building of a democratic society that cannot otherwise be had" (Nilsson 2004: 75, my translation). Folklife research was not to be conducted for its own sake; rather, researchers were to help planners of a modern welfare society to avoid mistakes committed in the past, for example during the breakup of traditional villages. Where modern planners ignored "the human factor," folklife scholars could step in to fill the gaps. In particular, the immense documentation of traditional housing and village structures undertaken by Erixon and his collaborators was, he maintained, highly useful when new housing was to be built for members of the rural proletariat who had moved to the cities in search of jobs.[4]

In order to further increase the supply of information, Sigurd Erixon and his colleagues began, in 1928, to send open-ended questionnaires to respondents all over Sweden, an activity for which substantial state funding had been obtained. These questionnaires resulted in lengthy essay answers on such diverse topics as village organization, laundry, male and female culture, midsummer celebrations, legends about Swedish kings, or beliefs in the supernatural beings of streams and forests. Actually, a great deal of that which today is singled out as Sweden's "intangible cultural heritage" was amassed during Erixon's era via this method, not only at the Nordic Museum but also at other institutions. This "intangible" past is now preserved in monumental and highly "tangible" archives containing massive collections of manuscripts and tapes (Klein 2007).[5]

However, with the exception of research devoted to Sámi culture, little was written by folklife scholars about the customs and traditions of "foreign" or "exotic" groups residing in Sweden. Indeed, the 1950s constituted a peak period for the idea that Swedes were extraordinarily homogeneous; its population was thought to be just about "complete" in its "national purity" (Appadurai 2006: 9). For example, in 1953, a widely read encyclopaedia stated that the Swedish population "with regard to race, language, and religion, is more homogeneous than the population of most other countries" (*Bonniers Folklexikon* 5, 1953: 491, my translation). Also, by this time, some of the diverse rural traditions brought together at Skansen and other museums had fused into easily recognized standardized forms. This was the case with Lucia and Midsummer celebrations, for example. Together with flags, selected literary works, archaeological remains, and other phenomena, they were now components in a prototypical cultural repertoire. Although the words, "cultural heritage," were hardly ever used, one might say that this was the era when a national Swedish heritage repertoire was truly consolidated. Together folklife museums and folklife scholarship had contributed to shaping a cultural repertoire capable of arousing deep feelings in Swedes—albeit feelings that among many were fraught with inner conflicts.

Although many folklife scholars who were active during the 1930s, 1940s, and 1950s were less interested in sociology and social planning than Erixon was, it is not far-fetched to view the discipline during this period as a reform project aiming to create citizens of a modernizing welfare state in which differences in income and social class were to be erased. The "folk" discipline went hand in hand with political efforts to shape a homogeneous "folk" home, and differences in terms of language, religion, or culture among such minorities as Sámi, Roma, Jews, and Finns were hardly recognized. Or, if differences were noted, it was taken for granted that, as a matter of course, they would disappear in the process of modernization. Furthermore, while the idea of human rights was fervently discussed after the forming of the United Nations in 1948 (Strzelewicz 2004), it appears that little was said about cultural expressions in the context of human rights, at least not in Sweden.[6] The question did not seem to have come up. Since minorities or distinctly different ethnic groups were not recognized, it seems to have been self-evident that all cultural expressions were Swedish and that Swedes had the sole right to them.

Getting Rid of the Folk Baggage: 1970–2000

In the 1960s and 1970s, some folklife scholars were even more involved than Erixon in social planning. Most radical of them was Åke Daun, who eventually was to take over the chair at the Nordic Museum and Stockholm University. His political influence was considerable during the 1970s, when he was engaged in community planning and housing policies and was highly visible in the media as a member of government committees. But where Erixon argued that folklife scholars were useful because of their familiarity with housing traditions of the past, Daun maintained they were useful because of their understanding of contemporary social life.

To Daun the "folk" terminology was detrimental to an academic discipline that wished to be taken seriously.[7] He and other scholars worked hard to bring about a name change that was eventually effectuated at all Swedish universities in 1972, when "Folklife Research" became "European Ethnology," or (in daily parlance) "Ethnology."[8] Furthermore, and not surprisingly, Daun and his followers hardly ever used such words as *kulturarv*, or "heritage." If they did, they did it ironically. In Daun's opinion, ethnologists were not at all in the business of preserving and presenting, neither folk culture nor any other kind of culture of the past or the present. Rather, the task of ethnology is to describe social life in order to bring about political change. To him, parts of the history of the field, in particular its links to national romanticism and its self-satisfied concentration on Swedish culture, are heavy burdens to be gotten rid of.

But also other, politically less radical researchers signaled a departure from the past. This is particularly true of Jonas Frykman and Orvar Löfgren, who, as young scholars in 1979, published a seminal book that has been translated into English as *Culture Builders: An Historical Anthropology of Middle Class Life* (1986). Combining British anthropological structuralism, historical sociology, and the thinking of Swedish folklife researchers into a fresh brew, the book inaugurated a special ethnological brand of cultural analysis that became highly influential during the 1980s and 1990s in many disciplines in Sweden. In principle, cultural analysis was not adverse to folklife museums or cultural history. Nevertheless, its practitioners distanced themselves from "the old folklife research" and spoke ironically about its moralism and its emphasis on an idealized version of "the old peasant society" (*det gamla bondesamhället*). Like Daun, Frykman, and Löfgren, many young scholars were embarrassed about the discipline's beginnings in folklife museums and called for a divorce between these museums and the field of ethnology, a divorce that also eventually took place.[9] But the divorce was only partial, since many employees in folklife museums or cultural historical museums were trained in European ethnology and many young ones have continued to be trained in the field. These employees are now working toward finding new approaches to exhibiting the immense holdings representing "the old peasant society."

Today, Swedish ethnologists work with themes, topics, approaches, and theories that recur in many disciplines within the human and social sciences the world over: gender, sexuality, identity questions, transnational migrations, the multicultural society, postcolonial theory. In the main, ethnologists are now carrying on a kind of qualitative social science that has its roots in the reform ideologies that prevailed during the height of the "folk home" era. Although the "social welfarist" (T. Bennett 1998) ideas of that era have been increasingly called into question during the last two decades, in Sweden as well as elsewhere, the ethnological ideals of Åke Daun and others have not been abandoned. Yet at the same time there are signs of renewed interests in ethnology in the arts, folklore, and other topics that were long the concern of a very small group of scholars.[10]

Furthermore, since the mid-1990s, these subjects are often addressed in terms of cultural heritage. Particularly striking is the frequent use of "cultural heritage," or *kulturarv*, to denote phenomena that not so long ago were called folklore. The concept of cultural heritage has found its way into the discipline from many directions including museums and a variety of national and international political arenas.

The Heritage Sphere and Contemporary Swedish Ethnology

Indeed, all of sudden, in the mid-1990s, *kulturarv* cropped up everywhere in Swedish life. A similar development appears to have taken place in some other countries; in some languages new words for "heritage" were invented. Of course, the ultimate impulse was the use of "cultural heritage" in English-speaking countries, which began with UNESCO's heritage initiatives and conventions after World War II and increased during the 1970s and 1980s. Nevertheless it is striking that it was as late as the 1990s that equivalents of this word began to be used in Sweden and some other countries outside the English-speaking world (Klein 2006). Why?

One source of the sudden use of *kulturarv* in Swedish museums was its appearance as a (fuzzily defined) key term in the final report of an official government museum inquiry from 1994. Here we can read that the most important role of Swedish museums is to "undertake a national rescue action on behalf of our cultural heritage" and to prevent "moths and mice" from deciding what we will remember.[11] The word *kulturarv* was now applied to all kinds of phenomena regarded worthy of preservation and protection: great literature, Bronze Age finds, royal castles, parish churches, natural landscapes, historic book collections, twentieth-century industrial parks, modernistic satellite towns, Swedish jazz, children's rhymes, the folklore archives. The "folk" heritage was just one part of a wide spectrum of possible heritage phenomena. Other, more or less subtle changes were effectuated. For example, in 1998, the Riksantikvarieämbetet (founded in the 1600s) changed the official translation into English of its name, from the Central Board of National Antiquities to the Swedish National Heritage Board. This was part of an official acknowledgment that not only antiquities are to be selected as heritage but a broad range of phenomena with "recourse to the past" (Kirshenblatt-Gimblett 1998a). Somewhat later, a professorship in Cultural Heritage and the Use of History (*historiebruk och kulturarv*) was instituted at Linköping University, in some respects following a British model.[12]

To employees at the folklife museums it seemed self-evident that *kulturarv* had "always" been a part of their vocabulary. To many it was now a matter of course that they work to discover, select, protect, preserve, and exhibit the Swedish cultural heritage and that they do so in order to serve democracy. By the late 1990s, *kulturarv* was also appropriated by members of the government and parliament to describe some of the most positive and morally praiseworthy forms of social action in a democratic society. Furthermore, officials now spoke about *kulturarv* in terms of human rights and sustainable development, and many people began taking for granted that all human beings have a right to their own cultural heritage. The word "heritage" was used in countless contexts, but few critical or conceptual debates materialized.

But why at this time? It seems to me that, in addition to government reports of the kind mentioned above, a true catalyst was the official recognition of the importance of the culture of immigrants and old minorities, a recognition that in Sweden did not take place until the mid-1990s. In 1995 (one year after the publication of the government museum inquiry mentioned above), all museums, as well as all other public cultural institutions, were given an official "diversity mandate" (*mångfaldsuppdrag*), according to which they were obliged to take into consideration in all their activities that Sweden had become multicultural. In other words, "cultural heritage" and "cultural diversity" made their first appearance in official and state publications at about the same time. This is crucial and entirely logical. Given the new emphasis on the idea that all human beings have a right to their own cultural heritage, it became necessary to admit, on an official level, that cultural heritages exist in the plural and that many heritages, as well as many different ways of life, can and must coexist within one and the same social order.

Indeed, it had to be admitted that in an era in which the individual person has become "sacralized" (Joas 2005), each and every human being has a right to his or her cultural heritage.[13] Certainly, there was no need to speak about cultural heritages in the plural at a time when Sweden imagined itself the most homogeneous nation on earth.

But how were the museums to act, considering that they had so long lived with the idea of a basic national cultural homogeneity and considering the lack of research concerning diversity in cultural expressions in a new multicultural Sweden? These and other questions were hotly debated in conferences and seminars, not least in conjunction with the planning of a new museum of world culture in Göteborg. Participants in the debates often pointed out that museums must and can help to counteract xenophobia and racism (see, e.g., Lundström and Pilvesmaa 1996), and several research programs materialized. Among them was a state-supported program entitled "Agenda kulturarv" and directed by the Swedish National Heritage Board (Lindvall and Johansen 2003). A main idea of the program was to inspire Swedish museums to take an interest in different cultural heritages in a new, pluralistic Sweden and to be "a meeting-place for analysis and discussion," a meeting place that would "gather the heritage sector in a joint effort" to shape the future (Aronsson 2004: 148). Many museums felt and still feel a need for this kind of forum in which important questions can be raised. Museum employees came to recognize that it is necessary to expand knowledge and insights if the complexity of a new multicultural Sweden in a world with new global interconnections is to be well represented. Curators and other museum employees had begun to become aware of the many difficulties involved when, for example, the practices and traditions of recent immigrants were to be exhibited in the old folklife museums.

However, the exhibitions and other museum activities attempted so far (or at least until very recently) have been highly problematic and demonstrate the need for further research. Often "diversity is celebrated" while real "difference is shunned" and a sort of "feel-good" diversity is established (Kurkiala 2002). Many museums (including the Nordic Museum) have been reluctant to single out or highlight distinct cultural or religious differences that are an outcome of the intense immigration during the last few decades. The reasons for this can be laudable: curators may wish to avoid stereotyping, essentializing, or exoticizing other people. Yet, the upshot can also be that other cultures, religions, and languages stand out as something disagreeable that must be avoided. Unfortunately, Swedish museum exhibitions still include examples of how the label "cultural heritage" can hide important differences in order to celebrate a happy, wholesome, and uncontroversial pluralism (Bendix 2000: 50–51).

The many problems have led museums to call for scholarship that probes more deeply than they themselves are able to do. Museums now acknowledge that they can benefit from the voluminous scholarship in ethnology, anthropology, history, political science, and other fields regarding not only migration, diasporic cultures, and the "multicultural society" but also regarding other aspects of social life in the past and present. In other words, the situation now differs a great deal from that which prevailed in the 1970s and 1980s, when there was mutual suspicion between folklife museums, ethnologists, and other scholars in the cultural fields. New demands in a new era are leading to a tentative rapprochement, and in many ways it is the concept and idea of cultural heritage(s) that has furthered this rapprochement. Indeed, there is a new recognition on the part of young scholars that the old folklife museums are interesting places, not least in terms of knowledge production.[14]

A Reform Ideology for Our Times?

If, as noted above, "having culture" was "one of the main duties of a modern state" in the late nineteenth century, it might be said that "having cultural heritage(s)" is a main duty of the state today. Moreover, if (as I think they are) Swedish ethnologists and representatives of other disciplines concerned with culture are now joining forces with the museums, the cultural tourism industry, and other parts of the heritage sector in new ways, they will have to confront, or become a part of, a reformist heritage ideology that is every bit as powerful and moralizing as the reformist nationalistic ideologies that inspired the creators of the folklife museums. It is also every bit as powerful and moralizing as the reformist ideologies that inspired the folklife scholars who took part in the shaping of the Swedish welfare state during the 1930s, 1940s, and 1950s.

But, of course, it remains to be seen what directions the new rapprochement will take. Will there be attempts to establish a new Swedish heritage arena that is essentially a variation of Hazelius's idea of an open-air museum representing a diverse but united Sweden? The only difference would be that now the diversity does not only consist of Swedish regions and dialects but also of a multitude of cultures and ways of life with roots in all parts of the globe. Or will the powerful heritage ideology, with its links to global preservation issues and human rights issues, make Swedish ethnologists and other scholars more open to the world at large than it was during most of the twentieth century?

Both these and other developments are possible and even likely. But, in my view, one most desirable development would be the establishing of a long-term critical forum involving museums, other heritage institutions, universities, local communities, and others. Such a forum would be devoted to wide-ranging reflections concerning the many large and difficult questions inherent in the contemporary notions of cultural heritage and heritage activism. Indeed, history, politics, and, not least, the buzzword character of the concept of cultural heritage teach us that caution is advisable. Is the preservation and protection of cultural heritage always morally good and valuable? Could it also be a liability or a smoke screen preventing the highlighting of other even more pressing issues? Is it always a human right to "have" or "possess" a cultural heritage (Brown 2004a)? Perhaps, as Talal Asad (2003: 180) emphasizes, in European countries today it is much less urgent to be concerned with multiple identities or multiple heritages and much more of a need to open up space and time for multiple "ways of life." And (to add to Asad's remarks) in these many "ways of life," the intangible rights to feel, to imagine, and to identify would naturally be a part. The extent to which such intangible rights intersect with issues of cultural heritage would then be a secondary question. Indeed, in the current preservation mania and the current cults of heritage there are risks of heritage inflation to such an extent that the real needs and rights of many peoples around the globe will be shunted away or ignored.

Chapter 5

Balkan Romani Culture, Humans Rights, and the State: Whose Heritage?

Carol Silverman

Roma, Europe's largest minority, provide an illuminating viewpoint from which to probe problematic issues of the definition, ownership, and control of heritage in a historic framework of discrimination. The human rights of Roma are routinely violated, the very existence of their own culture is often denied, and they usually are excluded from the category "nation." At the same time, their music enjoys worldwide fame in forms appropriated by non-Romani commercial forces. Via four case studies of Balkan Romani music, this chapter analyzes how states, global markets, human rights activists, and international institutions like UNESCO ignore, erase, or reframe Romani culture.

Examining the construction of forms of intangible heritage for nationalist projects, I show how Balkan states as well as ethnic identity movements deploy symbols for strategic aims. My focus on Roma highlights the tension between inclusion and exclusion: heritage, as configured to represent national folk culture, excludes Roma as well as other minorities in part because of its reliance on bounded notions of one national organic folk community (Noyes 2006). On the other hand, although Roma object to exclusionary state practices, they rely on similar essentialist assumptions in their own mobilization toward a Pan-European human rights movement. Activists, then, attempt to construct nationalist symbols of Romani culture that can unify disparate groups. Roma pose the question of belonging; they interrogate the framework of "nation" while employing it for strategic reasons. Inspired by Michael Herzfeld's concept of cultural intimacy (1997), I investigate the complex performative relationship between Roma, the state, and the market.

My performance approach embraces identity issues through the senses and the imagination. Roma play an especially relevant role because in the European imagination, they are known as iconic consummate performers; through the senses, especially music and dance, they are said draw out their patrons. Often they are credited with eliciting in their patrons "the soul of the nation" through music. Although they may "embody" the nation through music, they have a problematic relationship with states in terms of rights, recognition, and resources. Furthermore, their music is often appropriated via transnational markets where non-Roma usually benefit.

Despite being associated with music, Roma have been plagued with the popular and scholarly notion that they have no folklore or heritage of their own, especially in the realm of music. They are known as inveterate borrowers, appropriators, and "cultural sponges" who take the "hosts' music" and sell it back with "Gypsy style." While it is accurate to highlight the historic service relationship between non-Romani patrons and Romani professional musicians, we should remember that non-Roma have also appropriated music from Roma. Hungary, Spain, and the Balkans provide historic examples of this two-way street. The recent global craze for Gypsy music is a further illustration of non-Roma appropriating from Roma.

The older typical Balkan scholarly attitude toward Romani music was one of contempt. For example, as early as 1910, Serbian music scholar Tihomir Djordjević disparaged Gypsies because, when adopting Serbian music, they "gypsified" it (1984 [1910]: 38); in 1977 Serbian scholar Adrijana Gojković wrote that Gypsies "corrupt not only national music of various countries but also new music, for instance, jazz" (1977: 48; my translation); and, as I discuss below, in the 1980s Bulgarian ethnomusicologists demonized Romani wedding music style as kitsch and foreign. In these accounts, "Gypsy style" usually meant improvisation and innovation, criticized because it was in opposition to preserving "authentic national folk music." Despite scholarly condemnation, Romani musicians have always been respected and hired by patrons.

I place these cultural negotiations into the wider current societal framework where Roma are reviled as criminals/vagrants but revered as musicians (Silverman 2012). The current craze for Balkan Gypsy music in festivals and clubs illustrates how globalization may reinforce hierarchies. Ironically, while many non-Romani musicians, DJs, and producers are now profiting from Romani music, Roma suffer gross human rights abuses and musicians are out of work. Furthermore, while Romani music proliferates on the Internet, Roma still have difficulty securing employment in the global Gypsy music market. Asking the thorny question "Who owns culture?" (Brown 2004b), I explore how Roma pose a challenge to heritage studies because of their historical role as appropriators, their exclusion from "the nation," and the global trafficking of their music.

In the framework of this volume, Romani music resonates with editor Deborah Kapchan's triptych of cultural rights: the right to feel, the right to imagine, and the right to identify. Music, as a multisensory genre, engages both the performer and the listener in the intimate act of feeling, both emotional, sensory, and cognitive. Music also appeals to the imagination in that it creates transformative worlds while being anchored to political realities. Music's contextual place in life cycle and calendrical ritual plus its profits in popular culture all ensure its imaginative viability. And finally, music is tied to ethnic and minoritized identities by, on the one hand, being regulated and prohibited by states while, on the other hand, being employed as resistance.

History, Human Rights, and Music

Linguistic evidence shows that Roma migrated westward from northwest India and reached the Balkans by the fourteenth century and western Europe a century later.[1] Initial curiosity about Roma by European peoples and rulers quickly gave way to hatred and discrimination, a legacy that has continued until today (Hancock 1987, 2002; Barany 2002; Guy 2001). In the southern Romanian principalities Roma were slaves from the fourteenth to the nineteenth century. Despite their small numbers, Roma inspired fear and mistrust and were expelled from virtually every western European territory. Bounties were paid for their capture, and repressive measures included confiscation of property and children, forced labor, prison sentences, whipping, branding, and so on. Assimilation was attempted in the eighteenth century in the Austro-Hungarian Empire by forcibly removing children from their parents and outlawing nomadism, traditional occupations, and Romani language, music, and dress; similar legislation was enacted in Spain after 1499 (Fraser 1992; Petrova 2003). In the Balkans, the policy of the Ottoman Empire toward Roma was, in general, more lenient than state policy in Western Europe, at least from the sixteenth to the eighteenth centuries (Marushiakova and Popov 2001). Perhaps the most tragic period of Romani history was World War II, when anywhere from 500,000 to 1.5 million Roma were murdered, between one-fourth and one-fifth of their total population (Lewy 2002; Hancock 2002).

The communist regimes in Eastern Europe defined Roma as a social problem. They were targeted for integration into the planned economy, forced to give up their traditional occupations, and assigned to the lowest skilled and lowest paid state jobs (e.g., street cleaners). Specific policies varied by country and by decade, with forced sterilization common in Czechoslovakia until the 1970s; nomadic Roma were forcibly settled, settled Roma were forcibly moved, and aspects of their culture, such as music, were prohibited, as I will discuss below.

In the postsocialist period, harassment and violence toward the Roma of Eastern Europe have increased dramatically, along with marginalization and poverty. Numbering 8–12 million in Europe, they have the lowest standard of living in every country, with unemployment reaching 80 percent in some regions. Today Eastern European Roma face inferior and segregated housing and education (including tracking of children into special schools for the disabled) and poor health conditions, specifically higher infant mortality and morbidity, shorter life expectancy, and higher frequency of chronic diseases. Discrimination is widespread in employment and the legal system, and even educated people routinely express disdain for Gypsies. Hate speech and racial profiling are common in the media. Perhaps most troubling are the hundreds of incidences of physical violence against Roma perpetrated by ordinary citizens and also by the police.[2]

In response to historic discrimination and recent abuses, a Romani human rights movement has mobilized in the last twenty years via a network of activists and nongovernmental organizations such as the European Roma Rights Centre (ERRC), the European Roma Information Office (ERIO), the International Romani Union, the Roma National Congress, the European Roma and Travellers Forum, and European bodies such as the European Union, the Council of Europe, and the Organization for Security and Cooperation in Europe (Klimova-Alexander 2005; Acton and Klimova 2001). This movement has drawn much public attention and funding to the plight of Roma, but material conditions have hardly improved.

Recently, a rising tide of xenophobia and anti-Romani sentiment has surfaced all over Europe. According to the ERRC, Roma remain to date the most persecuted people of Europe; in fact, the *Economist* titled an article "European Roma: Bottom of the Heap" (2008: 35). Observers have shown that rather than being the purview of extremists, anti-immigrant and anti-Romani sentiment is becoming more mainstream. For example, in 2008, the Italian government started to fingerprint all Gypsies living in camps in an effort to crack down on crime; and in 2010 France deported European Union Romani citizens back to Bulgaria and Romania. All over Europe, nationalist parties are growing (often under the guise of populism) and the population is becoming more polarized.[3]

In contrast to negative stereotypes invoking criminality, violence, and lying, positive stereotypes depict Roma as genetically endowed "natural" artists. This attractive yet dangerous coding of Roma hinges on their romanticization by non-Roma as free souls (outside the rules and boundaries of European society), their association with music and the occult, and their proximity to nature and sexuality. Using Edward Said's concept, we can claim that Roma are "orientalized" and exoticized (1978).[4] Katie Trumpener emphasizes the association of Roma with an ahistoric, timeless nostalgia: "Nomadic and illiterate, they wander down an endless road, without a social contract or country to bind them, carrying their home with them, crossing borders at will" (1992: 853). Simultaneously they are reviled as unreformable untrustworthy liars and rejected from civilization. "Feared as deviance, idealized as autonomy" 854), Roma serve as Europe's quintessential others.

In economic terms, Roma adapted to their exclusions and became indispensable suppliers to non-Roma of diverse services such as music, entertainment, fortune-telling, metalworking, horse dealing, woodworking, and seasonal agricultural work. For hundreds of years, Balkan Romani professional musicians have performed for non-Roma (as well as Roma) in cafés and at events such as weddings, baptisms, circumcisions, fairs, and village dances. This professional niche, primarily male and instrumental, requires Roma to know the regional repertoire expertly and interact with it in a creative manner. A nomadic way of life, often enforced on Roma through harassment and prejudice, gave them opportunities to enlarge their repertoires and become multimusical and multilingual. In addition to nomadic Roma, numerous sedentary Roma in major European cities professionally performed urban folk, classical, and/or popular music (Silverman 1999). This musical niche is still somewhat viable today, although employment has greatly diminished. Several Balkan Romani performers are profiting from the recent boom in Gypsy music, but most of the fame and profits tend to go to non-Romani arrangers, producers, and DJs, as I will discuss later. In sum, despite discrimination, Balkan Roma have maintained their association with professional music. Scholars and states, however, have contested the relationship of Romani music to the nation.

Bulgarian Wedding Music: Nationalism, Socialism, and Postsocialism

Moving from Europe in general to the Balkans specifically, I note that the terms "heritage," "tradition," and "folk" had great weight in nineteenth-century Eastern European nation-building projects; indeed, they were used to culturally define the nation, which was assumed to be a community composed of homogeneous folk. Heritage was configured to represent the majority national culture, thereby excluding Roma as well as other minorities. It is no accident that the discipline of folklore arose during the age of romantic nationalism and became a tool for nation building (Bendix 1997; Abrahams 1993; Kirshenblatt-Gimblett 1988). According to Johann Gottfried Herder, the architect of "romantic nationalism," every nation was an organic entity with its own native cultural institutions and pure spirit that are best reflected in the folklore of the peasants (W. Wilson 1976). Language, religion, customs, and music were central elements of the folk spirit; likewise, Benedict Anderson showed nations were "imagined communities" constructed through narratives and symbols of identity (1983).

In the Balkans, folklore emerged at the nexus of valorizing peasant culture; the preoccupation with language/dialects, rural life, and regional variation surfaced in music, especially in collections of rural folk song texts. Donna Buchanan (2006: 36) comments that *narodna muzika*, defined as simultaneously folk, national, people's, and popular music, emerged as both inclusive (of all things Bulgarian) and exclusive (of all things non-Bulgarian); this could be termed a classic case of ethnonationalism in music. Bulgarians (and other Balkan peoples) view their pre-nationhood past as a time of foreign (eastern) domination (Buchanan 2006: 37; Herzfeld 1982). The Ottoman period of "slavery" is contrasted with the fight for "freedom" for the nation-state. Here I will not contest the validity of this depiction, but merely note that most of the populace still today assumes it is factual. Suffice it to say that respected Balkan historians agree that at least in the early centuries the Ottoman Empire was tolerant.

Roma have never been counted under the rubrics "folk" and "peasant," defined in Eastern Europe as locals, persons "from here," tied to the land usually through ownership. Roma were constructed by locals as "others": they were assumed to be nomadic, even though many were sedentary rural dwellers; they did not own their own land; and many of them practiced Islam, which was conflated with Ottoman domination and Turkish culture and thus marginalized. Their culture was assumed to be foreign, different, Eastern, although it actually shared many characteristics of Balkan culture.

A central task of the scholars of the emerging nation-state became proving that Bulgarian culture was pure, untainted by years of Ottoman domination. In fact, until recently, historians and folklorists depicted Bulgarian folklore as a refuge from Turkish domination. Music was a prime area to display the supposed purity of folk culture, untainted by foreign influence (Silverman 1989). Until 1989, almost every scholar claimed that Turkish music left hardly a trace in Bulgaria. This claim is clearly absurd, considering not only the history of Bulgaria but also its location as a crossroads between the Middle East and Europe. Historian Maria Todorova points out that the dominant view of the Ottoman past characterizes it as a "religiously, socially, institutionally, and even racially alien imposition" (1997: 162).

Because folk music became a politicized symbol of the Bulgarian nation, its definitional borders were carefully patrolled to exclude "foreign" musics. Romani music, then, has never been performed in public ensembles, festivals, or music schools under the rubric "folk." Furthermore, Romani music was never specifically collected during the period of nation building or the socialist period. During the socialist period, village music of the Slavs was reaffirmed as authentic folk music, to the exclusion of urban music and the music of minorities, whether they lived in villages or towns (Rice 1996; Buchanan 2006). Furthermore, despite the high level of talent among young Romani musicians, very few were admitted to state-sponsored music high schools, universities, and institutes of music that were the training ground for ensembles. The exclusion of Romani students from music schools occurred not only because of structural discrimination but also because state officials were afraid that Romani music would "pollute" the "purity" of heritage.

As Kapchan pointed out in the introduction to this volume, cultural exclusions often serve as an index to human rights violations. Thus, during the socialist period, Romani and Turkish Muslims were subjected to forced name changes (Muslim to Slavic names), forced changes in their song texts and prohibitions of their customs such as circumcision and costumes such as *shalvari* (Muslim women's wide pants). The instrument *zurna*,[5] exclusively played by male Roma since the fourteenth century, was prohibited in 1984 because the government claimed it was Turkish. Officials and scholars alike claimed Turkish and Romani musics were "foreign" to Bulgaria and were corrupting official folk music. The new genre called "wedding music" was seen as the culprit for the decline in folk music (Silverman 1989, 1996; Buchanan 1996).

Loud, electrified, and displaying a modern aesthetic akin to rock music, wedding music typically utilizes clarinet, saxophone, accordion, guitar, bass, and drum set. Disparate elements, such as jazz and the musics of other cultures (e.g., Indian, Serbian, Greek, Turkish), are combined, and eclecticism and improvization are valued. Wedding music is characterized by melodies with wide ranges, syncopations, daring key changes, fast tempos, and chromatic and arpeggio passages. These practices threatened the socialist establishment because they represented a stylistic abandonment of the official folk music formula. Furthermore, wedding music was often coded as "ethnic" because Roma created the style, and the Romani and Turkish genre *kyuchek* (a genre of music showcasing improvisation and danced solo with torso and abdomen movements) represented a large part of the repertoire. *Kyuchek* became a musical emblem of the suppressed ethnicity of Roma and Turks; the more the government regulated *kyuchek*, the more Roma and Turks demanded to dance and hear it. Everyone in Bulgaria was supposed to identify as Bulgarian: the ethnic and Muslim threat as expressed through music had to be erased.

Wedding music was also a social threat to the establishment because it was a mass movement of young fans of all ethnicities who made music, rather than socialist jobs and loyalty to the state, the center of their lives; they followed famous musicians and spent money on expensive underground recordings and on lavish three-day weddings. In addition, wedding music posed a political threat because it inherently defied the socialist order; it was unofficial, countercultural, and even subversive.

The 1980s was the era of socialist attempts to harass and intimidate wedding musicians. Famous musicians were jailed for playing *kyuchek*; their heads were shaven, they had to break rocks, and their cars were confiscated by the police. Note the comments of Romani wedding musician Yuri Yunakov:

> Unfortunately, Bulgarian politicians mixed music with politics. According to me, music has nothing to do with politics; I think music

> remains music. Our politicians made music political. . . . Imagine yourself in a big field, in a tent where we hold our weddings, and you see fifteen police cars coming. . . . They arrested the sponsor of the wedding also, and, if we were in a restaurant, the owner too. . . . But in spite of this, we played Romani and Turkish music anyway. Jailing us was the most shameful thing for our country and everyone learned about it via newspaper and radio. They put us, the most famous, in jail, so other musicians would see. They made examples of us so others would be afraid.

Yunakov's comments suggest that playing *kyuchek* was not a deliberate antigovernment rebellion, not conscious resistance, but rather a strategic life choice based on his beliefs. Yunakov vividly remembered strategies for avoiding arrest, for example, posting a lookout on the roof to scout for the police, stylistically morphing a *kyuchek* into an approved musical genre, and developing intuition for approaching police officers. Many times wedding musicians ran away even before the police arrived. These strategies are performative responses to discrimination; they underscore how resistance creatively finds appropriate genres of expression (Slymovics 2005; Silverman 2007a).

According to Sherry Ortner (1995), the literature on resistance tends to be "thin" because it is not grounded in thick ethnography. Ortner calls for fieldwork that moves beyond the binary domination versus resistance and investigates cultural ramifications. Resistance needs to be grounded in the subjectivity and agency of actors who are individuals with unique motives and histories (Ortner 1995, 1999). Thus, Yunakov's strategy of performing *kyuchek* in the face of sanctions made sense to him in aesthetic, cultural, and economic terms: it was the music of his community, plus he was making a good living from it.

Yunakov's resistance, however, should neither be romanticized nor elevated to heroic defiance, because in several arenas he (as well as other wedding musicians) accommodated to the socialist government. For example, he ran away from the police, he did not resist the name changes even though his relatives ostracized him, and he recorded sanitized, censored versions of his music so it could be disseminated via the state media. James Scott suggests that in public spaces, "public transcripts" are performed to flatter elites, while backstage "hidden transcripts" express grievances (1990). Indeed, wedding musicians courted favors with communist officials so they wouldn't be driven out of business. Yuri even recalls private parties where socialist officials requested *kyuchek*! Collaborations with the dominating order exist side by side with acts of resistance.

Unfortunately, after the fall of socialism in 1989, the performative valor of wedding musicians was not rewarded. Romani music continues to be excluded from school curricula, folk festivals, ensembles, and other official Bulgarian state institutions; *zurna*, for example, is not taught in the schools. In the 1990s wedding music was no longer prohibited, but it declined in popularity when the market was flooded by *chalga*, a commercial pop/folk fusion. More recently, however, fatigue with *chalga* has surfaced, and a tame form of wedding music that excludes the Romani genre *kyuchek* is making a comeback in media channels as a symbol of "folk heritage." It is being contrasted to the superficial glitz and the artificial formulas of *chalga*, which is criticized as too Romani, too Eastern, and simultaneously too Western, too much like Europop. Ironically, wedding music received the very same criticism in the socialist period, but now it is hailed as quintessential folk music. Wedding music is becoming an ideological symbol of patriotism and monoethnism in a period where Bulgarian identity seems precarious. Nationalist parties rail against *chalga* as corrupting the historical core values of Bulgaria; they encourage patriotic Bulgarians to support folk music, and for private media companies folk music means wedding music. Thus the popularity of wedding music today, just as in socialist times, is informed by a highly politicized environment where the meaning of Bulgarian heritage and identity is debated and the historical politics of the music has been inverted (Silverman 2007a, 2012).

UNESCO and Macedonian Cultural Heritage

My second example of how Romani music contests the category of heritage comes from the Republic of Macedonia, which declared independence from Yugoslavia in 1991. In 2002 Macedonia applied to UNESCO to have the traditional wedding from the village of Galičnik declared a Masterpiece of Oral and Intangible Heritage of Humanity.[6] This UNESCO competition responds to the 1989 initiative titled Recommendations on the Safeguarding of Traditional Culture that advocates preserving cultural heritage that is "in danger of disappearing due to cultural standardization, armed conflicts, tourism, industrialization, the rural exodus, migrations, and the degradation of the environment" (UNESCO 2001: 3). Although I do not have the space here to interrogate all the problematic notions that underpin this UNESCO project and similar proclamations by the World Intellectual Property Organization (WIPO), I wish to point out that heritage is assumed to be coterminous with bounded territorial groups, so-called "communities," and rural culture (Noyes 2006). Cultural heritage comes from "living communities with a sense of continuity" (UNESCO 2001: 5). These agencies have resurrected narratives of the impending loss or survival of selected items of authentic folklore that have rejected "unwanted hybridization" and "alien cultural forms" (Kirshenblatt-Gimblett 2004).

Note that only nation-states can submit applications in the competition for the Masterpieces List. Thus the "humanity" designation elides into the "nation" which must choose some aspects of its culture as masterpieces and reject other aspects. Needless to say, minority culture can be problematic here. On the other hand, UNESCO specifically advocates for the "preservation of cultural diversity" and "the tolerance and harmonious interaction between cultures," so one might expect cultural communication between ethnic groups to surface in applications. Not so for Macedonia's application for the Galičnik wedding. Although the entire wedding is too complicated to describe here, note that at the turn of the twentieth century up to fifty weddings took place simultaneously on Petrovden, July 12. As a collective ceremony of many couples, the wedding dramatized community values; this was especially important in Galičnik, where men migrated out to work for most of the year. Today the wedding has such an iconic place in Macedonian folklore that it appears prominently in a 2009 tourist advertisement.[7]

What is relevant here is that fact that whereas Galičnik is an Eastern Orthodox ethnic Macedonian village, all the musicians who provide music for the week-long ritual are Muslim Roma from nearby cities. These *zurla* and *tapan* players (all from the Majovci clan based in the town of Debar) intimately know the native dance repertoire and signal every important ritual moment with appropriate melodies. There is even a proverb that says "no wedding will take place in Galičnik unless the Majovci family plays" (Kličkova 1996 [1951]). Thus Roma are not only integrated into the Galičnik wedding, but the villagers are dependent upon them for their ritual, dance, and processional music.

Despite the above facts, the UNESCO application from Macedonia hardly mentions Roma at all and nowhere mentions them in relation to the goals of affirming cultural identity and preserving traditions. Roma are merely described in a few sentences as musicians. The great potential in this project for recognizing and promoting the cultural exchange between Roma and Macedonians is ignored. Similarly, Roma are omitted from the section on training the next generation in folk practices. For example, one tangible way Roma could benefit is by UNESCO facilitating the learning of the ritual repertoire by young Romani *zurla* and *tapan* players, many of whom have few professional opportunities.[8]

In fact, for the past few years the *zurla* and *tapan* players at the Galičnik wedding have not been from the Majovci clan but have rather have been Roma from the capital city of Skopje who are employed by national dance ensembles. Furthermore, since the 1960s and the depopulation of the village (for economic reasons), the ritual has been enacted in a two-day condensed version by summer returnees to the village and by members of the Skopje-based Kočo Racin dance ensemble in a specially built amphitheater. Thus the wedding is a revival staged by ensemble members. Sometimes a couple actually gets married, but for the most part, the wedding is a staged "re-creation" of the earlier ritual.

The UNESCO application was submitted by the Union of Macedonian Folklore Ensembles, whose stated aim is "to preserve, protect, support and present Macedonian folklore which reflect [*sic*] . . . the heritage and traditions of the Macedonian people and the nationalities who live in the Republic of Macedonia." The submitted list of "custodians of the know how," however, excludes Roma and is dominated by ensemble leaders and folklorists. The UNESCO application consists of florid language, lauding the Galičnik wedding as "a masterpiece of human creative genius," embodying authentic folklore and national heritage. Referencing the organic tropes of romantic nationalism, the application implies the wedding embodies the soul of the nation that finds expression in rural folklore. All this is quite paradoxical considering that the wedding is a re-creation. Ironically, while Romani living traditions are excluded or minimized, the staged folklore of the majority is coded as authentic.

As Barbro Klein points out (in this volume), states use UNESCO (and heritage policy more generally) to protect the privileged category of "national culture." The coveted UNESCO list of intangible masterpieces deliberately avoids communities like Roma who are not coterminous with states. Heritage may appear to be "safe" conflict-free folk art, but, under the surface, it is often precisely about conflict, nationalism, and human rights. Bill Ivey similarly interrogates the role of states and, furthermore, underlines its obligation to counter forces of corporatization (2008). However, we must also keep in mind the dubious role of states in failing to protect human and cultural rights of minorities. Remembering socialism, Eastern Europeans tend to be either wary of state policy or long for its paternal protection.

Unity/Diversity, Heritage, and the Romani Human Rights Movement

Roma have been dispersed for over a thousand years in a diaspora over several continents. They constitute a rich mosaic of groups that distinguish among themselves culturally and do not intermarry. Discrimination is sometimes the only thing that seems to unify Roma, and this is precisely what they seek to eliminate. Unified neither by language, religion, territory, nor culture, Roma face a huge challenge in mobilizing a Pan-European human rights movement to redress past and present injustices. Activists, then, attempt to construct a cultural heritage that can unify disparate groups. Simultaneously, they recognize the diversity of Roma and grapple with its political implications: "While East European administrators tend to look for the 'uniqueness' and the unity of a people's culture as a prerequisite for promoting distinct cultural entities . . . the Romani people is presenting itself as a huge diaspora embracing five continents, sharing the citizenship of a multitude of states, while lacking a territory of its own" (Gheorghe and Acton 2001: 55–56).

Will Guy similarly explains: "in view of the diversity of Roma experience, it would be more accurate to talk of a constellation of Romani cultures and . . . a cluster of varying and related identities rather than a homogeneous identity" (Guy 2001: 28). However, Nicolae Gheorghe and Thomas Acton also realize that the "multiculturality" of Roma can be a drawback to political mobilization: "it is still difficult to imagine how multiculturality and multi-territoriality could become the basis for the cultural affirmation and development of people . . . which strive to identify themselves . . . in terms of unity and specificity" (2001: 56). While Andrzej Mirga and Nicolae Gheorghe (1997) have suggested adopting the term "transnational minority,"[9] other activists use the terminology "ethnogenesis" (Guy 2001: 19) and "nation." The International Romani Union's 2000 Declaration of a Nation states: "Individuals belonging to the Roma Nation call for representation of their Nation, which does not want to become a State. . . . We share the same tradition, the same culture, the same origin; we are a nation" (Acton and Klimova 2001: 216).

Similar to indigenous rights movements that have utilized symbols for unification (such as the powwow of Native North Americans), the Romani rights movement has created a unifying label (Roma), a singular narrative of Indian origin, the Holocaust as a symbol of oppression, an anthem, a flag, and a literary language. Each is a trope that inscribes the legitimate historical place of Roma; each corresponds to the dominant European tropes of defining a singular nation. This is no accident, as the Romani movement seeks to legitimize the place of Roma in European politics. The term "Roma" is used as an in-group label by Roma who speak Romani, but these Roma constitute only about half the world's Roma. Other designations, such as Sinti, Tsigan, Gitano, and Gypsy, have regional provenance but are rarely accepted in Pan-European activist forums. Roma has emerged as the unifying term even in regions where it was never used.

The Indian origin of Roma is solidly supported by historical linguistics, but the precise time, location, and nature of the exodus is contested (Hancock 2002). Indeed, Roma might not have been a unified ethnic group that left India at one time. Activists often use dubious historical connections to prove cultural ties to India, such as claiming certain Romani musical scales or dance steps come from India (Fonseca 1995). Furthermore, Gypsy music festivals are usually modeled on the documentary film *Latcho Drom* (The Good Road), which depicted linear nomadic migration from India to Spain. Festivals and concerts begin with Rajasthani music and then travel westward, ending with flamenco music. This conveys the simplistic linear message that Rajasthani music today represents what Romani music sounded like a thousand years ago. Furthermore, not all Roma are nomadic; historically, Roma in Eastern Europe have tended to be more sedentary than Roma of Western Europe due to government polices.

Elena Marushiakova and Vesselin Popov claim that a significant part of Romani nationalist ideology is "emphasizing the Holocaust" (2001: 49). Indeed, the new Romani word for the Holocaust, *porrajmos*, is now widely used in Romani circles. The Holocaust has become a symbol of Romani oppression for several reasons: the fact that Roma were targeted is still not widely known; no Roma received compensation; and, most important, Romani activists have had to fight to be included in Holocaust museums and commemorations (Hancock 1987, 2002).

Unlike the Holocaust, which is a badge of suffering, the Romani anthem and flag are positive affirmations of Romani heritage. Both were adopted at the first World Roma Congress, which took place in 1971. The flag is composed of a green lower portion (the earth), a blue upper portion (the sky), and a red wheel in the middle (migration); some activists claim the wheel is an Indian spiritual sign, a mandala. The anthem "Dželem Dželem" (I traveled. I traveled) combines a melody in oral circulation in the Balkans and a text about nomadism and persecution composed by a Serbian Romani singer (Marushiakova and Popov 1995: 11–21). The anthem now has a ceremonial function among activists at conferences but is only found in some Balkan Romani communities. Finally, the formation of a Romani literary language and the production of a Romani dictionary were mandated several years ago by the International Romani Union, but progress has been slow. Many Romani dialects exist and the language has changed in relation to surrounding languages. Deciding which dialect of Romani to elevate to the literary language is problematic, as is deciding which orthography to use.

In sum, although Roma have been excluded from the dominant tropes of national folklore, they have constructed their own symbols of heritage as part of a strategizing process in European politics. As Herzfeld points out, states *and* citizens both depend on the semiotic illusion—that identity is consistent; they both create or constitute homogeneity and produce iconicities (1997: 31). Although "essentialism is not exclusively a state activity," Herzfeld explicates that "states do have a rich variety of devices [and I would add institutions] for essentializing—law, etc.—it seems like common sense" (31). On the other hand, marginalized ethnic groups like Roma often engage in what Gayatri Spivak has termed "strategic essentialism" (Spivak 1988) in the cause of mobilization. Herzfeld reminds us that "powerful state agents and humble social actors all engage in the strategy of essentialism to the same degree." In fact, "social poetics is the analysis of essentialism in everyday life" (1997: 31).

Herzfeld rightly draws our attention to essentialism, a concept that has been so demonized in cultural theory that Pnina Werbner called it "the bogey word of the human sciences" (1997: 226). In fact, perhaps the concept of hybridity became so fashionable in cultural studies because it seemed like the perfect antidote to essentialism. The demonization of essentialism is quite unfortunate because we can never understand identity politics without it. Furthermore, as scholars, we remove ourselves from the trenches of political struggle when we point fingers and assign accusatory labels. As Arif Dirlik writes: "It seems that any admission of identity, including the identity that may be necessary to any articulate form of collective political action, is open to charges of essentialism" (2000: 188). Similarly, bell hooks welcomes a critique of essentialism but warns that "This critique should not become a means to dismiss differences or an excuse for the ignoring of experience. It is often evoked in a manner which suggests that all the ways black people think of ourselves as 'different' from whites are really essentialist, and therefore without concrete grounding. This way of thinking threatens the very foundations that make resistance to domination possible" (1990: 130). Both hooks and Dirlik remind us of the irony that postmodern/postcolonial intellectuals have the luxury to repudiate essentialized identities. They encourage scholars not to dismiss cultural and historical claims to collective identity as mere essentialisms, but to analyze them as works in progress in a hierarchical political playing field that has real consequences.

Although we may be tempted to label Romani nationalist symbols essentialist "invented traditions" because they are newly created, we fall into several traps by employing the term "invented." Eric Hobsbawm and Terence Ranger (1983) first used the term to refer to symbols and practices that figured prominently in European nationalist discourse but were of recent historical provenance. They therefore implied that some traditions were authentic while others were invented, hence inauthentic. Richard Handler and Jocelyn Linnekin (1984) and Allan Hanson (1989) broadened the argument to claim that all traditions and authenticity itself are invented in the sense that they are social constructions. This position fell squarely into the 1980s postmodernist critique of bounded notions of culture but couldn't have been more ill timed in terms of world politics.

Indeed, the 1980s were precisely the era of the emergence of identity politics, when marginal groups were finally taking center stage and defining their own histories and symbols. James Clifford explains that exactly at the moment when radical poststructuralisms became popular, "a whole range of formerly marginal and excluded peoples and perspectives were fighting for recognition: women, racial and ethnic minorities, new immigrants. These groups, for the first time entering the public sphere, often felt the sophisticated cultural critics to be, in effect, telling them, 'Oh yes, we understand your gender, race, culture and identity are important to you, but you know, you're just essentializing' " (2003: 64). Indigenous scholar/activists such as Haunani-Kay Trask rejected "the implication that dynamic traditions were merely politically contrived for current purposes" (Clifford 2004: 156); they criticized constructivists as neocolonial outsiders who were thwarting the legitimate political agendas of marginalized people. Other scholars analyzed the confrontation between these two sides, arguing that we should simultaneously abandon the loaded language of "invention" and interrogate all positions as to motivations, agendas, and funding (Briggs 1996).

Taking Charles Briggs's suggestion, my task is to elucidate how the concept of heritage/tradition can be pried from its narrow historical moorings so we may understand the symbols of the Romani human rights movement as historically placed responses to marginality. The symbols discussed above (the flag, the language, the Holocaust, and Indian origins) are all drawn from European models but have profound significance for many Roma. As Toby Miller writes, culture "provides the legitimizing ground on which particular groups claim resources and seek inclusion in national narratives" (2006: 110). At the same time, an expanded notion of heritage can help us widen bounded notions of national culture to embrace multicultural and hybrid forms. Indigenous heritage movements such as those of various Native American groups can serve as useful comparisons to Roma. As Clifford notes, indigenous leaders are simultaneously loosening and reclaiming the notion of authenticity; sometimes authenticity can be "a straitjacket, making every engagement with modernity (religions, technologies, knowledges, markets, or media) a contamination, a 'loss' of true selfhood" (2004: 156). Rejecting their emplacement in the past, native leaders are asserting their legitimate place in modernity through global displays of media, technology, and legality. Simultaneously they are claiming land, reviving languages and rituals, reclaiming sacred objects and burials from collections, building cultural centers, and representing themselves in museums. Similarly, Roma are starting to establish cultural centers, design exhibits, produce films, and publish their own histories and ethnographies. Sometimes these artifacts and sites are awkward hybrids or essentializing efforts, but they are all "zones of contact" (Clifford 1997: 188), "whereby authenticity thus becomes a process—the open-ended work of preservation and transformation. Living traditions must be selectively pure: mixing, matching, remembering, forgetting, sustaining, transforming their senses of communal continuity" (2004: 156). To examine what Roma and other marginalized groups are doing in constructing their current identities is to implicitly interrogate and rethink notions of heritage and authenticity. These terms do not necessarily indicate fixed boundaries and recognizable content, although stable identity is always an issue in politics.

Clifford claims that "what is at stake is the power to define tradition and authenticity, to determine the relationships though which . . . identity is negotiated in a changing world" (2004: 157). The challenge is to reject both a pro- and anti-essentialist position and to embrace an anti-anti-essentialist position. As Clifford writes:

> The two negatives, do not, of course, add up to a positive, and so the anti-anti-essentialist position is not simply a return to essentialism. It recognizes that a rigorously anti-essentialist attitude, with respect to things like identity, culture, tradition, gender . . . is not really a position one can sustain in a consistent way. . . . Certainly one can't sustain a social movement or a community without certain apparently stable criteria for distinguishing us from them. These may be . . . articulated in connections and disconnections, but, as they are expressed and become meaningful to people, they establish accepted truths. Certain key symbols come to define the we against the they; certain core elements . . . come to be separated out, venerated, fetishized, defended. This is the normal process, the politics, by which groups form themselves into identities. (2003: 62)

Roma have, thus, defined and defended key symbols of "the we against the they," even if these symbols are mutable and emergent.

Stuart Hall, in "Who Needs 'Identity'?" (1996: 4), makes the point that identity politics arise precisely around issues of representation: "Though they seem to invoke an origin in a historical past . . . actually identities are about . . . using the resources of history, language and culture in the process of becoming . . . ; not 'who we are' or 'where we came from' so much as who we might become, how we have been represented, and how that bears on how we represent ourselves. Identities are, therefore constituted within, not without representation" (also see Hancock 1997).

Hall's concept of identity rejects an unchanging traditional core; it emphasizes the emergent; it "does *not* signal that stable core of the self, unfolding from beginning to end through all the vicissitudes of history without change. . . . Nor . . . is it that collective or true self hiding inside the many other, more superficial or artificially imposed 'selves,' which a people with a shared history . . . hold in common." Rather, identities are "never unified, and . . . increasingly fragmented and fractured; never singular but multiply constructed across . . . intersecting and antagonistic discourses, practices and positions" (Hall 1996: 3–4). For Roma, identities are always emergent, constructed, fragmented due to the changing constraints of marginality. Moreover, Romani cultural identities have always been construed in relation to hegemonic powers such as patrons of the arts, state folklore officials, and market forces.

According to Clifford, "tradition is not a wholesale return to past ways, but a practical selection and critical reweaving of roots" whereby " some essentialisms are embraced while others are rejected (2004: 157). Tradition should not be read as "endless reiteration but as 'the changing same,' . . . not the so-called return to roots but a coming-to-terms-with our 'routes' " (Hall 1996: 4). Here Hall is referencing Paul Gilroy's useful formulation of tradition as the "changing same" (1993: 101). Gilroy advocates that the term "tradition" be used "neither to identify a lost past nor to name a culture of compensation which would restore access to it" (198). The "lost past" is sometimes conceived by African American writers and activists as the African homeland, whereby "Africa is retained as one special measure of their authenticity" (191). But, according to Gilroy, this ignores the important place of the diaspora in forging African American identities. Similarly for Roma, Indian origins, whether historical, linguistic, or cultural are valorized as deep cultural symbols, but on the ground, diasporic flows and cultural circulations define the Romani experience in practice.

Gilroy, Clifford, Hall, and Briggs all urge us to analyze specific identity projects in their historical contexts, paying special attention to inequalities and hierarchies. Just as the project of African American identity making was forged in the crucible of slavery and diaspora and the project of Native American identity making was forged in the crucible of genocide and displacement, similarly the project of Romani identity making was forged during centuries of discrimination and diaspora. The marginal position of these groups has led to an urgency of cultural matters tied to human rights and global entitlements. Heritage sits at the center of these political debates.

Romani Music, Appropriation, and Cultural Rights

My last example concerns the global musical landscape of Balkan Romani music that has expanded dramatically in the last two decades (Silverman 2007b). Whereas in the early 1990s, Balkan Romani music was admired by a small group of fans, by 2002 *Time* magazine's music section proclaimed "Roma Rule" (Purvis 2002: 70–71) and in 2007 *Newsweek* wrote "The World Embraces Gypsy Culture" (Brownell and Haq 2007). In 2006 Balkan Romani music exploded on the *Borat* movie soundtrack, and today youth dance to Gypsy remixes played by DJs in cities such as New York, San Francisco, Brussels, Frankfurt, Berlin, Vienna, Paris, and Amsterdam. What does all this mean for the cultural rights of Romani musicians? Before we celebrate too glibly we need to investigate representational and performance issues, the flow of international capital and media attention, and how power relationships are implicated in these exchanges.

In my introduction I discussed how Roma have been characterized as the ultimate music appropriators; while is true that Balkan Roma have taken numerous musical elements from co-territorial peoples, we must also remember that Roma borrow selectively, and, furthermore, they creatively rework whatever they take. Balkan Roma have also contributed many musical elements and genres to the music of other ethnicities. Their major role in the Balkan genre *kyuchek* and in Bulgarian wedding music has been mentioned; similar contributions to Romanian and Hungarian string bands and Spanish flamenco are documented.

When Roma appropriate, however, their class relationship to others is rarely altered. No matter how powerful their music, they have not become powerful politically. They may provide a desirable commodity, but they still have not lost their stigma. Furthermore, they still need patrons who are more privileged than they are. Even the most famous Balkan Romani performers today tend to be managed by non-Romani managers and recording companies.[10] I underscore, then, that appropriations by the powerful from the marginal are different from appropriations by the marginal from the powerful. When more powerful groups take from the marginal, the marginal artists often lose; in addition, often they can't fight back in terms of ownership or copyright.

Goran Bregović is a good example of a non-Romani appropriator who has become more famous and wealthy than any Roma. He is often an object of wrath to many Balkan Romani musicians and is even described by some as a thief. Born in Bosnia of mixed heritage, Bregović dared to perform rock/folk fusions of all the ethnic groups in Yugoslavia in the 1970s. In the 1980s he became internationally famous for his musical scores for Bosnian film director Emir Kusturica, whose films deal with Romani themes. Bregović's film scores, albums, and concerts prominently feature Serbian brass bands composed of Roma, but he copyrights the material under his name (as arranger/composer) and has not credited any sources. In fact, at Romani music festivals, he gets top billing, above his sources.

We may clearly place Bregović in the "celebratory camp" of synthetic music practitioners. Steven Feld notes the divide between "anxious narratives" and "celebratory narratives" of world music appropriation. Celebratory narratives valorize hybridity, feature hopeful scenarios about economic fairness, and "even have romantic equations of hybridity with overt resistance" (Feld 2000: 152). Anxious narratives fret over purity and underline the economics of exploitation. I believe that we need to interrogate both types of narratives. Celebratory scholars and musicians eschew ownership and valorize the fertile artistic exchange of musical styles. George Lipsitz, for example, shows that appropriations create cultural zones of contact where intercultural dialogue between ethnic groups can happen; he says hybridity produces "an immanent critique of contemporary social relations" (1994: 17).

On the other hand, Lipsitz may "overstate the relative cultural power of these musics" (Born and Hesmondhalgh 2000: 27) to effect change.[11] Celebratory tales espouse a "democratic vision for world music," which then becomes part of the marketing scheme. When audiences observe the incredible diversity of music available, they see it "as some kind of sign that democracy prevails, that every voice can be heard, every style can be purchased, everything will be available to everybody" (Feld 2000: 167). But, in celebrating diversity, we shouldn't confuse the flow of musical contents with the flow of power relations (Feld 1994: 263). Often music critics and fans pay too much attention to the sound aspects of world music and not enough to the hierarchical social, political, and economic relationships that produce and shape them.

Aside from Bregović, there are many DJs in western European countries who have profitable careers remixing Romani music and/or playing Gypsy remixes in clubs. Remixes such as *Electric Gypsyland* 1 and 2 (Crammed Discs 2004 and 2006) were high on the European pop music charts but have hardly helped Roma. Very few Romani musicians have contracts with Western labels, and among those that do, fewer are fair. Most Roma jump at the chance of any contract whatsoever due to their lack of commercial contacts and employment. Once the rare Western contract is secured, the label has complete control over permissions and distribution. Depending on recording contracts, the label may or may not inform the artist and may or may not pay her/him if a DJ wants to do a remix or if a film wants to use a song. Most recording contracts do not give rights of distribution to performers. The music industry itself is very exploitative of most artists, whether Romani or not, except for the top pop stars. Although the Internet has opened distribution possibilities, this does not necessarily lead to Roma receiving profits from their music. YouTube may help a Romani performer increase his fan base, and music platforms like Soundcloud lead to DJs sharing their remixes, but, in general, Roma rarely profit from Internet music sharing.

Returning to legal rights, I note that Macedonian Romani singer Esma

Redžepova was quite upset at the use of her song "Čhaje Šukarije" (Beautiful Girl) in the film *Borat,* but she had no cultural rights and no legal case. The film properly credits Redžepova, and the producers asked proper permission from the label (Times Square/World Connection), but the label never asked her. In fact, the packaging of her album now proudly features an advertising sticker proclaiming "In Borat!" Note that in *Borat*, Gypsy music tends to be played when the scenes depict Kazakhstan, hence backwardness. Furthermore, the Kazakh village featured in *Borat* is actually Glod, a Romani village in Romania. The primitiveness was somewhat staged (e.g., animals were brought inside homes), but the poverty and marginality were all too real. In fact, the villagers were outraged when they found out how the footage was used. They too were unable to sue successfully sue because permissions were obtained from non-Romani officials.

Thus, when we see hordes of youths dancing to Balkan Romani music remixes in clubs, and even when we see selected Romani artists attracting huge live audiences, we should not assume that Romani musicians are directly benefiting. True, there are more consumers of Romani music. But the global market is mediated by record companies, managers, festivals, and clubs; these institutions and sites are mostly controlled by non-Roma.[12] Only a handful of Romani artists have achieved world acclaim while equally talented performers languish due to lack of international ties. It is clear, then, that the contemporary Balkan Romani music scene should not be judged by the international appearance of success.

Conclusion

Heritage, cultural rights, and human rights are entwined in historical layers of meaning and representation. States, as well as markets, scholars, activists, and international organizations such as UNESCO all play important roles in defining, controlling, and evaluating culture. In the Balkans, heritage played an important role in state building and in establishing official socialist arts; in the postsocialist era, states and markets continue to police boundaries of the nation in a heightened atmosphere of xenophobia. The case of Balkan Roma highlights how multiple marginalizations can make a group especially vulnerable to exclusions of state policy; creative performative resistance, however, can serve to mobilize ethnicity around cultural rights, such as music and dance. Moreover, historical and contemporary human rights violations have spearheaded a Pan-European Romani movement that constructs symbols of heritage for strategic political aims. Finally the globalization of Gypsy music poses complex questions of who owns, profits from, and performs Romani arts, and whether minority artists have a voice in terms of cultural rights in the world music market.

Music, then, as an embodied, sensory, performative, and highly symbolic genre traces a highly nuanced relationship to heritage. Both states and markets have used music to define categories of people and art as legitimate or illegitimate, depending on political and economic agendas. When the genre of music is combined with the historical stereotypic baggage associated with Roma, a powerful combination ensues. Via state and local exclusions and inclusions of music we can see how Roma have been alternately scripted into and out of definitions of the nation. Balkan Roma have been denigrated as corruptors of national folk music or hailed as geniuses of innovation; today their music is branded for global consumption yet they rarely benefit from this fame. Romani music, then, poses significant questions of human and cultural rights.

Chapter 6

Intangible Rites: Heritage Sites, the Reburial Issue, and Modern Pagan Religions in Britain

Sabina Magliocco

June 20, 2006: the night of the summer solstice, Stonehenge. Thousands of Britons of all ages and from all walks of life have assembled on the grounds of this UNESCO-designated cultural heritage site, with the consent of the authorities, to await the dawning of the sun on the summer solstice and participate in what has become an all-night rave. Druids and drummers mingle with police and vendors, who purvey everything from Mexican and vegetarian food to the glow sticks that have become ubiquitous to all nighttime public celebrations. As the night wears on, a light drizzle begins; the crowds attempt to take shelter under the stones. Some doze, while others drink, dance, and seek ecstasy on this, the shortest night of the year. At last, sky begins to lighten, and the crowd's energy picks up again. As the sun's rays crest over the heel stone at the henge's northeast edge, and the crowd begins to cheer. The roar grows up from the ancient temple toward the rising sun, and at that moment the New Agers, Druids, Goths, ravers, and drunken partiers touch, for a second, the point in the space-time continuum at which all other humans have celebrated this astronomical event at this place, in all times, like the apex of an arc, or light concentrated by a prism.[1]

August 25, 2008: Stonehenge again. A coalition of modern Druids, part of the Council of British Druid Orders, is present to bless excavations undertaken by archaeologists Mike Parker Pearson and Julian Thomas, accompanied by their colleagues Mike Pitts and Julian Richards, as part of the Riverside

Project, whose purpose is to explore the connections between Stonehenge and a neighboring site where ancient peoples may have camped and lived.[2] Today, the archaeologists are reopening a pit previously excavated during the 1920s where cremated human remains had been deposited after having been discovered by early archaeologists. The scientists want to subject them to DNA testing and mineral analyses to reconstruct early human life ways and kin relations that could shed light on the history of the monument. Because very little skeletal material remains from the late Neolithic, the study would make significant contributions to knowledge about the lives of these early Britons. The event is attracting a great deal of publicity: BBC cameras are rolling as white-robed Druids and archaeologists in field attire stand over the plotted area, about to kick off the dig.

Suddenly one of the Druids who is to conduct the blessing discovers that the excavation will be unearthing early human remains, a fact not previously known to him. Instead of conducting the blessing, he begins to shout abuse at the archaeologists, calling them "grave-robbers" and other slurs. He cancels the blessing and calls on the other Druids present to join him in protesting the excavation as an "insult to our ancestors."[3]

* * *

This chapter deals with the emerging conflict over access to prehistoric stone monuments, many of which are world heritage sites, and the disposition of human remains found in or near them, between different stakeholding groups in Britain during the first decade of the twenty-first century.[4] It addresses the competing claims and heritage discourses of archaeologists and heritage managers, on one hand, and those of a small group of Neopagans, on the other.[5] At its heart is the constructed nature of heritage itself, and the centrality of the imagination to that construction. It is imagination that creates intangible heritage, and that constructs "heritage" from places, objects, and events. In that sense, the human right involved in this issue is freedom of imagination—the right to imagine one's relationship to the past and construct a sense of identity based upon it. While seemingly frivolous in comparison to more vital human rights, the right to imagine actually stands at the center of the process of identity creation, as all cultural entities construct themselves with reference to the past—more often than not, one that is recast in terms of present needs and exigencies. We can thus think of the right to imagine as central to all cultural groups, whether ethnic, national, religious, or based on some other shared characteristic. Narratives of a group's imagined history, however, may come into conflict with the historical accounts of academic experts and scholars, whose authority is recognized by the dominant culture and the state. This clash between lay and expert notions of heritage lies at the heart of the conflict over access to stone monuments and reburial of human remains found therein.

The postcolonial critique of the sciences and decolonization of archaeology radically altered the relationship between archaeologists and stakeholding communities in the public they serve. Archaeologists in North America and Australia have increasingly had to engage with indigenous groups on a number of levels. Indigenous claims about the sanctity of certain locations have resulted in bans against their development or excavation by archaeologists (Jones and Harris 1998: 253; Haley and Wilcoxon 1997). Legislation such as the 1990 Native American Graves Protection and Repatriation Act (NAGPRA) "provides a process for museums and Federal agencies to return certain Native American cultural items—human remains, funerary objects, sacred objects, and objects of cultural patrimony—to lineal descendants, culturally affiliated Indian tribes, and Native Hawaiian organizations."[6] Associated state laws[7] mandate the presence in archaeological excavations of native representatives whose role is to participate in the examination of any human remains unearthed, help determine their origins, and ensure their return to the proper tribal organization for reburial. As a result, indigenous communities and archaeologists are cooperating to an unprecedented extent (Jacobs 2009).

At the heart of this endeavor are the religious rights of indigenous communities. Many Native Americans, Native Hawaiians, and Australians have specific extant beliefs about the proper disposition of human remains and sacred objects and the harmful results to the living if these are ignored or violated. These materials had often been obtained violently as part of the process of colonization, in a way that abused the human rights of indigenous communities. The fact that museums and curation facilities were infringing upon not only the human rights but the religious beliefs of indigenous peoples was finally recognized as violating the ideal of respect for minorities that is at the center of modern, liberal democracies and lent weight to the moral force of indigenous demands (Powell, Garza, and Hendricks 1993; Rosenblum 2009).

Since the late 1990s, a small minority of British Pagans, many of them Druids, have borrowed indigenous discourses to contest the excavation of heritage sites and the storage and display of prehistoric human remains in curation facilities and museums (Blain and Wallis 2007b). Drawing on arguments successfully used by indigenous peoples in North America and Australia, they claim that the scientific study of these remains violates the rights of ancient peoples to rest in peace as their funerary customs and traditions demanded. This has led to increasing conflicts between British archaeologists, heritage managers, and members of the public over access to, and interpretation of, archaeological sites, and over the reburial of human remains found at or near those sites. The problem is not simply one of religious beliefs versus the scientific establishment, however. Modern Pagans themselves are anything but unanimous on the issue; as I will illustrate, they take a range of attitudes, from full support of archaeologists and heritage managers, to uncompromising calls for immediate reburial of all human remains held in museums and curation facilities. Moreover, a growing sector of the public is disturbed by the exhibition of human remains in museum displays, and with the treatment of human remains, especially prehistoric ones, by archaeologists (Blain and Wallis 2007a: 15). Scientific professionals are likewise divided on the issue: some have reacted to Pagan demands with disdain, while others have been willing to engage more closely with stakeholding communities, taking into account a variety of site interpretations and becoming involved in the repatriation and reburial of artifacts and human remains.

Among the most important rights recognized by the Universal Declaration of Human Rights is the freedom of religion; "this right includes freedom to change . . . religion or belief, and freedom, either alone or in community with others and in public or private, to manifest . . . religion or belief in teaching, practice, worship and observance."[8] The majority of Western democracies strive to respect these rights, even in the case of minority religions and new religious movements. But as the editor of this volume reminds us, at stake is not only the freedom of minority groups to conduct religious ceremonies at heritage sites and hold religious beliefs different from those of the majority. Kapchan argues that the right to feel, the *freedom of imagination*, is just as central to cultural heritage as the right to tangible cultural property (Introduction, this volume). At the heart of the conflict, as I discussed above, is the freedom to imagine one's heritage, relationship to the past, and identity. But there are other rights involved as well: the rights of the ancient dead to rest in peace and have their burials respected; the rights of archaeologists to pursue scientific research in accordance with national laws; and the rights of other Britons to learn about their history.

The demands of a small group of Druids intentionally challenge our notions about proper relationships between present and past, between tangible and intangible heritage and the right to determine the use to which tangible heritage is put. By using the language of religious freedom to stipulate how heritage sites and human remains may be treated, they push the limits of liberalism in Western democracies. Using this as a test case, this chapter will engage a number of questions at the heart of the argument of human rights and heritage, both tangible and intangible. These include who has the right to decide the disposition of prehistoric human remains, and how arguments for the rights of prehistoric humans are constructed. In order to understand these within the context of the modern Pagan movement, I will examine how Pagans understand and interact with heritage sites, how they construe their relationship to, and right to determine the disposal of, ancient human remains, what they understand by respectful treatment of human remains, and more broadly how they interpret and use archaeological evidence. At the core of these issues is the question of how humans imagine and relate to the past, and what happens when competing stakeholders disagree on interpretations of the past and the right to determine the fate of historical materials associated with heritage.

My larger aim is to understand why some modern Pagans are choosing to engage in this polemic at this particular historical juncture. In exploring this, I seek to situate the reclamation of paganism in a more political framework in order to theorize how European pagan heritages are currently being imagined and reinterpreted.

Modern Pagan Religions

Modern Paganism, sometimes called Neopaganism, encompasses a number of religions that attempt to revive, re-create, and experiment with pre-Christian polytheism in a contemporary context. It is one of the fastest-growing new religious movements in the world. According to a 2002 estimate by the Pagan Federation, there are 50,000–200,000 self-identified Pagans in Britain.[9]

Modern Pagan religions emerged from the crucible of Romanticism in the late eighteenth and early nineteenth centuries as a form of rebellion against the increasing urbanization and industrialization of the Western world. In the traditions of their ancestors and the practices of indigenous peoples, they sought a more authentic relationship with nature, the sacred, and community, which would provide a needed counterbalance to the alienation and secularization of modernity. Modern Pagan religions often refer to themselves as "nature religions," in the sense that they see divinity as immanent in the natural world, rather than transcending it. They draw their principal sacred metaphors, symbols, and narratives from observation of the natural world, and some have animistic beliefs in which all aspects of the natural world are regarded as having a consciousness or soul (Harvey 2005). For Pagans, the landscape is alive, animated by a variety of spirits, which can include goddesses, gods, ancestor spirits, "land wights," or nature spirits, and "energy," or forces inherent in natural objects. The idea of the divine feminine is central to many forms of modern Paganism: most revere goddesses as well as gods, and for some the earth itself is a manifestation of the female generative principle in nature—literally, a "Mother Nature" upon which all forms of life on earth depend for sustenance and survival. Modern Pagan religions do not share beliefs about the nature, or even the existence of, an afterlife. There is no sense of otherworld rewards or punishments for behavior; instead, the emphasis is on human potential and development in the present life. They are united by the practice of ritual as their principle form of worship and artistic expression. Most rituals mark significant seasonal transitions. The most widespread festive calendar, adopted by the largest percentage of Pagan religions regardless of denomination, celebrates the solstices, equinoxes, and the days falling roughly between each solstice and equinox (February 1, May 1, August 1, and November 1).[10]

Pagan foundation legends portray these modern religions as unbroken continuations of ancient pre-Christian practices. Even when Pagans accept the academic view of their religions as a form of cultural revival or reclamation, the linkage to a pagan past is of vital importance to their identity and is frequently used as a way to authenticate their religious practice. Especially in Europe, where the connection between contemporary practitioners and their forebears has not been interrupted as it has for those in the New World, Pagans feel a strong link with their ancient ancestors. That bond need not be only genealogical; many believe that their practice, their view of the land as sacred, and their concept of an inspirited universe link them to past practitioners in a special way, and to a greater extent than modern Britons who do not share their religion and worldview. They may identify closely with these ancient ancestors, viewing themselves as their modern descendants and representatives.

There are numerous varieties of modern Paganism, many inspired by the traditions of a particular ancient culture.[11] In Britain, these may include Wicca, Druidry,[12] Heathenry,[13] and modern Shamanism. Among the most visible in the controversy over the disposition of British heritage sites and human remains are Heathens and Druids. Heathenry is inspired by the religions, literature, and folklore of the Germanic peoples of Northern Europe, as it is portrayed in works such as the Icelandic sagas and the *Poetic Edda*. Organized in small, family-based groups called "kindred," they may follow a Norse or Saxon pantheon (Blain 2005: 188). While the revival of Norse or Germanic paganism was tainted by its use as racist propaganda by the Nazis during World War II, the majority of modern British Heathen do not see themselves as racist. They perceive their religion as a product of a particular culture, landscape, and historical time—"indigenous to place but not tied to blood or race categorizations" (Blain 2005: 193). Landscape and place are therefore particularly important to Heathen. There are various subgroups of British Heathenry, including the Odinic Rite, Odinshof, and the Ring of Troth, but the majority of Heathen do not affiliate with any of these organizations (191). Heathens are smaller in number and much less conspicuous in the British Pagan scene than the more publicly visible and vocal Druids.

Druidry belongs to a class of religions more broadly known as Celtic-Based Spirituality (Butler 2005: 91), in that it consciously makes reference to a Celtic past. The druids were the priestly class of the ancient Celts in Gaul and Britain. As they left no written record of their spiritual beliefs and practices, what we know of them comes exclusively from the Romans, who conquered the lands in which they practiced and had every reason to make them appear savage and bloodthirsty. Because so little is known of the druids' real beliefs and practices, they have become, through the ages, a perfect blank canvas on which successive political and cultural groups have projected their fantasies, both positive and negative, of what ancient Celtic culture and spirituality were like. The figure of the druid was reclaimed in Britain for a variety of political and philosophical ends beginning in the late Renaissance, transforming the ancient priests into wise keepers of knowledge and national heroes (Hutton 2007: 8–23). Modern Druids see themselves as the spiritual descendants of these earlier practitioners. Historian Ronald Hutton, who has conducted the most thorough research to date on both the historical use of the druid trope and on modern Pagan Druidry (Hutton 2007, 2009), identifies two principal strains of it in Britain today. Both types share a view of nature and the land as sacred, and a penchant for celebrating public rituals in stone circles while dressed in colorful costumes. In other ways, however, they differ markedly.

The first is directly descended from fraternal Druid orders dating to the seventeenth and eighteenth centuries. It is represented by two main groups: the Universal Bond, founded in the late 1800s by George Watson McGregor Reid and revitalized in the 1960s by Ross Nichols, and the Order of Bards, Ovates and Druids (OBOD), founded by Philip Carr-Gomm, a pupil of Nichols, in the 1970s. The OBOD is now the largest modern Druid order, with 12,000 members, a home-study course, and "groves" through most of the English-speaking world. More a spirituality than a religion, it is open to members of all faiths. Its members are dedicated to philosophical and humanistic debate, distilling the wisdom of many different cultural and religious traditions for the benefit of humankind, and the pursuit of human development through liberal ideals. Their model of the Druid is that of a peacemaker and bridge builder between the natural and spiritual worlds, as well as between many different human cultures and traditions (Hutton 2008a). Several additional orders have peacefully split off from the OBOD, but retain cordial relations with it (Hutton 2007: 196–97).

A very different kind of Druidry grew out of the festival culture that developed around Stonehenge in the middle years of the twentieth century. Since the early twentieth century, members of the Universal Bond, with permission of the authorities, would gather, robed in white, at the heritage site on the summer solstice to carry out their rites. In the 1960s and 1970s, they were increasingly accompanied by a festival in the adjacent field, where hippies, drummers, musicians, and other free spirits gathered to celebrate, play music, drink, and welcome the dawn. From 1979 on, festival-goers mingled with Druids inside the stones, often culminating in rowdy, booze-soaked, all-night revels. Concerned for the preservation of the monument, English Heritage closed Stonehenge to the public completely in 1985 (Hutton 2007: 192). A popular movement protesting this closure then arose, incorporating the older Druid orders (the Universal Bond and OBOD), who wanted to continue to be allowed to celebrate there, and leading to the formation of three new orders expressly dedicated to the political cause of granting public access to the stones on the day of the solstice. These were the Loyal Arthurian Warband, led by Arthur Pendragon; the Secular Order of Druids, founded by the late Tim Sebastion; and the Glastonbury Order of Druids, headed by Rollo Maughling (Hutton 2007: 198). These much more radical Druids share a countercultural, politicized model of the Druid drawn from Tacitus's representation of druids as leaders of an anti-Roman resistance, seeing themselves as modern-day freedom fighters battling the bureaucratized, impersonal British state (Hutton 2008a).

Conflict between the public and the establishment over access to heritage sites is hardly new. During the late 1800s, for example, Stonehenge had become a gathering site for locals to assemble and watch the sunrise on the summer solstice, with attendant drinking and celebration (Hutton 2007: 174). Throughout the early part of the twentieth century, two Druid orders, the Ancient Order of Druids and the Universal Bond, held rituals there, with full support of the Ministry of Works, the government agency that predated English Heritage in supervising the site (187–90). With the increasing professionalization of archaeology during the twentieth century, concern grew over the possible degradation of the monument, and a number of archaeologists began to lobby to get the Druids out of Stonehenge (190). It did not help the Druids' cause that archaeologists saw them as silly. But it was the growth of the more countercultural folk festival, with its hippie contingent and representatives of alternative lifestyles, that really aggravated the archaeologists and heritage managers, leading to the total closure of the monument.

In this case, the joint efforts of the various Druid groups were successful. The two branches of Druidry jointly formed the Council of British Druid Orders (CoBDO) in 1989, in part to further their project of lobbying for open access to Stonehenge. Since 2000, English Heritage has allowed "managed open access" to Stonehenge on June 20, permitting entrance to up to 20,000 visitors to eat, drink, dance, and celebrate among the stones as they await the midsummer sunrise (Blain and Wallis 2007a: 2). But the more radical Druid orders were not content to stop with access to Stonehenge and other prehistoric stone circles, such as Avebury, another popular ritual site. Instead, toward the end of the 1990s, they began to shift their focus from lobbying for site access to advocating for the reburial of human remains found in or near prehistoric heritage sites.

Pagan Religions and Heritage Sites

Druids became associated with Stonehenge and other prehistoric stone circles through an error of early scholarship. The seventeenth-century English antiquarian John Aubrey theorized that the stone circles that dot the British landscape had in fact been constructed by the Celtic priests, who allegedly had possessed the superior technological knowledge to erect them and had used them as temples (Hutton 2007: 53). The development of professional archaeology and the advent of radiocarbon dating in the twentieth century definitively disproved this hypothesis: while the stone circles were erected in the late Neolithic period (3000–2500 BCE), the druid priests belonged to the Iron Age (800 BCE–40 CE). The Celts could not possibly be responsible for the erection of Stonehenge or any other stone circles. Nevertheless, this idea, which had gained ground during the eighteenth century, continued to be part of the popular imagination. The fraternal Druid orders of the eighteenth and nineteenth centuries used the stone monuments for some of their ceremonies, further strengthening this relationship in the public's mind. It was not until the mid-twentieth century that the notion that druids had built stone circles finally began to fade among the public at large (Hutton 2007: 67).

There is no similar set of notions linking Heathen to stone circles. However, a number of archaeological remains were constructed by the Anglo-Saxon occupants of Britain; Heathen may feel a particularly strong connection to them and their earlier residents. More broadly, because of the link between spirituality and the land, British Heathen often feel an attachment to certain features of the landscape, including prehistoric monuments and heritage sites.

British Pagans have a multivocal, diverse, and complex relationship with heritage sites. The most comprehensive study of this relationship has been undertaken by Jenny Blain and Robert Wallis in their Sacred Sites, Contested Rites/Rights project. Blain, a cultural anthropologist, and Wallis, an archaeologist, conducted a five-year intensive research study using participant observation and reflexive ethnography to understand how modern Pagans relate to "sacred sites" (Blain and Wallis, 2007b: 7). The term "sacred sites," applied to prehistoric stone monuments, is itself significant for two reasons. First, it creates intentional parallels with the language used by indigenous communities to express their right to access and utilize parts of the landscape they consider holy. But it also has implications for a range of stakeholders, from archaeologists and heritage managers to museum conservators and curators, who must contend with the notion that materials previously regarded simply as relics from the past must now be seen as having religious significance (Blain and Wallis, 2007a: 3). The borrowing of terminology from indigenous peoples is part of an overall pattern of intercultural borrowing that is a well-established component of the Neopagan movement (Magliocco 2004: 215–18). In their quest to reimagine and revive the practices of ancient peoples, modern Pagans often draw inspiration from the practices of today's indigenous peoples, who are thought to have a closer relationship to nature and the land. Their spiritual and religious practices are imagined to be closer to those of early European peoples. While this tendency has drawn fire from indigenous groups, who perceive it as appropriation or downright theft, for Pagans, it is part of a strategy to reenchant the world in the face of a secularizing dominant discourse (Blain and Wallis 2007a: 4). They view nature as animate, perceive the landscape as inhabited by spiritual beings, and speak of prehistoric Britons as "ancestors." Blain and Wallis call modern Pagans "new indigenes," building on Michel Maffesoli's concept of "neo-tribes" (5). They argue that Pagans' constructions of the past are as legitimate and valid as those of other stakeholding groups.

According to Blain and Wallis, Pagans visit sacred sites for a variety of reasons. Many see them as being intrinsically sacred, which is why ancient peoples chose them as locations for stone monuments. They may perceive them as places where deities, ancestors, and nature spirits are present and communicate with humans. At key times during the year they perform formal or informal rituals there, either alone or in groups. Many rituals are seasonal in nature, although sacred sites are also used for rites of passage, such as "handfastings" (weddings), child blessings, and memorials. Through ritual, Pagans seek to connect with the builders and earlier users of the sites. The repeated use of a sacred site during key times of the year for occasions that arouse powerful feelings, such as weddings and memorials, creates strong emotional associations for its users and aids in the formation of a link between modern and ancient practitioners. Of course, unlike the stones themselves, the rituals performed there in prehistoric times remain intangible; they must be imagined and are thus open to being imagined in different ways by different stakeholders, including archaeologists. However, this only highlights the importance of freedom of the imagination in the larger issue of human rights and intangible cultural property.

Pagans often draw on their understandings of archaeology and history to construct their own folkloric narratives about sacred sites, featuring spirits, land wights, Neolithic shamans, and goddesses (Blain and Wallis 2003: 307), although these understandings may not adhere to current academic norms. They share personal narratives of their own spiritual experiences at the sites with one another through oral tradition, as well as email listservs, blogs and publications; these in turn become part of an emergent folklore about sacred sites in the British Pagan community, and inform how other Pagans relate to them (308–11). Modern Pagans are thus creating their own intangible culture about sacred sites and contributing to the formation of a national intangible cultural heritage surrounding megalithic monuments and other archaeological remains.

Their direct interactions with sacred sites run the gamut from quiet contemplation and private rituals to wild parties, vandalism, and the leaving of what Blain and Wallis call "ritual litter": candle wax, joss sticks, and nonbiodegradable offerings (2007a: 5). Pagan site use is not always based on current archaeological interpretations or an understanding of what practices may be damaging to the site or offensive to other users. In one case, a group repositioned the stones in a circle because they thought the original builders had positioned them wrong (Blain and Wallis 2003: 310). However, this is an extreme case. The majority of Pagans see themselves as stewards of the sacred British landscape. Many groups have worked with heritage managers to clean up litter (ritual and otherwise), maintain and preserve the sites (310).

Pagans and heritage managers may differ, however, on how they interpret the meaning of the term "sacred site." Some of the latter have adopted the term enthusiastically because of its implications for the preservation ethos: to them, the idea of sacred is informed by a Protestant concept of sacrality, commonly applied to locations such as churches and graveyards, where the proper demeanor of visitors is one of quiet reflection. Such an attitude would help preserve them for future generations (Blain and Wallis 2003: 316). While some Pagans accept this ethos, others reject it. For them, sacredness encompasses sites as meeting places, loci of "tribal celebrations," music, altered states of consciousness, ecstatic experience, and all-night revelry. Partying, in this context, becomes a political act: an act of protest and a link with past celebrations that are imagined to have occurred at these places. From this perspective, partying *is* spiritual and sacred; it connects present partiers with past ones (317), as well as with nature, the landscape, and spiritual entities thought to dwell therein. Commenting on English Heritage's attempts to control the solstice celebrations at Stonehenge, one partier commented: "What they [English Heritage] want is tame Druids" (318). He and other like-minded Druids aligned themselves with a more carnivalesque idea of celebration. The use of Stonehenge as a party site, a place for rituals and celebration, ironically parallels some archaeologists' interpretations of Stonehenge as "a place for ritual feasting, rites of passage and the maintenance of ancestral connections" (Blain and Wallis 2007b: 121). However, Pagan interpretations of sacredness often run counter to those of archaeologists and heritage managers. They "challenge the passive and normative approaches to the sites encouraged by heritage management," the current axis of power/knowledge, and thus demand to be engaged with (2003: 314). Both concepts of sacredness—archaeologists/heritage managers as well as modern Pagans—draw on and parallel postcolonial indigenous discourses. In cases of rights to natural and human-made landscapes, the concepts of sacredness and sacred sites are key, because of the centrality of the idea of religious rights in modern multicultural nation-states. Modern Pagans find the construction attractive because it fits with their worldview and suits their political aims.

The Reburial Controversy

In the late 1990s, Paul Davies published a piece in *The Druid's Voice: The Magazine of Contemporary Druidry*, in which he advocated for the reburial of human remains found in archaeological sites and museums. He wrote, in part:

> Every day in Britain, sacred Druid sites are surveyed and excavated, with associated finds being catalogued and stored for the archaeological record. Many of these sites include the sacred burials of our ancestors. Their places of rest are opened during the excavation, their bones are removed and placed in museums for the voyeur to gaze upon, or stored in cardboard boxes in archaeological archives. . . . I believe that we, as Druids, should be saying 'Stop this now. These actions are disrespectful to our ancestors.' . . . When archaeologists desecrate a site through excavation and steal our ancestors and their guardians . . . it is a theft. We should assert our authority as the physical guardians of esoteric lore. We should reclaim our past. (Davies 1997)

Davies's piece was the opening salvo in what became the reburial controversy. It eventually led to the splintering of the CoBDO, the foundation of at least three new Pagan interest groups, and a number of encounters and joint ventures between the Pagan and archaeological communities over the issues of site access and reburial, which I will outline below.

Blain and Wallis have called attention to the similarity of Davies's discourse with that of Native Americans and other indigenous communities, arguing that the borrowing of native spiritual practices lays the groundwork for the adoption of other native perspectives, such as the disposition of human remains (Blain and Wallis 2007b: 194).[14] The use of terms such as "ancestors," "sacred burials," "desecration," "stealing," and "theft" in the context of archaeological excavations echoes that of Native American activists such as Vine Deloria (1969), and pits modern Druids against archaeologists in a conflict in which Druids take on the role of an oppressed minority whose heritage has been violently pillaged by agents of colonialism. Implicit in his argument is the idea that contemporary Pagans are the descendants—actual or spiritual—of prehistoric peoples, and therefore have some claim to their remains. According to this line of reasoning, they also possess knowledge of their spiritual beliefs about burial and the afterlife, which would give them the right to advocate in favor of reburial. In a later issue of the same magazine, Davies continued in the same vein, citing his beliefs that "bones are living people and should therefore be respected and ceremonially reburied" (1998/9: 11).

Davies's argument raises a number of questions, foremost among them the definition of "ancestors." In the context of indigenous discourse, this word usually has a literal meaning. When Native American communities reclaim human remains from museums and curation facilities, they must follow specific legal procedures that require them to prove they are the likely descendants of the remains in question. Because colonialism in North America is a fairly recent phenomenon, in the majority of cases, evidence can be found linking remains to contemporary claimants, whether it is historic and geographic (the remains were found in areas known to be historically occupied by a particular federally recognized tribe), cultural (the remains were found with artifacts that clearly link it to a particular cultural group), or genetic (DNA evidence links the remains to a particular family or tribal group). Similar guidelines regarding ownership of human remains are in vigor in the United Kingdom. The Royal College of Surgeons revised its policy on the return of human remains in 2001, following requests from indigenous communities in Australia and North America. Their recommendation that all claims on human remains be assessed by an independent panel of experts was approved by the World Archaeological Council in 2002. However, the College made no specific recommendations regarding prehistoric British material, because of a widely held assumption that there are no "indigenous" peoples in Britain (Blain and Wallis 2007a: 7). The British Association for Biological Anthropology and Osteoarchaeology (BABAO) has guidelines for determining the legitimacy of claims to human remains, which usually rely on DNA evidence of direct family relationships. It considers Pagan claims frivolous because they lack the requisite kind of evidence (Blain and Wallis 2007a: 14): it is unlikely that Davies and other modern Pagans advocating for reburial are any more (or less) directly related to the excavated human remains than the archaeologists doing the excavation. Based on these guidelines, the Department of Culture, Media and Sport in 2005 developed its own set of rules for the treatment of human remains in museums, *Guidelines for the Care of Human Remains in Museums*, now known popularly by the acronym DCMS (DCMS 2005; see also Swain 2007: 194). These acknowledge the special nature of human remains and specify that they must be treated with care and respect during the processes of research and conservation, especially when a museum makes the decision to display them to the public—a decision that should not be undertaken without careful consideration. It also provides a rubric for the handling of claims for the return of human remains. Legitimate claims must present clear evidence of genealogical, cultural, or national continuity, although some claims can also reference the spiritual or religious significance of the remains. Other important factors include the age of the remains and how they were acquired in the first place, that is, whether they were taken under contentious circumstances. The DCMS states, in part, that claims on remains older than five hundred years are unlikely to be successful, as it is difficult to prove genealogical, cultural, or ethnic continuity beyond that point.

In 2007, jurisdiction over the exhumation of human burials and remains was transferred from the Home Office to the Ministry of Justice, which decided in 2008 that the most appropriate legislation to govern this issue was the Burial Act of 1857. It stipulates that exhumed human remains are to be reburied within a period of two years "in an accepted place of burial"—in other words, a cemetery. While the law is hardly new, it had not previously been applied to archaeological excavations. The Burial Act was written during a period of unprecedented urban development in Britain, during which cemeteries were being dug up for new construction at record rates, leaving the problem of the recently buried being exhumed practically before the eyes of their immediate families. Its intent was to ensure that urban expansion did not trump the rights of families to guarantee a permanent resting place for their dead. It was never intended to deal with archaeological excavations and the discovery of prehistoric human remains. The result, however, has been an outcry of protest from archaeologists, who feel the law is being misapplied, as it does not give them adequate time to study human remains before having to rebury them.[15] Some Pagans, however, have welcomed the new application of the Burial Act as honoring the wishes of their forebears, albeit unwittingly.

In addition to civil legislation, the United Kingdom also has religious rules governing the treatment and disposition of human remains. The Church of England has issued guidelines specifying that human remains found in Christian burial grounds ought to be treated "with dignity and respect," and all attempts should be made to trace living relatives and dispose of the remains in accordance with the customs and wishes of the deceased (*Guidance for Best Practices for Treatment of Human Remains Excavated from Christian Burial Grounds in England* (Church of England and English Heritage 2005; quoted in Blain and Wallis 2007b: 193). No such guidelines exist for prehistoric burials, which constitute the majority of human remains unearthed by archaeological excavations. The Church of England and English Heritage also recommend that such remains be treated in a respectful manner, but obviously this implies a Christian understanding of respect. The customs and wishes of ancient peoples remain "intangible rites," thus invisible and negligible. Because of the strong identification modern Pagans feel with these forebears, it is understandable that some would feel a sense of outrage over the erasure of earlier cultural beliefs and practices implicit in the distinction between the recommended religious treatment of Christian versus pre-Christian burials, and the imposition of Christian standards upon remains whose owners had very different religious beliefs. The difficulty is, of course, that no one in the present time can say with certainty what those beliefs might have been.

Pagan definitions of ancestors differ from those of scientists in this context. As Blain and Wallis argue, they range from "family members" and members of restricted cultural groups, such as "Celtic" or "Saxon," to broad concepts such as "previous occupants of the land" (2007b: 195). Inevitably, references to ancestors as belonging to specific, bounded cultural groups involve notions of race and ethnicity. Although Britain today is a multiethnic, multicultural nation, some Britons feel they are more native than others, claiming Celtic, Anglo-Saxon, or Norse ancestry (191). The British Pagan community is overwhelmingly of white European descent, and includes a minority whose claims to native ancestry are couched in the discourse of racialism and nativism (Blain 2005: 193; Strmiska 2005: 27). But for most modern Pagans, cultural affinity is more important than ancestry in determining identity (Bowman 1996; Kaplan 1996; Magliocco 2004: 235). Pagans advocating for reburial argue that no blood relationship is necessary to claim a connection to prehistoric peoples; it is a *spiritual* inheritance that they are claiming. For them, it is sufficient that both they and the prehistoric inhabitants of Britain share a pagan practice. The use of the term "ancestors" in this context is clearly a political one: an attempt to authenticate and legitimate modern Pagan practice by linking it with both national heritage and the discourse of oppressed indigenes. Since the Civil Rights movement of the 1960s, the quintessential pattern for groups seeking to legitimize their identity is to model themselves after oppressed minorities who have suffered egregiously at the hands of a colonizing majority (Abrahams 2003; Magliocco 2004: 187). This pattern allows emergent groups to create oppositional subcultures that flip valences commonly held by mainstream culture: thus witches become surviving practitioners of an ancient feminist nature religion forced into hiding first by evil warrior cultures and later by bloodthirsty Christians. By the same token, pagans, heathen, and druids are transformed from shadowy pre-Christian cultists to oppressed indigenes, the first victims of British colonialism.

Davies's rallying call predictably brought forth a variety of responses from a range of perspectives within British Pagandom. The lack of a single, obvious leader and the multiplicity of voices and subgroups in the Pagan community make for a complicated political picture around the issue of reburial. Here I will summarize three positions evenly spaced along the continuum: that of the CoBDO, which has now split into several factions over the issue of reburial, but still takes a position at one extreme of the spectrum; that of Honouring the Ancient Dead (HAD), an association of Pagans dedicated to establishing a dialogue with heritage professionals to ensure the respectful treatment of prehistoric human remains; and Pagans for Archaeology, a group supportive of archaeological inquiry and opposed to the reburial of prehistoric human remains.

The CoBDO, an umbrella organization consisting of twenty-one Druid orders with several thousand members in Britain, takes the most radical position in favor of the immediate reburial of all human remains held in museums and curation facilities. However, in the CoBDO, different shades of this sentiment are present, each associated with a separate Druid order within it, often at odds with all the others over specific details. According to a statement on reburial published on the group's website, the CoBDO "believes that all over the world, in every belief, friends and relations handed bodies or cremated remains over to the earth, as part of the practice of saying goodbye and moving on. Therefore human remains found in the earth, belong to the earth. The earth has ownership. An ownership that should be reestablished. And this should be made common archaeological practice" (CoBDO 2009).

CoBDO bases its stance not on genetic links between its members and prehistoric remains, which it recognizes are no stronger than those of any other modern Western Europeans, but on spiritual ones: it "considers the claim for continuity of belief and customs, (if not language) with the human remains, to be of paramount importance." While it is not unaware of the scientific and educational value of human remains to non-Pagan Britons, and does not oppose the scientific analysis of remains at the moment they are found, it nevertheless argues firmly that all such remains should immediately be returned to the earth, "where friends and relations had put them, or as close thereby as possible . . . on humane grounds." It is adamantly opposed to the display of human remains in museums, as well as to their retention in curation facilities, although it concedes that remains should be reburied in a way that makes future study possible. The issue of museum display is one of "respect for ancestral remains. . . . It is a matter of common human decency to inter the bones of the deceased, not gawp at them in a glass case. Replicas or 3-D imaging can present the matter sufficiently well."

The issue of respect is echoed in the stance of Honouring the Ancient Dead, founded by Druid priestess Emma Restall Orr, which takes a more moderate position regarding reburial. According to its website, its goals are to ensure that "appropriate care is given by those involved in the unearthing, studying, storing and display of such remains. HAD works on the basis that, within modern British Pagan traditions, such remains are considered worthy of profound respect, and in many Pagan religions are felt to be sacred." HAD's approach is to work as a mediating organization between Pagans and heritage managers, ensuring that Pagan interests are accurately understood and respected. It seeks to educate archaeologists, heritage managers, site custodians, and other stakeholders about modern Paganisms in order to "promote appreciation and understanding of this country's heritage, across a wide range of communities."[16] The organization explicitly recognizes the interests of academics to study human remains and offers itself as a conduit to transmit the results of such research back to the Pagan community. In keeping with its restrained approach, HAD takes a moderate position vis-à-vis the reburial controversy. It does not call for mandatory reburial, but supports and facilitates consultation with stakeholding communities on the part of publicly funded organizations. In cases where all stakeholders agree that reburial is called for, HAD works to bring it about with the performance of the requisite rituals by a priestess or priest in the Pagan community.

At the other end of the spectrum of Pagan opinion is the group Pagans for Archaeology (PFA), founded by Wiccan priestess and Druidess Yvonne

Aburrow. The purpose of PFA is to refute the arguments of Pagans who criticize archaeology. Predictably, PFA's stance on site access and reburial closely matches that of archaeologists and other heritage professionals. Its blog states:

> We're Pagans who love archaeology and believe that it has contributed hugely to our knowledge of our ancestors and the religions of the past. Without archaeology, people would still think ancient peoples were fur-clad smelly cannibals and that ancient paganism involved frequent human sacrifice. In addition, we are opposed to the reburial of ancient human remains, and want them to be preserved so that the memory of the ancestors can be perpetuated and rescued from oblivion, and the remains can be studied scientifically for the benefit of everyone. Of course we want human remains to be treated with respect, but respect does not automatically mean reburial. Respect should mean memory, which involves recovering the stories of past people. . . . We are also vehemently opposed to people leaving tealights, candles, crystals and other non-biodegradable "offerings" at sacred sites. (Pagans for Archaeology 2008)

On its website, members post testimonials expressing their enthusiasm for archaeology, citing its value to Pagans in distinguishing fantasies about the past from verifiable facts, its contributions to contemporary Paganism by revealing details about ancient practice, and the importance of understanding the past to Pagan reverence for the wisdom of the ancestors. The site further expounds the case in favor of studying human remains, displaying them in museums, and not reburying them. While much of the text reaffirms the official academic position, some statements reflect a uniquely Pagan perspective, for example, arguing that displaying the dead and their grave goods in museums helps to perpetuate their memory—something ancient pagans apparently wanted, since they built elaborate memorials to their dead. Museums are interpreted as Pagan shrines, or "temples of the Muses," although the authors acknowledge "okay, so the proprietors of the museums may not see it that way, but we can choose to do so." In June 2009, PFA organized the conference Pagans and Archaeology at the University of Bristol, which featured papers by academic scholars and archaeologists as well as representatives of the Pagan community. Spokespersons from the CoBDO were not, of course, invited to participate.[17]

What all Pagan positions have in common is a shared concern that prehistoric human remains be treated with respect; but there is little consensus around what constitutes respectful treatment. For members of the CoBDO, it is nothing short of immediate return to the earth, where they can lie undisturbed and eventually become one with the sacred landscape. They find the display of ancient remains in museums offensive, believing it violates the wishes of the ancient ancestors to have their bodies return to the earth. PFA, in contrast, argues that the display of remains in museums, or their storage in curation facilities, does not violate ancient concepts of respect for the dead, since many burials were not private and allowed community access to the remains after interment. Martin Smith, an osteoarchaeologist at Bournemouth University who presented at the "Pagans and Archaeology" conference in Bristol in 2009, argued persuasively that prehistoric peoples might have in fact preferred the cardboard and plastic containers in which curators store human remains to holes in the ground; because they do not easily decay, they may even have thought them magical.[18]

Because so little is known about the afterlife beliefs of prehistoric peoples or the rites that accompanied their burials, it is obviously impossible either to reconstruct treatments that would respect all their wishes or to achieve consensus among the various Pagan organizations as to what constitutes respectful treatment. While modern Pagans see themselves as the spiritual descendants of prehistoric Britons, we cannot know, based on material remains alone, to what extent their beliefs and customs regarding the dead are similar to those of ancient peoples. Only a relatively small percentage of human remains from ancient times have survived to the present, and it is difficult to extrapolate from them, since there is no telling whether these remains are typical. What we do know about ancient praxis suggests that a wide variety of attitudes and beliefs surrounding death existed in prehistory. In the Neolithic period, it appears that human remains were treated in a variety of ways. In some cases, bodies were subject to excarnation, followed by crushing and mixing of the bones with those of other humans, probably members of the same kin group (C. Jones 2007: 125). These remains would then be interred in or near megalithic monuments. In other cases, it appears that cremation was used, while in still others, humans, often infants or toddlers, were buried whole in or near habitations. Then there are the famous "bog bodies," dating to the much later Iron Age, which appear to be ritually executed in a variety of ways before being tossed into a peat bog, where the acidity preserved them until they were unearthed, often by accident, in recent times. By the time of the Anglo-Saxons, wealthy elites were buried in barrows, or burial mounds, often accompanied by a rich trove of grave goods commensurate with their elevated social status. Finally, some human remains appear to have been casually treated, perhaps left to decompose on a field of battle, or dumped in a remote place to conceal the details of a murder. What emerges is a picture of a past populated by a very diverse array of cultures, each of which had complex beliefs and practices associated with death and the disposition of the dead, and all certainly different from those of modern Pagans, among whom there is likewise no uniform belief or practice regarding death.

Ironically, the idea that burial is the only appropriate disposition for the dead is a distinctly Christian one. Its roots can be found in Jewish burial customs, but also arise from the Christian parallel between the resurrection of Christ and the resurrection of the body at the time of the final judgment (1 Corinthians 15: 42). While Christian doctrine stresses that bodily resurrection will occur even if earthly remains have been destroyed (e.g., through cremation or decomposition), burial has always been regarded as an important part of Christian religious observance. Nonetheless, the notion of the sanctity of human remains appears to be a rather recent one, even in Christianity. In early Christian catacombs, for example, the bones of the dead were sometimes stacked and arranged in gruesome displays designed to remind the faithful of the fleeting nature of earthly life, compared with the greater importance of eternity. And until fairly recently in many parts of the Mediterranean, ancestral remains would periodically be swept up from family tombs and thrown into a common ossuary to make room for the more recently deceased (see, e.g., Danforth 1982).[19] Clearly, therefore, while the notion of respect for the dead appears to be universal to human cultures, how that respect is construed and expressed is culturally determined.

That begs the question of cultural relativism. Should all past beliefs and practices be respected, regardless of modern sensibilities? Should reburials reproduce historical, social, and gender inequalities out of respect for the beliefs of ancient peoples? If a body was disposed of disrespectfully in the past, should it be reburied in the same way? As Martin Smith argued in his conference presentation, the reburial debate appears to be not about honoring the desires of ancient ancestors, but about making the living feel good about themselves—and the living are deeply divided over how to achieve that.[20]

Pagans and Archaeologists: The Case of "Charlie"

The reburial issue came to a head over the fate of the prehistoric skeleton of a three-year-old child displayed in the Alexander Keiller Museum at Avebury, another stone circle and World Heritage Site not far from Stonehenge. Due to the site's prominence and the wide public recognition of the skeleton, this became a test case for the conflict between Pagans and heritage professionals over the disposition of human remains. In 2006, CoBDO member Paul Davies launched a demand for the reburial of the Neolithic child's skeleton, popularly called "Charlie," held by the Keiller Museum in Avebury. Davies, then reburial officer of the CoBDO, drafted a statement that read, in part: "The Council of British Druid Orders believes it would be beautiful to rebury the human remains of 'Charlie,' a 3 year old child currently displayed in the Alexander Keiller Museum, Avebury, along with the partial skeletal remains of 7 ancestors taken from the Kennet Avenue, Avebury. The Council feels, very strongly, that reburial is the most loving and respectful act for the sacred relics of our ancestral remains and is both morally desirable and spiritually important. We invite you all to be part of this process" (CoBDO 2008). According to the statement, Davies's request was based on three criteria: the ethical principle that the storage and display of human remains are disrespectful; the belief that human remains contain the ancestral spirit, which, through natural decay, becomes part of the landscape; and the fact CoBDO members consider themselves genetic descendants of the ancestor through mitochondrial DNA. The latter, of course, links all descendants of an unknown female progenitor; CoBDO members are no more or less related to "Charlie" through this line than any other modern human being from Northern Europe. Shortly thereafter, the CoBDO split into rival factions, each claiming to be the true CoBDO: one containing Rollo Maughling and the Glastonbury Order of Druids; the other, smaller one including Davies, now a member of the Secular Order. The latter group has become known as CoBDO West and remains most vocal in the reburial controversy.

In contrast, HAD continued to call for dialogue, mutual consultation, and shared decision making in the case. PFA, of course, supported the continued display of the remains in the museum, completely opposing reburial. Some Pagans felt outraged that CoBDO West presumed to speak for them. "CoBDO West have brought Paganism into disrepute," wrote one in response to a blog on which the issue was posted.[21]

Recognizing the importance of this as a test case because of Avebury's status as a World Heritage Site, English Heritage and the National Trust, the two public bodies in charge of "Charlie's" remains, called for a public consultation on the issue in the autumn of 2008. Input was solicited from a variety of stakeholders, including Pagans as well as the general public, through a consultation involving 73 groups and 567 individuals, as well as a survey administered by an independent professional polling company. In April 2010, the results of this survey were published, along with the final recommendations of English Heritage and the National Trust. The final determination was that the remains should stay in the Keiller Museum (see English Heritage 2010). Over 90 percent of the thousand individuals polled by the survey, and 89 percent of the groups and individuals who responded to the English Heritage and National Trust consultation request, said they were comfortable with keeping prehistoric remains in museums (BDRC 2009).

In addition to the weight of public opinion, English Heritage relied on two compelling arguments in formulating their response. The first was the value of leaving the remains accessible for future scientific study, which they thought outweighed the harm likely to occur from not reburying them. Leaving the remains in the museum was also the most reversible option. The second argument was based on the DCMS criteria. In this case, the age of the remains was such that conclusive evidence of genealogical, cultural, ethnic, or religious continuity could not be conclusively established (English Heritage 2010). Chief scientist at English Heritage Dr. Sebastian Payne said in the press release: "We respect the beliefs that have led to this request, and have taken the request seriously. These remains are important for our understanding of the past. We found that the public overwhelmingly support the retention and display of prehistoric human remains in museums, and that there is no clear evidence for genetic, cultural or religious continuity of a kind that would justify preferential status be given to the group which requested reburial" (2010).

Predictably, both HAD and CoBDO replied publicly to this statement by expressing their disagreement with and displeasure at the decision. HAD's response specifically criticized the DCMS guidelines as designed to deal with claims of groups whose remains had been obtained in the last five hundred years through the process of colonization, and thus inappropriate for adjudicating the claims of contemporary Pagan groups. It considered the decision invalid as a result and recommended development of "a process for inclusion of Pagan and other community groups in decision-making and programming around these (and other) human remains" Honouring the Ancient Dead 2009).[22]

Discussion

As this complex case makes clear, reburial is not simply an issue of religious beliefs versus scientific ones, or Pagans versus archaeologists, as the majority of British Pagans are not advocating for reburial. Instead, it illustrates the multi-faceted, contested meanings of cultural heritage, property, and human rights in a postcolonial, globalizing landscape. It also demonstrates the complex struggles that typify the decolonization of knowledge. The archaeological vision of the past is now one of many in the national discourse; in fact, it plays no small role in informing modern Pagan religious practice and belief. Prehistoric human remains are deeply meaningful to both scientists and Pagans, albeit in different ways. Blain and Wallis suggest that this postmodern, post-processual perspective necessitates reflexivity, openness, and transparency on the part of archaeologists and heritage managers, who should "open up their research/data to external scrutiny" (Blain and Wallis 200). To be sure, however, the latter already engage in this process on a regular basis. Archaeologists have always had to answer to both peers and the public regulating agencies that review and fund their research. Museum exhibition is part of the process of making those results available to the public—a public that includes Pagans among a large number of other constituencies. Furthermore, archaeologists adhere to an ethical code that mandates that they put the welfare of the communities they study above their own and protect the human rights of all categories of people affected by the research in which they take part (Powell, Garza, and Hendricks 1993: 6). Museums and heritage sites have also acted responsibly, as far as their responsibility is to allow people to engage with the past in their own way. But the right of a single group of stakeholders does not trump the rights of others merely because of its spiritual beliefs. In this case, a small faction of Druids was able to use the language of human rights to pressure heritage professionals to open a series of negotiations around the reburial of prehistoric human remains. The ethical view that all stakeholders deserve respect and hold legitimate claims compelled the scientific community to give Druids the recognition and legitimacy they crave. Yet taken to its logical extreme, this principle could ultimately allow other communities to make demands on the public sector that deprive other constituencies of the right to access their own cultural heritage. Pagans would not like it, I suspect, if Christian religious extremists used this argument to suppress information about the past because it violated their own notions of history. There is a need to balance the rights of community groups and individuals with those of the larger society.

I do not wish to imply by this that Pagans have no right to religious freedom, access to heritage sites, public respect and recognition, and the freedom to imagine their relationship to the past on their own terms. What I am arguing is twofold: first, that their rights are no greater or lesser than those of any other stakeholding group; and second, that at heart, the reburial controversy is about power: the power to determine whose values have primacy in narrating a nation's past, whose intangible heritage is recognized as legitimate, and who therefore has a right to its tangible heritage. Until the end of the twentieth century, the academy maintained control over this process. The decolonization of the academy and the recognition of the existence, in multicultural nations, of multiple stakeholding communities with competing interests and points of view have fragmented that monolithic hold, challenging the primacy of academic discourses and allowing minorities a greater stake in the control of heritage, both tangible and intangible. The reburial controversy in Britain is part of that process.

Respect has emerged as a central issue in Pagan discourse on reburial, transcending internal divisions between the various factions (Blain and Wallis 2007a: 16). The focus on respect suggests that in this very political struggle, the ancient dead and their artifacts are in fact key symbols: they have become stand-ins for modern Pagan religions themselves. Pagans want their religious viewpoints to be taken seriously; like other religions, they want the respect and recognition of society, especially of the scientific community, which holds one of the highest quotients of esteem in modern Western states. Many Pagans justifiably feel that they are not respected by mainstream society, especially by representatives of the academic and scientific establishments. We have already seen how hostility on the part of archaeologists played a role in the closing of Stonehenge to the public in 1985, and how the official statement of BABOA calls Pagan reburial demands "frivolous." The political effort to gain access to sacred sites and have human remains reburied is part of a larger struggle for recognition and legitimation in the eyes of society. By linking their religious practice with that of ancient ancestors in this very tangible and political way, modern Pagans assert the validity of their spirituality and compel powerful sectors of society to recognize them as a legitimate faith. In this, they have largely been successful. While "Charlie" remains in the Keiller Museum, English Heritage has agreed to the reburial of other, undocumented (and thus less scientifically useful) prehistoric remains, and to give special access to Pagan groups wanting to conduct rites to honor human remains in its custody. Some archaeologists have also been sympathetic to Pagan demands, for example, encouraging Druids to bless the excavations at Stonehenge during summer 2008.

What makes Pagan demands particularly vexing to heritage professionals is the relatively recent nature of Pagan spiritual identity and the lack of provable continuity between Pagans and the forebears whose cause they have passionately adopted. It should be remembered, however, that even in the case of colonized indigenes, links to the past are often contested, and traditions that are presented as age-old are revealed to be of fairly recent origin. Yet this has not prevented such groups from successfully claiming sacred territory and repatriation of cultural property (Haley and Wilcoxon 1997; Rosenblum 2009). In fact, the argument could be made that cultural groups undergoing transition "require continuous edification through symbols and tradition" (Jacobs 2009: 84) to a much greater extent than groups whose identity is well established. While all traditions are in a constant state of emergence, those of more recent provenance have a particularly high stake in connecting to the past; historical symbols and artifacts provide an especially valuable means to do so (Hobsbawm 1983). As emergent traditions, modern Paganisms have a vested interest in highlighting their connection to heritage; in an increasingly multicultural state, a connection to ancient ancestors, be it genealogical or spiritual, is a powerful vehicle for creating identity and legitimacy. The use of the pagan trope in this context challenges widely held notions of the relationship between past and present that tend to distance us from the remote past, using time in order to objectify long-dead humans and create anthropological objects (Fabian 1983; Lowenthal 1985).

To return to the issue of intangible rights with which this volume is concerned, it is clear that groups cannot be denied rights as a result of the constructed (or recently constructed) nature of their identity, for that would deny the rights of everyone. It is also clear that Pagans, as well as other cultural groups, have the right to freely imagine their relationship to the past, including to heritage sites and prehistoric human remains associated with them. It is therefore incumbent upon a liberal democracy that strives to respect the rights of all its citizens to facilitate relationships between modern Pagans, heritage sites, and human remains that allow full expression of religious belief, while at the same time preserving heritage for other cultural groups. This may mean revising existing protocols to take into greater account the special position of modern Pagan groups vis-à-vis the past, permitting some access to certain sites and objects for the purpose of ritual expression, and allowing the reburial of undocumented prehistoric remains, as English Heritage was willing to do in the Avebury case. For Pagans, it means remembering that Pagan exceptionalism is just as noxious as any other kind, and that their imagined past is one of many lenses through which heritage can be interpreted. In the negotiation of intangible cultural heritage, all groups deserve a place at the table.

PART III

Making Sense of Human and Cultural Rights

Chapter 7

Intangible Heritage in Transit: Goytisolo's Rescue and Moroccan Cultural Rights

Deborah Kapchan

> The proverbial difficulty of listing all the things that space engenders knickknacks, miscellaneous utensils, odds and ends swept along narrow streets and main arteries by a violent maelstrom: countless objects of every sort and description wherever the eye happens to land: an utterly mad proliferation of useless goods: advertisements and images of consumer products to entice the possible buyer
> patiently setting down nouns, adjectives one after the other, parts of speech fighting a losing battle with the perfect simultaneity of the photograph: chasing after the same effect in vain, like a traveler who misses the train and stands on the platform panting grotesquely till he runs out of breath
> artifacts, gadgets, products filling the vacuum, materially occupying the entire urban landscape, pouring out in a cloying stream from bazaars and stalls, overwhelming the visual field to the point of nausea
> pyramids of almonds and walnuts, dried henna leaves, Moorish shish kebabs, steaming caldrons of harira, sacks of broad beans, mountains of sticky, filthy dates, carpets, water jugs, mirrors, teakettles, trinkets and baubles, plastic sandals, woolen caps, gaudy lengths of cloth, embroidered sashes, rings, watches with colored dials, faded postcards, magazines, calendars, cheap paperbacks, fat sausages . . .
> the conception of wearing apparel as symbol, reference, disguise: the variety and the splendor of the dress permitted in the brief parenthesis of a holiday

> celebration: the temporary shedding of one's ordinary garments and social personality: changing one's clothes so as to change one's skin: being, for a few short hours, a nabob, a world traveler, a king: staging a performance for oneself and others
> (elderly men dressed in white from head to foot, girls with silver earrings and bracelets, delicate, transparent almaizales, a profusion of new sashes and slippers, turbans like gracefully coiled serpents)
> a theatrical spectacle: the calls of muezzins in the minarets of the mosques as an accompaniment in the background: shoddy footlights, stage sets, backdrops: joining in the rejoicing of the chorus bidding farewell to the fast of Ramadan
> the fierce rivalry of the halca: multiple, simultaneous attractions: the frank abandonment of this or that spectacle by a crowd continually in search of novelty, the infectious excitement of the knot of onlookers gathered together a few steps farther along: the need to raise the voice, argue, polish up the come-on, perfect the gesture, exaggerate the grimace that will capture the attention of the passerby or irresistibly unleash his laughter: capering clowns, agile tumblers, Gnaua drummers and dancers, shrieking monkeys, the pitches of healers and herb-sellers, the sudden bursts of sound from flutes and tambourines as the hat is passed: immobilizing, entertaining, seducing an eternally drifting audience seeking only to be diverted, magnetizing it little by little and attracting it to one's particular territory, wooing it away from a rival's siren song, and finally extracting from it the shiny dirham that will be the reward for physical strength, perseverance, cleverness, virtuosity.
>
> —Juan Goytisolo, *Makbara*, 2008

This is Juan Goytisolo's list of things observed in Jmaʿ al-Fna square in Marrakech. I begin with this length of tangible heritage to illustrate the porous membrane between language and object, between ether and solid in his project of "listing all the things that space engenders." But I also use this literary endeavor to illustrate the ways imagination flows between the personal and the public, permeating and deeply affecting both.

Juan Goytisolo is celebrated as Spain's most famous living writer. He does not live in Spain, however, but splits his time between Paris and Marrakech—where this, my story, unfolds. In particular, I tell part of the story of Goytisolo's rescue—his intervention (as told by him to me) in the saving of the Jmaʿ

al-Fna square. It is a story about cultural and fictional imaginations, and how they intertwine and determine each other. It is also the story of how personal biographies determine regional, national, and, ultimately, international landscapes.

Jmaʿ al-Fna

In 1999, Goytisolo wrote a letter to UNESCO requesting special status for Jmaʿ al-Fna square in Marrakech. Goytisolo, who has lived in Marrakech for decades, sits in the Café de France almost everyday around four o'clock. From his chair (and it is reserved for him), he can observe many of the performers of Jmaʿ al-Fna—traditional herbalists, clairvoyants, jugglers, musicians, storytellers, and comedians. I went to meet Mr. Goytisolo that same year.

Jmaʿ al-Fna has always been a crossroads of performance, travel, and exchange. The herbalists who sell their traditional remedies are from the Sahara, and many of their fathers actually crossed the desert regularly in the caravan trade of spices, textiles, and other goods. "Our fathers did this," said herbalist and verbal artist Abdelnacer Boutkrine to me in 1994, "and our grandfathers' grandfathers" (*jdud jdud-nah*). The herbalists I have worked with since 1994 have spent their lives going back and forth between Tata and Marrakech, bringing goods from the Sahara to Marrakech to sell, and bringing money back to Tata to build homes and raise families.

Perhaps most notable in the square, however, are the verbal artists and musicians. They perform in a space called the *halqa*, literally, a "link" (of a chain) or a "circle." From above, Jmaʿ al-Fna is an agora, a forum of disconnected and adjacent circles, where people congregate around artists (called *hlayqiyyin*, people of the *halqa*), who stand in the middle. The *halqa* is the most iconic of performance spaces in Morocco (Kapchan 1996). Not only does the word denote the place of performance, but it also implies the *mode* of performance—which is interactive, unruly, and often bawdy. The *halqa* is a space of license and the carnivalesque, a space of humor, but also a space of transgression. The herbalists, for example, sell potions to cure spells of sexual impotence as well as other sexual ailments, and they discuss the symptoms in graphic terms.

Despite the sometimes risqué nature of the topics in the *halqa* (or perhaps because of it), these performances have become iconic of Moroccan folklore. Indeed when Moroccan theorists of theater were looking for a particularly indigenous form of performance after independence in 1956, writers like Abdelkrim Berrechid designated the *halqa* as that form. It was then taken up by playwrights like Taieb Saddiqi and others. The tradition of *halqa* performance became the touchstone for a national Moroccan theater (Amine 2001; Kapchan 1996).

As Goytisolo notes "Markets, squares, public spaces, constituted the ideal place for . . . festive germination" (2003: 7). For Goytisolo, the performance square of Jma' al-Fna is one such festive space. But not too long ago, he felt that it was under siege—both by the disgust of the Moroccan bourgeoisie who saw its disorder as threatening, and by the neglect of city and state officials who wanted to tear it down to build more lucrative (for developers) enterprises. "Today, it is no longer possible to deny that all cultural richness, which sowed the seeds of what we call 'high culture,' will be swept away if we do not rush to its rescue," warns Goytisolo, adding that "the illiterate storytellers were my professors."[1]

This chapter examines the effects of Goytisolo's "rescue"—including UNESCO's 2001 decision to designate Jma' al-Fna as one the "masterpieces of intangible heritage." Based on interviews with performers from 1990 onward, I document the transformations wrought in cultural and intangible rights as tourism and heritage-making created "intangible heritage in transit."

Tradition, Heritage, Patrimony

Tradition, heritage, and patrimony have one thing in common: the notion that things, whether tangible or intangible, property or practices, are transmitted from generation to generation. The three words, while linked, have nonetheless come to have very different usages. While it is clear that traditions are not static but are "invented" in every generation (Hobsbawm 1932), the word "tradition" still has popular currency that equates "what is done now" with "what has been done in the past," usually in a relationship of continuity. Tradition is often equated with the face-to-face and with a temporality that is (somehow) always slower than the one we inhabit now. Yet tradition is thought to leach into the present with the force of precedent. Through repetition and mimesis, tradition plods on.

Patrimony, on the other hand, resonates with institutions. There is a tinge of privilege to patrimony (not least in the male bias of the word) connected to the official—the patrimony of the church, of the state, of the upper class. As used in France, however, the word *patrimoine* has become the virtual synonym of what is referred to as heritage in the Anglophone world.

Historically the word "heritage" arises from the notion of inheritance—what is acquired by virtue of genealogy, and, implicitly, as a result of someone's death. Heritage is what belongs to and stays within the family, whether nuclear, extended, communal, religious, national or even, as is the case of "world heritage," the "family of man." Heritage is transferred from one proprietor to another at moments of transition. Because heritage outlives its owners, however, it seems to strain toward the eternal. This is particularly true of tangible heritage like architectural monuments, or delicate and rare instruments, but also extends to intangible culture, such as storytelling or local festivals. For preservationists and others in the business of culture, heritage will disappear if it is not given proper stewardship. Constructing the imminence of the death of tradition is thus necessary to the project of heritage (Kirshenblatt-Gimblett 1998a). Indeed, the relationship between heritage and its stewards is not unlike that between a deity and its devotees: the deity needs the worship of mortals to exist. Heritage therefore must be protected and conserved if it is not to disappear like gods forgotten by their worshippers (Kapchan 2009; Lowenthal 1998; see also D. Miller 1998).

Heritage is tradition me(ta)morialized and metamorphosed, while authenticity is as necessary to heritage as advertising is to the market; indeed, we live in a "market of identifiable authenticities" (Bendix 1997: 3). The irony in this now global heritage market is that authenticity is fabricated in order to be "sold" to tourists, travelers, and funding agencies. It is in part the ability to transform the "authentic" objects of tradition into commodities of heritage that defines a world order based upon information and consumption.

Vignette 1

I had been told that Juan Goytisolo sat in the Café de France everyday around four o'clock, and so I went to see him. The Café de France looks over Jma' al-Fna square, where musicians, jugglers, fortune-tellers, herbalists, and others perform for mostly Moroccan crowds. Jma' al-Fna borders the Semarin market in the Marrakech medina, a labyrinth of twisting, raffia-covered streets. Both the market and the performance square have existed for centuries and both are in view from the Café de France.[2]

When I got there, Goytisolo hadn't arrived yet, and the waiter told me to come back in about an hour. I did. Goytisolo greeted me warmly. We spoke in Moroccan Arabic. Why not? I didn't know Spanish, and he spoke Arabic fluently. Knowing his interest in traditional performance, I had come with some of my articles on the *halqa*. He told me that he was deeply involved in trying to get UNESCO to recognize Jma' al-Fna as a "masterpiece of intangible heritage." We spoke about the changes that we had both witnessed over the years—the regulation of the performers, the reconfiguration of the space, but also the increased pollution as buses, taxis, and mopeds zoomed through the thick throngs of pedestrians. He congratulated me on my Arabic, clearly delighted to have a conversation in Arabic with a non-Moroccan, and he told me to come by the next day, when he would bring me photocopies of his own writings on the *halqa*.

Vignette 2

An herbalist sits on a blanket that he has laid on the asphalt in the main square in Marrakech, called Jma' al-Fna. This square is known for its performance traditions. In the evenings there are jugglers, storytellers, clairvoyants, acrobats, and snake charmers. The audience for these performances is largely Moroccan and the language used in the square is Moroccan Arabic. During the day, however, there are fewer performers. Abdelnacer Boutkrine and his brother Abderrahman Boutkrine sit under a large umbrella in the square waiting for customers. They are Sahraoui, people from the Sahara, but they make their livelihood in Marrakech selling medicinal herbs, potions against magic, and other ritual goods—lizard skins, amber and other resins used as incense, ostrich eggs, whalebone. I sit with them in the mornings, observing their interactions with regular customers who, upon seeing me, whisper their problems discreetly to Abdelnacer and wait as he mixes herbs and creates amulets. He is a ritual specialist, a kind that is fast disappearing from Moroccan culture due to the increasing popularity of allopathic medicine. Abdelnacer's father was in the caravan trade and brought spices from Timbuktou to Marrakech. Abdelnacer and his brothers no longer travel great distances to get their goods, which arrive by air now, but they do move back and forth between their desert home in Tata and Marrakech (see Figure 2).

At night Abdelnacer performs. He hawks his herbs to the crowds on the street, describing the ailments that they cure and giving social commentary on the processes of modernity as well. He mixes Qur'anic verses in classical

Figure 2. Abdelnacer and Abderrahman with their father's scale in Jma' al-Fna, Marrakech. Photo Deborah Kapchan.

Arabic with proverbs from the Moroccan oral canon, talking animatedly, and providing a choreography of gesture that glues his audience to his words and being.

> He who sees is better than he who doesn't see
> For the person who is ill or "closed" [impotent due to magic]
> Those struck by the eye
> Because the Messenger of God said, "All of you have the [evil] eye
> except those who have blessing [*baraka*]."
> Wake up with incense and the "wood-of-the-cross."
> Here, we've spoken.
> If my Lord brings healing, who knows . . .
> The doctor has his share [of truth] and we have our share.
> You see, we're called Arab doctors.
> We were in the beginning of time.
> I took this scale from the hand of my father.
> This year, sir, forty-nine is the age of this slave.

This year, sirs, traveling, buying, and selling . . .
This is Ramadan and loved ones meet together.
There are those who never go out
One has a store, one has a bakery,
One has a business, one has a café, one has a hotel.
He doesn't have time to wander around.
Us [Saharans], we go out.
Here it is.
You have here the news about saffron.
Yes, when Arabs stopped using saffron!
Oh Arabs!
Saffron is used in tea.
Here, two sprigs.
It's Ramadan. You drink it.
Put two sprigs, simmer them with tea or milk.
If you're eating innards, or if there's some tajine.
I have no meat.
Wa! Meat today is 1200 riyals [a kilo]!
I don't have any meat.
I can bring tea.
Simmer them with tea.
And it's good for the kidneys.
You know all about it.
It's good for the cold [in the body],
Whether in a woman or a man.
The woman is an inkwell, the man a pen.
The man is a tractor, the woman is soil.
Man, a blanket, woman a bed.
Man is the sky and the woman earth.
Saffron is used by men or women.
I remember, in Morocco . . .
Let's not hurry with medication.
When a woman gives birth we give her saffron.
When a woman gives birth we give her chicken.
But today times have changed.
Time has turned upside down.
I remember myself when our women used henna.
Women didn't have high blood pressure.

I remember when our women used *sanuj*,
For men and women.
I remember our women would use henna to fight high blood
pressure . . .
The wise men and interpreters talked about the black seed, *sanuj*.
Look, today, without gain or loss:
You're my brother and I'm your brother.
You're my arms and I'm your arms.
Because whoever teaches his brother one letter will go to paradise.
That's what Saharans are all about.
This [Jma' al-Fna] is the place of gain.
This is the sea. It's called the sea.
For example, it's called a television.
For example, it's called a video . . .
What are we, children?
In the name of God, the healer is my Lord
The curer is my Lord
And the slave is just the vehicle [lit. *reason*].
A person can either take a risk or call or choose.
The first Arabs said,
"Don't go unless you are decided.
Don't venture out if you don't have honor."[3]

It is interesting to note that Abdelnacer, who is technically not an Arab, nonetheless discursively constructs "Arab" identity in the context of postcolonial Morocco. What's more, in his discourse Saharans are also "Arab doctors," no doubt by virtue of their long coexistence in Morocco. Indeed, Saharans have been in Morocco much longer than the Arabs who invaded in the sixth century. Abdelnacer himself speaks a dialect of Tamazight (Berber), not Arabic, with his family. Nonetheless, he constructs his authority through an Arab genealogy he distinguishes from the Western allopathic tradition: "The doctor [*tabib*] has his share [of truth] and we have our share. You see, we're called Arab doctors. We were in the beginning of time." For Abdelnacer, Arab doctors (as opposed to doctors trained in the Western tradition) have existed from time immemorial.

While Abdelnacer discursively aligns himself with Arab medicine and identity, he nonetheless distinguishes himself as a Saharan with Saharan characteristics. Unlike other professionals (bakers, tailors, café managers),

Figure 3. Abdelnacer selling to a client in Jmaʿ al-Fna. Text recorded, translated, and transliterated by Deborah Kapchan. Photo Deborah Kapchan.

Saharans travel. "Us [Saharans], we go out." Saharans make it their business "to wander around." This reference to a nomadic past sets Abdelnacer apart from his Arab brothers and privileges him in terms of knowledge and expertise. Talking to his primarily Arab audience, Abdelnacer discursively aligns himself with them (with phrases such as "our women"; and "You're my brother and I'm your brother. You're my arms and I'm your arms"), while creating a space of distinction and specialization for the knowledge and identity of the Saharan. For after all, "the first Arabs said, 'Don't go unless you are decided. Don't venture out if you don't have honor.'" It follows then that as someone who does "venture out," Abdelnacer is a decisive man of honor, one who has accumulated the wisdom of experience.

This narrative is a highly self-conscious performance of a particular kind of modern subjectivity that distinguishes itself from some Western practices (medicine) while embracing others (media). It is also a subtle critique of modernity, for although he compares Jmaʿ al-Fna to a video and to a television, two "modern" forms of entertainment, his discourse is not free of nostalgia: "I remember when our women used henna. I remember when our women used *sanuj*" he says, lamenting that "time has turned upside down." "Yes, when Arabs stopped using saffron! Oh Arabs!"

As C. Nadia Seremetakis (1994) notes, nostalgia takes on a particular cast in modernity, one that mourns a past where the senses were more alive, a time when things tasted better. Abdelnacer mourns this as well. His comparison of Jmaʿ al-Fna to a video, to a television, is both a move to place the square in the same domain as these mediated events and an acknowledgment of their hegemony in the world of both healing and entertainment. It is unlikely that Abdelnacer would consider television to be "as vast as a sea."

Abdelnacer's verbal performances attract a primarily male Moroccan audience, some of whom buy his goods, but some who are there merely to be entertained. He is not merely a businessman, but a verbal artist who takes great pride in his abilities to affect and move an audience. Although he sells goods, his narrative as well as his gestural economy is what UNESCO would call "intangible heritage."

When I began working with Abdelnacer in 1994, UNESCO hadn't yet designated the "Cultural Space of Djamaa el-Fna Square" an intangible heritage site. That happened later (Hafstein 2004; Kirshenblatt-Gimblett 1998a; Kurin 2007). But the repercussions of this designation were nonetheless well under way. In 1997 Goytisolo and other scholars "proposed the idea of providing international recognition for . . . ephemeral forms of cultural expression" (Kurin 2007). Goytisolo was trying to rescue the square from plans to raze it and turn it into a parking lot for the thousands of cars that now roamed the Marrakech streets. By 1999 many things had changed for Abdelnacer. In preparation for the rehabilitation of the square, Moroccan authorities relocated all the herbalists to another, single section of the square; what's more, they were told to cease their verbal performances. Obviously, the cleaning up and "preservation" of Jmaʿ al-Fna in Marrakech required a codification of roles in the square, and since herbalists are not in the UNESCO categories of "storytellers, acrobats, or musicians," their own brand of verbal art was not recognized and was ultimately silenced.

Vignette 3

That same year, several performers in the square were given visas and taken to Paris where Jmaʿ al-Fna was recreated in the Tuileries Gardens in order to celebrate "The Year of Morocco" in France.[4] Due to the growing population of the conservative right in French politics (and its xenophobia), Jacques Chirac and the late King Hassan II of Morocco engineered a year of performances in France that celebrated the presence of Moroccans and Moroccan culture in France and that eased some of the intercultural tensions. The re-creation of Marrakech's famous performance square in the Tuileries Garden was a culminating point of this plan. It was an outdoor museum, a performance space of cultural tourism that allowed the French to experience exoticism at home. Moving the herbalists to Paris required yet another restriction on their practices, however; not only were their verbal performances absent, but (for tax reasons) no one was allowed to sell goods. Thus did the interactive and carnivalesque nature of the *halqa* become ossified in display. In the eyes of the French authorities, Abdelnacer's brother Abderrahman, as well as his younger cousin Brahim, themselves became exhibits to be visually consumed. Ironically, the Moroccans living in Paris still tried to buy the goods of the herbalists, and the herbalists sold them discreetly when the authorities were not present.[5]

As a social drama, the performances of the herbalists in Marrakech and in Paris differ considerably. Whereas the herbalist in Marrakech may be interpreted as taking his audience into the future by providing metacommentary on performance practices, comparing Jma' al-Fna to television, for example, and a critique of Western healing practices, in Paris he becomes an embodied icon of the past, displaying such items as *zuwwak*, a traditional stick toothbrush, pumice stones, and henna leaves—all "natural" commodities that predate modern cosmetics. (One of the recent restrictions imposed on the herbalists in Marrakech is that they can't sell henna; the authorities have given that privilege to the "new" performers in the square—the henna artists.) In Paris, that is, the social drama enacted transformed a modern performer into an emblem of the past, constructing the European spectator as situated within the present (Kirshenblatt-Gimblett 1998a: 7).

Vignette 4

In June 2009 I went to a conference on heritage, sponsored by the University of Cadi Ayad, and organized by scholars Ouidad Tebbaa and Ahmed Skounti (Skounti and Tebaa 2009). The participants came primarily from the United Kingdom, France, the United States, and Morocco to analyze the contingencies of heritage production. Laurajane Smith, author of *Intangible Heritage*, was there, as were researchers for UNESCO in Marrakech and in Paris.

Figure 4. Aberrahman as "herbalist" in the Tuileries Garden in Paris. Photo Deborah Kapchan.

The last day of the conference was devoted to Jma' al-Fna square. There was a panel of scholars, civic officials, and a *halqa* performer-storyteller, Mohammad Bariz, who came with his ten-year-old son. Mohammad Bariz is one of a handful of traditional storytellers still practicing in Morocco.[6] He sits not in Jma' al-Fna per se, but in the courtyard of the nearby mosque where the storytellers have recounted their epic tales of al-'Antariyya (Antar and Abla) and Alf Layla wa Layla (from the One Thousand and One Nights)

Mr. Bariz listened politely and attentively to the academics and public officials who preceded him. When it came time for him to speak, however, he was both passionate and angry. He was passionate because storytelling is his life. He was angry because, despite conferences and UNESCO designations, he is unable to support his family with the few coins he gets from telling stories. (Storytellers, like other performers in the *halqa*, rely on donations from audience members.) He was tired of being praised for his role as preserver of national heritage and yet uncompensated for that responsibility. Indeed, few children of *halqa* performers go on to become performers themselves. This is because deciding to become a performer is deciding for a life of relative poverty. Mohammad Bariz brought his son to the conference to demonstrate that there were some exceptions to this rule. The young boy spoke articulately about his love of storytelling, and then performed a section from al-'Antariyya (the epic of Antar and Abla), to great applause from the audience. Mohammad Bariz ended their presentation with a plea: that the Moroccan Ministry of Culture put him and the few others like him that still possess this knowledge and art on television. On television, he said, they would be seen as role models, the art would live on, and he could feed his family.

> This [Jma' al-Fna] is the place of gain.
> This is the sea. It's called the sea.
> For example, it's called a television.
> For example, it's called a video . . .

Analytical Openings . . .

The ability to reorder the senses has always been a tool of hegemony—whether colonial or capitalist. In observing the subtle and gross motion that the heritage industry produces, we observe also the transformations in sensory worlds so beautifully described by C. Nadia Seremetakis in her discussion of the diminishing sensory palette of modernity. Yet the term "modernity" is at once too charged and too easy a gloss to define the changes afoot here. Clearly the transitions in the herbalist's practices signal an association with global lines of power, but is the specular economy of global capitalism a necessary result? The themes do indeed enter into their own discourses—Jma' al-Fna is compared to a television, to a video. In the case of Abdelnacer, however, his performance transforms depending on who is directing the performance. When the square was less controlled by the government, his performances were more his own, though the genre of oratory that he employed is in the Moroccan oral canon. Now, however, he is silent—or rather, his soundscape is less publicly audible. He sells his goods and still dispenses private advice, but his performance is restricted to enacting the scenario of the "herbalist," a category of profession in UNESCO's list, and a genre of folklore for the tourist. He performs his personhood and his profession, but not his artistic medium (oratory). He, himself, becomes the object of the touristic gaze, a display item in the outdoor museum of Jma' al-Fna, an exhibition of himself. The specular remains, the oral is silenced, the kinetic and proprioceptive modes are diminished.

Just as the heritage industry alters the "relationship of practitioners to their art," UNESCO lists and categories *create*, rather than preserve or safeguard, the intangible heritage in question (Kirshenblatt-Gimblett 2006: 171). This alteration is evident in the examples above. The silencing of the herbalists in Marrakech speaks to what happens when international categories move into local institutions and change artistic practices. The "road show" to Paris is an example of the actual material itineraries of the bodies and goods associated with intangible heritage—the movement of the inheritees, so to speak. This transit, however, transformed the performances radically—virtually canceling all audible heritage and leaving only the tangible husk, the score so to speak. These alterations create a different sensory relation between artists and the spaces they inhabit, including the space of their own bodies. Sensory hierarchies change as a result, and, as Kathleen Stewart reminds us, "power is of the senses" (2007).

These four vignettes embody several different levels of cultural imagination—an international one (UNESCO), a national one, and several personal ones—that of Goytisolo, but also of the artists/herbalists themselves. All these moving imaginaries configure/conjure/conspire in the performance of "tradition," "heritage," and "identity"—whether Moroccan, Arab, Marrakshi, or global. And it is perhaps the porosity of these imaginations (along with contested claims to their ownership) that characterizes this historical moment where "patrimony" comes to belong to "humanity" at large.

But what of Juan Goytisolo's rescue?

Goytisolo has lived and thrived in Marrakech for many years. He took refuge there during the Franco years (his mother was killed by a bomb in the war) and has remained ever since. He is admired and accepted by his friends in Marrakech, where he and his partner live with their adopted children. Despite the fact that he lives with a man, the love of his life, he says, was a woman—Monique Lange, an editor at Gallimard Press who knew Sartre, de Beauvoir, and Duras. Goytisolo is a protean artist, and he celebrates the protean aspects of Marrakech and its culture. Indeed, the ability to change skins is one of the aspects that Goytisolo most values in Jmaʿ al-Fna: Let's not forget his own words: *the temporary shedding of one's ordinary garments and social personality: changing one's clothes so as to change one's skin: being, for a few short hours, a nabob, a world traveler, a king: staging a performance for oneself and others.*

The ability to change one's skin has been important to Goytisolo. His personal biography as a son of the haute bourgeoisie in Spain, a political exile, and bisexual have determined his own loves and causes. Jmaʿ al-Fna is one of them. Fernanda Eberstadt (2006) in her *New York Times Magazine* article on Goytisolo refers to him as the "anti-orientalist." Yet he writes in a publication presciently entitled "The Oral Patrimony of Humanity" (2003: 8):

> The universe of cheapjacks and charlatans, beggars and water-sellers, tinkers and artisans, . . . lunatics, women of scant virtue, . . . quacks, preachers, doctors of homespun science, that entire motley world of free-and-easy commerce, once the marrow of Christian and Islamic society—much less differentiated than people think— . . . was swept away gradually or at one foul swoop by a nascent bourgeoisie whose State grid-ironed cities and lives, lingering on as a hazy memory in their technically advanced and morally empty nations. The empire of cybernetics and the audiovisual flattens minds and communities, disneyises children, atrophies their powers of imagination. Today only one city upholds the privilege of sheltering the extinct oral patrimony of humanity, labeled contemptuously as "Third World" by many. I refer to Marrakech and the square of Djemaa el Fna, next to which, on and off, for some twenty years, I have joyously written, meandered, lived.

Like Paul Bowles (to whom Eberstadt compares him), Goytisolo celebrates the plebeian and (often the) seedier sides of Moroccan life. His writing on the square is infused with a nostalgia for what he feels is fast disappearing—a world of "doctors of homespun science, that entire motley world of free-and-easy commerce [which was] once the marrow of Christian and Islamic society." As a writer, he says that he is indebted to the illiterate performers of Jmaʿ al-Fna. But surely he would not have them stay poor and illiterate. What Goytisolo bemoans is a lost world, one that he transforms into a sort of literary utopia wherein the interactions of the *halqa* and the freedom that it signifies become primary touchstones of a liberatory past. And indeed, had he not intervened—this one man of international repute—Jmaʿ al-Fna might not be there today. Yet it lives on in a very different way: the entire site is off-limits to cars, taxis, and other wheeled vehicles. Only horse coaches can cut through the throngs of people there on summer nights. The musicians, the jugglers, and the snake charmers are all there. But is the imagination in a state of atrophy or is it not a matter of new imaginations emerging from the old?

Goytisolo himself posits a competitive relation between the descriptive power of words (the breath) and the static perfection of the specular economy (the image): "patiently setting down nouns, adjectives one after the other, parts of speech fighting a losing battle with the perfect simultaneity of the photograph: chasing after the same effect in vain, like a traveler who misses the train and stands on the platform panting grotesquely till he runs out of breath."

This narrative inhabits a space of anxiety wherein worlds of sense, breath, odor, and taste risk obliteration by regimes of objectifying display and cybernetic representation. And in fact, despite Goytisolo's efforts, the storytellers, those masters of word and breath, die off one by one. With rare exception, their sons and daughters do *not* replace them. They have their sights on university education and more lucrative professions. The clairvoyants and palm readers would also prefer to make better money. Their seductive lures verge on begging, yet they are there.

We must not lose sight of the irreducible paradox and irony produced by cultural agents like Goytisolo and cultural agencies like UNESCO.[7] It is not accidental that Mohammad Bariz feels that his only hope is in the very "empire of cybernetics and the audiovisual [that, for Juan Goytisolo,] flattens minds and communities." Despite all good intentions, every attempt to conserve, constrains; every attempt to display, deadens; every attempt to define, ossifies—at least somewhat.

"The dazzling incandescence of the word prolongs its miraculous reign," says Goytisolo, "But sometimes I am worried by the vulnerability of it all and my lips tremble fearfully with a single question: 'For how long?'" (Goytisolo 2003: 12).

Coda

The trembling lips of Goytisolo have moved nations so to speak. Jmaʿ al-Fna is not a parking lot, but a thriving performance space. But imaginations do not remain static. Like Goytisolo who bemoans the *difficulty of listing all the things that space engenders*, international organizations like UNESCO, as well as analysts of culture, share much in common with the *traveler who misses the train and stands on the platform panting grotesquely till he runs out of breath.*

Are we also breathless, running after a departed train?

Ironically, the local authorities in Marrakech have asked Abdelnacer to start orating again. Apparently they have had a change of heart and think it would be good to animate the herbalist's corner of the square.

"I don't want to start performing again," Abdelnacer told me. "I'm tired. I'm ready to retire."[8]

Notes

Introduction. Intangible Rights: Cultural Heritage in Transit

1. Pateman (2002: 23): "If rights are so closely associated with ownership, then neglect of the concept of property in the person is all the more surprising. The category of the 'person' has been fundamental to the very lengthy and bitterly contested process of democratization, and the universalization of rights and political standing, in Anglo-American countries. The concept of the 'self,' while central to moral argument, has not had the same legal and political significance as 'person.'"

2. "the idea of property in the person . . . [is] a political fiction, but a fiction with a powerful political force" (Pateman 2002: 21).

3. UDHR, art. 17: "(1) Everyone has the right to own property alone as well as in association with others. (2) No one shall be arbitrarily deprived of his property."

4. Serres posits that from the earliest days, humans have delimited their property by where they could pollute (excrete, fertilize soil). He asserts that today our pollution is not only ecological but extends to the symbolic realm—in the form of advertising and signs of all kinds that circulate for global consumption. The spread of this cultural imperial pollution is largely, according to Serres, a result of the notion of property, a political fiction that has outlived its efficacy. The answer? For Serres, detach from the notion of property. We are all renters on earth, he says. Professor of public policy and author of *Beyond Outrage*, Robert Reich writes in his blog: "I'll believe corporations are people when Texas executes one." Reich, "Why BP Isn't a Criminal," *Huffington Post*, November 16, 2012.

5. The first biases that must be addressed are those of the analyst herself (Mahmood 2005), and then those of her culture (whether it is the culture of academia or the political fictions that inform a national sentiment). Positing the universality of anything is tricky business.

6. Speaking of the poet Robert Duncan, Stephen Collis (2005: 45) says he worked from a "notion of the poetic commons . . . in his poetics, all poetry, all language, is derived from the commons."

7. Like notions of "democracy," WIPO assumes definitions of the self that concur with the practices and commonly held beliefs of contemporary society: "The job of political theorists becomes that of finding moral justification for accepted interpretations of the principles that form part of a taken-for-granted institutional background. The assumption then follows that political theorists can begin their arguments from intuitions, considered judgments, or fixed points of agreement about, and received understanding of, the ideas and principles inherent in those institutions. The possibility is eliminated that accepted forms of interpretation may systematically rule out an adequate understanding of the authority structures of institutions, and an appreciation of the political force and significance of major concepts" (Pateman 2002: 40).

8. Of course the seeds for this display were sowed with the displays of open-air museums and the folklife movement in Sweden (Yoder 1963).

9. See David Panagia 2009 for an analysis of artisanal cheese and chocolate-making as heritage productions.

10. Particularly as embodied in their contribution to the well-known popular groups Nas al Ghiwan and Jil Jilala (Kapchan 2007).

11. Essaouira Gnawa Festival of World Music (Festival d'Essaouira Gnaoua Musiques du Monde, http: //www.festival-gnaoua.net/festival_essaouira/pages/index.php, accessed June 13, 2013).

12. There are of course exceptions to this. In performances at the Divan du Monde in Place Pigalle, Paris, the Gnawa employed women (members of the family in fact) as "trancers" on the stage. The women loosened their hair, swung it around, and danced in front of strangers. This also happens frequently on the stages at the Essaouria Festival of Gnawa Music. While effectively displaying the feminine body on stage, these performances do not valorize women's role as anything other than marginal and exotic, thus reinstating traditional patriarchal values in a public context of spectacle. Indeed, at one concert in France I heard an audience member exclaim, "Why is that woman on stage? She isn't doing anything."

13. Festival website; what Victor Turner 1969 called "communitas."

14. Indeed, master musician Abdellah El Gourd along with African American composer Randy Weston were honored by King Mohammed VI for bringing Moroccan music to the attention of the international community. They stand in for the encounter of their respective communities—the Gnawa in Morocco and African American jazz musicians in the United States.

15. See "Human Rights at the Heart of UNESCO Programming" 2005.

16. Crediting Jason Baird Jackson and Merrill Kaplan.

17. In the days of early capitalism in the United States, the language of the marketplace—with its lures, exaggerations, seductions, and outright lies—represented the antithesis of legal language, a purportedly "purer" and certainly more arcane language (St. George 1998).

18. See Statement to UNESCO Clubs and Associates: "UNESCO and Israel—the sudden 'Politization' of UNESCO," http: //unesdoc.unesco.org/images/0001/000111/011184EB.pdf.

19. On "musicking," see Small 1998.

Chapter 1. Protection as Dispossession: Government in the Vernacular

The research on which this chapter is based was partially supported by the HERA (Humanities in the European Research Area) Fund, by Rannís (Icelandic Centre for Research), and by the University of Iceland, where I serve as associate professor of folklore and ethnology. I would like to thank my coauthors in this volume for sharing their insights; the anonymous referees for their helpful suggestions and their insistence; and especially Deborah Kapchan, the volume's editor, for her subtle editing, her forbearance, and her perseverance in seeing the volume through. I am also grateful to my colleagues Pertti Anttonen, Regina Bendix, Alan Dundes, Barbara Kirshenblatt-Gimblett, Terry Gunnell, Barbro Klein, Kristin Kuutma, John Lindow, Leah Lowthorp, Stein Mathisen, Dorothy Noyes, Ólafur Rastrick, Marteinn Helgi Sigurðsson, Martin Skrydstrup, and Tok Thompson for their generosity in critiquing and discussing the contents of this chapter on various occasions; to my fellow fellows at New York University's International Center for Advanced Studies in 2005–2006 who read and helped me shape the first draft version of the chapter: Jangam Chinnaiah, Munir Fakher Eldin, Ilana Feldman, Forrest Hylton, Nivedita Menon, Timothy Mitchell, Tavia Nyong'o, Arzoo Osanloo, Leshu Torchin, and Alexei Yurchak; and to audiences who listened and responded to shorter or longer oral presentations of the evidence, analysis, and argument of this chapter at UNESCO's International History Conference on the occasion of its sixtieth anniversary in 2005, at Harvard's Weatherhead Center for International Affairs in 2006, at a meeting of the Institut für Kulturanthropologie/Europäische Ethnologi of the Georg-August Universität in Göttingen in 2006, at the annual meeting of the American Folklore Society in 2007 (on a panel organized by Deborah Kapchan), and at Berkeley's Folklore Roundtable in 2008.

1. In article 2(1) of the 1970 convention, the states parties "recognize that the illicit import, export and transfer of ownership of cultural property is one of the main causes of the impoverishment of the cultural heritage of the countries of origin of such property and that international co-operation constitutes one of the most efficient means of protecting each country's cultural property against all the dangers resulting there from." See Skrydstrup 2009; Bendix and Hafstein 2009.

2. The third session of the Intergovernmental Meeting of Experts on the Preliminary Draft Convention for the Safeguarding of the Intangible Cultural Heritage took place June 2–14, 2003. It met in a large conference room in the basement of UNESCO headquarters, Place Fontenoy in Paris. According to the Secretariat Report, 249 participants representing 103 member states took part, in addition to ten delegates from UNESCO's three permanent observation missions, and representatives from two intergovernmental organizations and five nongovernmental organizations. In fact, no more than half that number of people actually took part and I only noted one NGO (Traditions for Tomorrow) in the room.

It should be noted that official figures count the delegates announced in advance by member states. Nevertheless, it is fascinating how wide the gap can be between official reports and what one actually observes at these meetings; the number of participants is only mentioned here as an illustration. Reports such as this tend to gloss over conflicts, omit confrontations, downplay disagreements, all the while emphasizing points of convergence and insisting on consensus, even in its absence. They are, in fact, instrumental in creating the convergence that they portray as though it had actually taken place. Having observed such discrepancies, one soon learns not to take the official presentation at face value but to read against the grain of these documents. What I gathered from participant observation and personal communications is therefore fundamental to my understanding of the process.

Officially, I attended this meeting in the capacity of an "expert" on the Icelandic delegation. As such, I was alphabetized by state (Islande) and sat to the right of the Indian delegates (the Iranians were absent, as were the Iraqis, who did not command a sovereign state at the time). On my right sat Guðný Helgadóttir, the head of delegation and only other delegate in attendance from Iceland. Although there was a microphone on the desk in front of us, I never took the floor during the meeting. Guðný was in charge; I was there at her discretion and by special permission from the Icelandic UNESCO commission, to observe the debate, take my own notes, and draw my own conclusions.

3. The law defines this culture as "the sum total of cultural properties, created by the entire nation (etnos), passed from generation to generation and constantly renewed, which makes it possible to preserve the national identity and consciousness and uniqueness of ethnographic regions" (art. 2, para. 4).

4. I have a hard time making sense of some diplomatic alliances, this being one of them. It is important to bear in mind, however, that a great deal of horse trading went on behind the well-lit scenes of the meeting room at Place Fontenoy, out of earshot from microphones and multilingual headsets. Discussions and negotiations took place during coffee and lunch breaks, and over decked Parisian dinner tables. Over coffee or drinks or *steak frites*, alliances were formed and broken over

the major issues at stake in this convention, but in many cases such alliances also involve affairs completely foreign to intangible heritage.

Chapter 2. Heritage, Legacy, Zombie: How to Bury the Undead Past

Along with the individuals mentioned in the text, I thank Ilana Gershon, Deborah Kapchan and the two anonymous readers, Bogdan Popa, Ned Lebow, and the attendees of "The Form of Value in Globalized Traditions" at the Ohio State University, March 2009, and "Local Knowledge and Open Borders: Creativity and Heritage" at the University of Tartu, July 2009, for their comments. The chapter was completed amid the collegial stimulations of the Shelby Cullom Davis Center for Historical Studies at Princeton University.

Epigraphs: James Dickey, *Deliverance*, 1970, 126; Goethe, *Faust* Part II, Act V, 1832, trans. Philip Wayne (Harmondsworth: Penguin, 2005).

1. For Faust as archetypal developer, see Berman 1982.

2. Eric Mortensen, personal communication.

3. For example, in intellectual property rights, increasingly held by corporations rather than individuals, and in the United States in the right for corporations to spend freely on political campaign ads, determined by the Supreme Court in 2010 to be protected by the right to free speech.

4. The usage dates from 1930, according to the OED.

5. The OED is again the source. I owe the larger account of the historical and organizational context of the term to Michael Krippendorf.

6. The six-year, $5 billion aid package called Plan Colombia was judged by a Government Accounting Office report to have improved human security but to have failed, despite record aerial spraying, in its goal of halving illegal narcotics production. Coca cultivation increased by 15 percent during the 2000–2006 effort, and moved from larger, more centrally located plots to more numerous, remote, and scattered ones (Forero 2006; "Colombia Aid Failed" 2008).

7. Afghans practice the inverse kind of distancing. The word in Dari and Pashto for what we call a warlord places the phenomenon squarely in European modernity: *kommandán* (Margaret Mills, personal communication).

8. All quotations come from "Taliban, Opium in Afghanistan Difficult to Contain" 2007.

9. Note that Wood invokes Afghan culture in the singular, reflexively assuming the isomorphy of state and culture.

10. To be sure, Afghan directors have other ideas, at least for the moment: the current reference points for aspiring Afghan filmmakers are Tehran in the artistic vein and Bollywood in the commercial one.

11. Some commentators see the fashion as the visual correlate of a larger project, "selling Brand Karzai" (Herold 2006).

12. Needless to say, the burqa is not becoming world fashion. While Afghan men's dress is incorporable, women's dress is treated as the emblem of medieval repression to be eradicated.

13. Catholics have always left town when possible; there is a traditional flood over the border on July 11. Protestant disaffection can also be read in the decline of Orange Order membership from 93,447 in 1968 to 35,758 in 2006 (Geoghegan 2009).

14. The burning of Irish flags, the mockery of Catholic victims of sectarian violence, and more direct forms of aggression by drunken participants are familiar features of the bonfires, as are regulatory struggles over environmental and safety issues. So too, of course, are their beauty and spectacularity and traditionality.

15. For a dramatic extension of the market idiom of branding to address North-South

inequality and national development by creating "intangible value" through cultural resources, see Anholt 2005.

16. I oversimplify for clarity: the carnival, like traditional festivals in general, including the Orange Order parades, is of course celebration as well as political action and many other things. As per my introduction, rebranding foregrounds the cultural dimension to the exclusion of all others.

17. See http://www.ulsterscotslanguage.com/.

18. See, for example, a testy discussion on the Wikipedia "talk" page, http://en.wikipedia.org/wiki/Talk:Ulster_Scots_people#Culture.3F_Language.3F, accessed July 5, 2010.

19. An Ulster-Scots grammar was published in 2007, but after several iterations the academy would appear to be on hold: a revised development strategy was published in June 2013 by Northern Ireland's Departure of Culture, Arts, and Leisure, http://www.dcalni.gov.uk/index/language-cultural-diversity-r08/ulster-scots_academy_development_and_research_strategy_consultation.htm, accessed August 26, 2013.

20. See, e.g., http://www.ulsterphotography.co.uk/; Anthony McCann, personal communication.

21. "Get Ready to Party for Orangefest," http://liammacuaid.wordpress.com/2009/07/07/get-ready-to-party-for-orangefest/, accessed July 5, 2010.

22. Similarly, Paul Krugman speaks of "zombie doctrines," ideologies that have failed in practice and yet presist in influencing policymaking (2009). This usage of "zombie" by economists derives from George Romero's horror movies, not from the origins of the term in Haitian vodou belief. By contrast, the IT concept of a "zombie computer," one that has been compromised and redirected to distribute spam or viruses without the owner's knowledge, is closer to the original conception but less relevant to my discussion here. www.ulsterphotography.co.uk/; Anthony McCann, personal communication.

23. The following discussion draws extensively on conversations with Willard Tucker as well as Geoffrey Smith and other students in the course "American Regional Cultures and Global Transition: Appalachia, Louisiana and the Texas Border Country," which I taught in spring 2009 at Ohio State.

24. Fly ash, which contains heavy metals such as arsenic, lead, nickel, manganese, and chromium in concentrations far higher than the EPA rates as dangerous, had been left unregulated by the EPA in 2000 because of industry pressures: the potential cleanup costs for utilities at that period were estimated at more than $5 billion.

25. As a crude measure of comparison, a LexisNexis Academic search for "Tennessee coal spill" between December 23, 2008, and January 31, 2009, found 22 newspaper stories about the spill and its aftermath (calls for regulation, congressional investigation, TVA announcements, concerns about slurry ponds elsewhere, and so on). A search for "Katrina" between August 25 and September 30, 2005, revealed 818 stories; for "Exxon Valdes" between March 24 and April 30, 1989, 444; for "Three Mile Island" from March 29 to May 5, 1979, 496.

26. To be sure, the Big Branch mine explosion of April 2010 did excite significant national attention. Where immediate, dramatic mortality makes cause-effect relationships tangible, the stakes are higher.

27. Respectively www.flickr.com/photos/hypostylin/2918292560/ and www.myspace.com/hillbillyzombiehunter.

28. Summaries and quotations refer to the film rather than the novel unless otherwise noted.

29. www.facebook.com/pages/Hillbilly-Zombies.../1213308479. This project appears never to have been realized,

30. Scott Ashlin argues plausibly that most 1970s exploitation film genres developed from mainstream movie prototypes and describes the influence of *Deliverance* on "the hillbilly horror strain," http://www.1000misspenthours.com/reviews/reviewsa-d/deliverance.htm. This influence has become so pervasive as to provoke metaparody: the trailer to Ruben Fleischer's 2009 *Zombieland* features two allusions to emblematic moments of *Deliverance*.

31. The particular context for *Deliverance*, especially the novel, is Cold War nuclear anxiety, stressed as much as the environmental change. The character Lewis, consumed with survivalist fantasies, values the river as a place of testing and refuge. Not yet incorporated into the national infrastructure and its concomitant real estate and recreation industries, upland Georgia is still a training ground for the moment when "machines are gonna fail" (Osborne 2007).

32. Except, dare one say, to fight legacy warlords, each anomaly helping to cancel out the other . . .

33. Regional activists occasionally point out that extreme othering of the hillbilly is more socially permissible than blatant stereotyping of African Americans or even Arabs. Outrageous representations of rural whites are still fair game in public settings in the United States. This othering, however, seems to betoken identification rather than rejection on the part of middle- and working-class white people. The white trash image provides an idiom for carnivalesque self-inversion now that racial minstrelsy is no longer socially acceptable, and for some racially polarized whites no longer desirable.

34. Since the initial framing of this chapter, the hillbilly's revenge on the suburbanite has made some progress. The euphoria for fracking—hydraulic fracturing to capture underground shale gas—has made coal country still less visible, while greatly extending the range of rural areas forced to choose between risky extraction and economic inanition. With the mortgage crisis, suburbs, like rural towns, have seen homes abandoned. And while we continue to ponder the disappearance of the middle class, zombies have completely overrun our popular culture. We are all Appalachia now.

35. As academics and cultural practitioners, we too have our place in this field of interested actors.

Chapter 3. The Right to Remain Cultural: Is Culture a Right in the Neoliberal Caribbean?

An earlier version of this section on "The Economic Problem" appears in the author's "Uneasy Heritage: Ambivalence and Ambiguity in Caribbean Heritage Practices," in *Heritage Regimes and the State*, ed. Regina F. Bendix, Aditya Eggert, and Arnika Peselmann, 79–96, Göttingen Studies on Cultural Property 6 (Göttingen: Göttingen University Press, 2012), reprinted by permission.

Epigraphs: Walcott, "What the Twilight Says," in Walcott 1999: 7; Fribourg Declaration on Cultural Rights, May 2007, article 1 (reference to cultural communities)

1. There has recently been some compelling scholarship critiquing the notion of "collective origins" for folk culture, which should redouble our focus on the contemporary political implications of the uses of that notion (see Hafstein 2004b)

2. For discussion of the development of the concept, see, for example, Bratich, Packer, and McCarthy 2003; Dreyfus and Rabinow 1983; Martin, Gutman, and Hutton 1988; Burchell, Gordon, and Miller 1991.

3. I take this term from a common expression used in relation to the Trinidad Carnival. Participation in any of the many masquerade groups, or "bands," is generally referred to as "playing." Hence, one "plays" in a "band." It does not mean performing in a musical group in Trinidad in this context.

4. The exception to this focus on local production is the economic colonization of Caribbean territory for free trade zones and the like, in which foreign capital takes advantage of low wages and governmental incentives, which amount to the suspension of local authority in favor of capitalist enterprises that yield little for the region (and even this is often sold to investors along with a cultural component, such as "friendly workers" or "literate populations"). That is, investors are lured both by economic incentives and persuasive portraits of a cultural milieu in which workers are educated, friendly, and hardworking.

5. For a similar perspective on Trinidad, see Ramcharitar 2008.

6. The idea of the national economy being tied to a new national identity is not restricted to the Caribbean. James Ferguson documents a similar phenomenon in Zambia (2007: 124–33).

7. Much discussion on Caribbean culture, tourism, and heritage has revolved around the notion of "place" and land. The literature is too vast to address here, but a key issue early on concerned a kind of anxiety over the lack of "authentic" culture in the Caribbean given the history of its population as displaced and consequently "de-cultured." Although some of this has been addressed by describing and celebrating Caribbean culture as, in turn, syncretic, creolized, or hybridized, the issue of land and place within a discourse of culture as rooted in places persists. See, for example, D. Bennett 2005; Olwig 1999.

8. Derek Walcott saw with great clarity the role the state must take with regard to culture in his essay "What the Twilight Says": "If the old gods were dying in the mouths of the old, they died of their own volition. Today they are artificially resurrected by the anthropologist's tape recorder and in the folk archives of departments of culture. . . . To believe in its folk forms the state would have to not only hallow its mythology but rebelieve in dead gods, not as converts either, but as makers" (1999: 7). The point here is not that what anthropologists and folklorists do is somehow unworthy, but that the appropriation of this work by the state is an indication that they are not continuing a tradition, but remaking it in the service of a culture economy.

Chapter 4. Cultural Heritage, Human Rights, and Reform Ideologies: The Case of Swedish Folklife Research

1. I once coined the term "folklife sphere" to emphasize that a great number of persons and activities worked toward similar goals at this time: the folklife (or cultural historical) museums, the homecraft movements (*hemslöjdsrörelsen*), the folk music movements, the local history movements (*hembygdsrörelsen*), the researchers and, eventually, a scholarly discipline. They were all part of one and the same reform project (Klein 2000a).

2. In 1910, another field, *folkminnesforskning*, or "folk memory research," was founded at Lund University. Through the establishing of these two related fields, the basis was created for an often uneasy relationship between the study of spiritual or "intangible" culture on the one hand and material or "tangible" culture on the other (Klein 2008).

3. The term was proposed by radical conservatives in their efforts to unite Swedes. In 1928, the "folk home" became a powerful and lasting metaphor for the efforts of a succession of Social Democratic governments (Wittrock 2004: 56).

4. To Erixon and his colleagues, the first task of folklife scholars was to investigate the life of rural and urban common people during the approximately two hundred years preceding their own time; the scholars were to try to reach back to "the oldest structure of the contemporary period" (Nilsson 2004: 71). It is fascinating to think about how this objective went hand in hand with social planning, modernization, and urbanization.

5. These collecting efforts have continued. In the 1940s and 1950s, the activity was broadened

so that questionnaires were sent to urban and industrial workers who were asked to write down their reminiscences of industrial work. During the last few decades, questionnaires have focused on topics deemed to be of interest to contemporary correspondents (such as friendship, hygiene, and death). Some 400 people tend to respond to each questionnaire.

6. Further research is needed here. For example, it would be important to study Alva Myrdal's attitudes to cultural issues. As Sweden's representative at UNESCO's social science division in 1951–1955, she would have been in a position to introduce discussions of human rights in relation to the cultural sphere. Yet, to my knowledge, she did not do this.

7. My comments on Daun are, in part, based on his fascinating recollections of the development of Swedish ethnology during the 1960s and 1970s (Daun 2003).

8. Folklorististics, or *folkloristik* (which essentially meant the study of verbal traditions), was included in European ethnology.

9. This was effectuated in Stockholm as late as 2001. At other Swedish universities, the discipline was less closely connected to a museum and tensions between academe and museum were far less pronounced.

10. Among the recent works in this vein are books on World Heritage Sites (Turtinen 2006); objects and sites of memory (Frykman and Ehn 2007); and the narratives of Iranian-Swedish women (Farahani 2007).

11. My translation from Statens offentliga utredningar (SOU) 1994: 97–99. The title can perhaps be translated as "Memory and Education: The Mandate and Organization of Museums."

12. Peter Aronsson held the position in 2001–2012; a new holder is expected to be announced within the year.

13. In 2000, Sweden recognized five official minority languages: Finnish, Mienkielä (a Finnish language spoken along the northern border between Sweden and Finland), Romani, Sámi, and Yiddish. This was one of the more visible results of the "diversity mandate."

14. An additional factor may be involved here, the very real possibility that such new disciplines as Heritage Studies will replace ethnology. Even if it is doubtful that this will happen in the near future, a few Swedish ethnologists realize it might be wise for them to rejoin the museums and go back to their beginnings. After all, these beginnings give ethnology a somewhat clearer profile than it has now. To the world at large, the discipline is nowadays often merely one more among several other vaguely defined enterprises concerned with culture, history, and the media.

Chapter 5. Balkan Romani Culture, Humans Rights, and the State: Whose Heritage?

Portions of this chapter were delivered at the Cultural Circulations Conference, Ohio State University, 2005. Some parts are reprinted from Silverman 2012 with permission of Oxford University Press. Fieldwork took place in Macedonia and Bulgaria in 1980–2011 and in Romani communities in New York in 1988–2011.

1. The English term "Gypsy," a shortened form of "Egyptian," derives from the erroneous belief that Roma originally were from Egypt. "Gypsy" is often used as an ethnic slur, and "to gyp" means to steal or cheat. Appellations in European languages, such as *tsigan*, are similarly derogatory.

2. For detailed information on these topics see the World Bank reports by Ringold 2002; Ringold, Orenstein, and Wilkins 2004; Petrova 2003; Barany 2002; the European Roma Information Office website (www.erio.net); and various issues of *Roma Rights*, the journal of the European Roma Rights Centre.

3. For discussion of recent xenophobia, see Ghodsee 2008 and Stracansky 2009.

4. Maria Todorova, discussing whether the Balkans are orientalized in reference to the rest of

Europe, points out that we are not dealing with a colonial situation (1997); nevertheless, the Balkans are posed as "other" to Europe, and Roma are posed as "other" to the Balkans. Ken Lee specifically extends Said's argument to Gypsies: "Whilst Orientalism is the discursive construction of the exotic Other *outside* Europe, Gypsylorism is the construction of the exotic Other *within* Europe—Romanies are the Orientals within" (2000: 132).

5. A *zurna* (known as *zurla* in Macedonia) is a double reed pipe often played in pairs, one drone and one melody. A *tapan* (large two-headed drum) accompanies the *zurna*. These are the main instruments for dance in Macedonia, and southwestern Bulgaria and Roma have a virtual monopoly of them (Silverman 1996).

6. Note that this designation is accompanied by seed money, not to mention prestige. A 1955 film of the wedding can be seen at http://www.youtube.com/watch?v=zjWsgbGqg5U (part 1) and http://www.youtube.com/watch?v=Z7Q2O2cNlHo (part 2). A 1999 performance can be seen at http://www.youtube.com/watch?v=mfXNtcNG2SE.

7. See "Macedonian Timeless" video clip, http://www.youtube.com/watch?v=eIx1jCrL3Sg&feature=related.

8. I would like to thank Mark Levy, who was a reviewer of the Macedonian UNESCO application, for sharing some of these insights.

9. Mirga and Gheorghe contrast a transnational minority to a national minority in the fact that national minorities seek rights in a nation-state framework, whereas transnational minorities seek rights on a wider (e.g., European) scale (1997). Some Romani groups, then, such as the Sinti of Germany, see themselves as a legitimate historic German minority and reject the label Roma.

10. Romania is an exception; in Romania, unlike Bulgaria and Macedonia, some Roma manage their own production companies.

11. African Americans may provide a useful comparative example in that they are a marginal group with musical power. What does the popularity of African American musics mean for the socioeconomic position of Blacks? Simon Jones (a celebratory scholar) asserts that when white British youth adopt Black musical styles they are implicitly rejecting racism (1988). But other authors focus on how Black music never lost its imputed exoticism and primitiveness even when taken into white commercial forms (Born and Hesmondhalgh 2000: 22–23). In jazz, white musicians have tended to receive greater rewards and prestige; similarly in rock, "its white stars have generally been paid much more attention than black innovators" (23).

12. In commenting on Third World musicians, Charles Keil claims corporations and privileged people profit the most from collaborations: "with the high-quality recording and distribution and all the rest, ninety percent of the money winds up going to white people . . . who are already in positions of power: the gatekeepers, the copyright holders, and the distributors" (Keil and Feld 1994: 317). But Feld says the same moves that are read as "cannibalizing" from an ethical point of view are also read as "empowering in various third-world locations" (315).

Chapter 6. Intangible Rites: Heritage Sites, the Reburial Issue, and Modern Pagan Religions in Britain

I wish to acknowledge the assistance of a number of colleagues in the preparation of this article. Cathy L. Costin first brought to my attention the conflict over site access between modern British Pagans and archaeologists; she was also invaluable in providing archaeological references that hugely helped me in my work. I was able to learn further details about archaeology through my conversations with two other departmental colleagues, Michael W. Love and Matthew Des Lauriers. I am deeply grateful to Ronald Hutton for the information he provided on the factions among the various Druid orders, the incident at Stonehenge with which I began this paper, the conference Pagans and Archaeology at the University of Bristol in June 2009, and the disposition of the controversy over "Charlie," as well as for making certain articles available to me that I would otherwise not have been able to access. I thank Jenny Blain for further stimulating my developing ideas on this topic through a paper she presented on my panel at the Societé Internationale d'Ethnologie et Folklore meetings in Derry, Northern Ireland, in June 2007, and Deborah Buchholtz for thought-provoking exchanges on the matter of Native American and British attitudes toward reburial. Finally I wish to thank Susan E. Parker for helping me realize the potential legal implications—both negative and positive—of this work, and for suggesting a possible resolution.

1. I am grateful to Jenny Blain for parts of the description; see also New Age U.K. Stonehenge Summer Solstice 2006 Pictures, http://www.new-age.co.uk/stonehenge-solstice-pics-2006.htm for photos of this event, and YouTube Summer Solstice 2006, http://www.youtube.com/watch?v=Zr6LXC6OIl0 for fire-staff dancing by participants.

2. See The Stonehenge Riverside Project Fieldwork 2008, http://www.shef.ac.uk/archaeology/research/2.4329/index for an explanation of the aims of the project.

3. I am grateful to Ronald Hutton for parts of this description (personal communication, August 2008). A BBC newsreel video was posted at http://www.bbc.co.uk/history/programmes/stonehenge/video.shtml?video=day2, but has since been taken down. It showed a Druid blessing of an earlier excavation at Stonehenge, associated with the Bluestones project, during the same summer.

4. Because this issue is currently unfolding, there is no published ethnography that fully covers every aspect of the controversy. I have interviewed several members of British Druid and Heathen organizations, but as these groups frequently publish and update their views on their websites, much of my post-interview information is derived from Internet sources.

5. The term "Neopaganism" was coined in Britain in the late nineteenth century (Hutton 1999: 28–29) and is used by scholars of the movement to distinguish it from ancient paganisms. This fact has made many modern Pagans reject it as a self-designation, especially in Britain. This chapter will use "modern Paganism" or "Paganism" for Neopagan religions; the capitalization indicates it is the name of a religious movement (cf. Christianity, Judaism). Similarly, terms for denominations within modern Paganism, such as Druid and Heathen, will be capitalized, while references to these as historical terms (druids, heathen) will not.

6. National Park Service, U.S. Department of the Interior, National NAGPRA, http://www.nps.gov/history/nagpra/.

7. E.g., CalNAGPRA in California.

8. On 24 June, 2013, the European Union adopted "Guidelines on the promotion and protection of freedom of religion and belief," which stipulate that member states must ensure the right of access to places of worship and burial for all religious groups. The full text of the declaration can be accessed at EU Guidelines on the promotion and protection of freedom of religion and belief, http://www.eu-un.europa.eu/articles/en/article_13685_en.htm.

9. BBC, "Religions: Paganism at a Glance," http://www.bbc.co.uk/religion/religions/paganism/ataglance/glance.shtml. The 2011 Census conducted by the Office of National Statistics found close to 80,000 self-identified Pagans in Britain; data available for download at http://www.ons.gov.uk/ons/rel/census/2011-census/key-statistics-for-local-authorities-in-england-and-wales/rft-table-qs210ew.xls.

10. For an account of the development of the modern Pagan festive calendar, see Hutton 2008b.

11. For an ethnographic treatment of modern Paganisms in Britain, see Greenwood 2005; for

a collection of essays that provide an overview of modern Paganism in Britain, see Harvey and Hardman 1995.

12. I follow Ronald Hutton in my use of this term rather than the earlier form "druidism," for much the same reason; see Hutton 2007: xiii–xiv.

13. See Blain 2005 for a discussion of the meaning and development of this term and an overview of British Heathenry.

14. This similarity was not accidental. In the late 1990s, Philip Shallcrass, head of the British Druid Order, visited the United States, where he met with a representative of a Native American tribe who informed him about their efforts to gain the repatriation of indigenous human remains and sacred artifacts held in museums, which culminated in NAGPRA. When he returned to Britain, he communicated this to a number of his followers, including Paul Davies and Emma Restall Orr, who in different ways took up the banner of reburial for British Druidry (Ronald Hutton, personal communication, June 2010).

15. See "British Archaeologists Urge Rethink on Reburial Law" 2010; see also Solon 2011.

16. HAD, "Statement of Intention," http://www.honour.org.uk/node/5.

17. Hutton, personal communication, July 2009.

18. Ibid.

19. This is also a practice I witnessed in my early field research in Sardinia in the 1980s, although by 2000 it was no longer customary.

20. From a description of Martin Smith's presentation at the "Pagans and Archaeology" conference at the University of Bristol, June 27, 2009 (M. Smith 2009); Hutton, personal communication, July 2009.

21. Jason Pitzl-Waters, "British Secularists Slam Druid Reburial Demands," *The Wild Hunt*, February 7, 2009.

22. "Had's Response to the English Heritage/National Trust Consultation on the Request for Reburial of Human Remains, Avebury, Wiltshire," http://www.honour.org.uk/node/283.

Chapter 7. Intangible Heritage in Transit: Goytisolo's Rescue and Moroccan Cultural Rights

Epigraph: Juan Goytisolo, *Makbara*, 2008. *Makbara* was originally published in Spanish (Barcelona: Editorial Seix Barral, 1980); trans. Helen R. Lane (New York: Seaver, 1981), reissued by Dalkey Archive, 2008. The portions quoted, 246–47, 250–51, are taken from the Dalkey reissue. Goytisolo says of the style of this piece: "My novels *Makbara* and *The Virtues of the Solitary Bird* privilege this latent orality that persists in writing though it is totally dissimilar to that of the bards of today's precarious oral tradition." From "Defending Threatened Cultures," http://www.unesco.org/bpi/intangible_heritage/goytisoloe.htm, accessed October 30, 2009.

1. Journalist Maya Jaggi (2000) notes in her interview with Goytisolo: "Scornful of the 'educated but uncultured' Moroccan bourgeoisie who look down on the low-life spinning fabulous tales on the square, he gleams with uncondescending pleasure at the paradox: 'The illiterate storytellers were my professors.'"

2. Under the French protectorate in 1922, and with the recommendation of Moroccan advisor, Muhammad al-Mukri, French General Hubert Lyautey signed a law that put Jma' al-Fna on the list of historic sites and monuments.

3. Text recorded, translated, and transliterated by Deborah Kapchan.

4. There is irony in the fact that Morocco—a former French protectorate—was celebrated in the Tuileries Garden, where the last remnants of royalty were violently abolished in a bloody

conflict. The Tuileries, in other words, have been the site of conflicting powers throughout history.

5. The dancers, musicians, and acrobats did reenact the *halqa* to a certain degree, as their art forms evoke embodied interaction on the part of audience members. Because the herbalists were silent and prohibited from selling or otherwise dispensing advice, however, their performativity was curtailed.

6. "Mohammad Bariz . . . is considered to be one of the most renowned Hala'iqis of Al-Fina' Mosque courtyard nowadays. He revives the souls and stirs up the memories of those who sit in circles around him to listen to the Antariya." From a 2005 "Andalusian Days Festival," http://boards.independenttraveler.com/archive/index.php?t-4387.html, accessed October 30, 2009.

7. Of these competing discourses, Goytisolo says, "culture and education are not identical terms, and consequently the holders of oral knowledge can be and at times are more cultured than their compatriots versed only in the use of audio-visual and computing techniques. But in a world subjugated by these ubiquitous techniques, oral culture, whether primary or hybrid, is seriously endangered and warrants an international mobilisation to save it from gradual extinction." Goytisolo 2001, "Defending Threatened Cultures."

8. Ironically Abdelnacer's sons are absent from the square. His young nephew is there, but he is not a verbal artist; he sells his herbs without words and his goods without advice to tourists without a clue.

Bibliography

Abrahams, Roger. 1993. "Phantoms of Romantic Nationalism." *Journal of American Folklore* 106 (419): 3–37.

———. 2003. "Identity." In *Eight Words for the Study of Expressive Culture*, ed. Burt Feintuch. Urbana: University of Illinois Press. 198–222.

Acton, Thomas, and Ilona Klimova. 2001. "The International Romani Union: An East European Answer to West European Questions?" In *Between Past and Future: The Roma of Central and Eastern Europe*, ed. Will Guy. Hatfield: University of Hertfordshire Press. 157–219.

"Afghanistan's 'Mr. Chic.'" 2002. *BBC News Online*, January 17.

"Africa 2009: Interview with Joseph King of ICCROM." 2001. *World Heritage Newsletter* 32 (October–November): 2.

Agrawal, Arun. 2005. "Environmentality: Community, Intimate Government, and the Making of Environmental Subjects in Kumaon, India." *Current Anthropology* 46 (2): 161–90.

Agrawal, Arun, and Clark C. Gibson. 2001. "The Role of Community in Natural Resource Conservation." In *Communities and the Environment: Ethnicity, Gender, and the State in Community-Based Conservation*, ed. Arun Agrawal and Clark C. Gibson. New Brunswick, N.J.: Rutgers University Press. 1–31.

Albro, Robert. 2005a. "The Challenges of Asserting, Promoting, and Performing Cultural Heritage." *Theorizing Cultural Heritage* 1 (1): 2–8.

———. 2005b. "Making Cultural Policy and Confounding Cultural Diversity." *Cultural Commons: The Meeting Place for Culture and Policy*. Cultural Comment. http://www.culturalcommons.org/comment-print.cfm?ID=26.

Amine, Khalid. 2001. "Crossing Borders: Al-halqa Performance in Morocco from the Open Space to the Theatre Building." *Drama Review* T170 (Summer): 55–69.

Anderson, Benedict. 1983. 1991 Rev. ed. *Imagined Communities: Reflections on the Origin and Spread of Nationalism*. London: Verso.

Anholt, Simon. 2005. *Brand New Justice: How Branding Places and Products Can Help the Developing World*. Rev. ed. Oxford: Butterworth-Heinemann.

Anttonen, Pertti J. 2005. *Tradition Through Modernity: Postmodernism and the Nation-State in Folklore Scholarship*. Studia Fennica Folkloristica 15. Helsinki: Finnish Literature Society.

Appadurai, Arjun. 1996. *Modernity at Large: Cultural Dimensions of Globalization*. Minneapolis: University of Minnesota Press.

———. 2000. "Grassroots Globalization and the Research Imagination." *Public Culture* 12 (1): 1–19.

———. 2006. *Fear of Small Numbers: An Essay on the Geography of Anger*. Durham, N.C.: Duke University Press.

Arnold, Matthew. 1998 [1869]. "Culture and Anarchy." In *Cultural Theory & Popular Culture: A Reader*, ed. John Storey. 2nd ed. Athens: University of Georgia Press.

Aronczyk, Melissa. 2008. "Living the Brand: Nationality, Globality and the Identity Strategies of Nation Branding Consultants." *International Journal of Communication* 2: 41–65.

Aronsson, Peter. 2004. *Historiebruk: Att använda det förflutna*. Lund: Studentlitteratur.

Asad, Talal. 2003. *Formations of the Secular: Christianity, Islam, Modernity*. Cultural Memory in the Present. Stanford, Calif.: Stanford University Press.

Augé, Marc. 1999. *The War of Dreams: Exercises in Ethno-Fiction*. London: Pluto Press.

Bahar, Saba. 2000. "Human Rights Are Women's Rights." In *Global Feminisms Since 1945: A Survey of Issues and Controversies*, ed. Bonnie G. Smith. New York: Routledge. 265–89.

Bakhtin, Mikhail. 1984. *Rabelais and His World*. Trans. Helene Iswolsky. Bloomington: Indiana University Press.

Balibar, Étienne. 2004. "Dissonances Within Laïcité." *Constellations* 11 (3): 353–67.

Barany, Zoltan. 2002. *The East European Gypsies: Regime Change, Marginality, and Ethnopolitics*. London: Cambridge University Press.

Barkan, Elazar. 2007. "Genes and Burkas: Predicaments of Human Rights and Cultural Property." In *Cultural Heritage and Human Rights*, ed. Helaine Silverman and D. Fairchild Ruggles. New York: Springer. 184–200.

Barthes, Roland. 1972. *Mythologies*. New York: Farrar, Straus and Giroux

Batteau, Allen. 1990. *The Invention of Appalachia*. Tucson: University of Arizona Press.

Baudrillard, Jean. 1994. *Simulacra and Simulation*. Trans.Sheila Faria Glaser. Ann Arbor: University of Michigan Press.

Bauman, Richard. 1984. *Verbal Art as Performance*. Long Grove, Ill.: Waveland Press.

———. 1986. *Story, Performance, and Event: Contextual Studies of Oral Narrative*. New York: Cambridge University Press.

Bauman, Richard, and Charles Briggs. 2003. *Voices of Modernity: Language Ideologies and the Politics of Inequality*. New York: Cambridge University Press.

Beckert, Jens. 2007. *Inherited Wealth*. Trans. Thomas Dunlap Princeton, N.J.: Princeton University Press.

Beckman, Svante. 1998. "Vad vill staten med kulturarvet?" In *Kulturarvets natur*, ed. Annika Alzén and Johan Hedrén. Stockholm/Stehag: Brutus Östlings/Symposion. 13–50.

Bendix, Regina. 1997. *In Search of Authenticity: The Formation of Folklore Studies*. Madison: University of Wisconsin Press.

———. 2000. "Heredity, Hybridity and Heritage from One Fin-de-Siècle to the Next." In *Folklore, Heritage Politics and Ethnic Diversity: A Festschrift for Barbro Klein*, ed. Pertti J. Anttonen, Anna-Leena Siikala, and Stein R. Mathisen. Botkyrka, Sweden: Multicultural Centre. 37–56.

———. 2009. "Heritage Between Economy and Politics: An Assessment from the Perspective of Cultural Anthropology." In *Intangible Heritage*, ed. Laurajane Smith and Natsuko Akagawa. London: Routledge. 253–69.

Bendix, Regina, and Valdimar Tr. Hafstein. 2009. "Culture and Property: An Introduction." *Ethnologia Europaea: Journal of European Ethnology* 39 (2): 5–10.

Benjamin, Walter. 1969. *Illuminations*. Trans. Harry Zohn, ed. and intro Hannah Arendt. New York: Schocken.

Bennett, David. 2005. "Global Tourism and Caribbean Culture." *Caribbean Quarterly* 51 (1): 15–24.

Bennett, Jane. 2010. *Vibrant Matter: A Political Ecology of Things*. Durham, N.C.: Duke University Press.

Bennett, Tony. 1995. *The Birth of the Museum: History, Theory, Politics*. London: Routledge.

———. 1998. *Culture: A Reformer's Science*. London: Sage.

———. 2000. "Acting on the Social. Art, Culture and Government." *American Behavioral Scientist* 43 (9): 1412–28.

———. 2001. *Differing Diversities: Cultural Policy and Cultural Diversity*. Strasbourg: Council of Europe.

———. 2003. "Culture and Governmentality." In *Foucault, Cultural Studies, and Governmentality*, ed. Jack Z. Bratich, Jeremy Packer, and Cameron McCarthy. Albany: State University of New York Press. 47–63.

Berliner, David. 2010. "Perdre l'esprit du lieu: Les politiques de l'Unesco à Luang Prabang (RDP Lao)." *Terrain* 55: 90–105.

Berman, Marshall. 1982. *All That Is Solid Melts into Air: The Experience of Modernity*. New York: Penguin.

Bhabha, Homi K. 1994. *The Location of Culture*. London: Routledge.

Björgvinsdóttir, Bryndís. 2010. "Menningararfur sem ásetningur." *Skírnir* 184 (1): 100–120.

Blain, Jenny. 2005. "Heathenry, the Past, and Sacred Sites in Today's Britain." In *Modern Paganism in World Cultures: Comparative Perspectives*, ed. Michael Strmiska. Santa Barbara, Calif.: ABC Clio. 181–208.

Blain, Jenny, and Robert Wallis. 2003. "Sites, Sacredness and Stories: Interactions of Archaeology and Contemporary Paganism." *Folklore* 114 (3): 307–21.

———. 2007a. "A Live Issue: Ancestors, Pagan Identity and the 'Reburial Issue' in Britain." In *Security of Archaeological Heritage*, ed. N. Petrov. Newcastle: Cambridge Scholars. 1–22.

———. 2007b. *Sacred Sites, Contested Rites/Rights: Pagan Engagements with Archaeological Monuments*. Eastbourne: Sussex Academic Press.

Blake, Janet. 2001. *Developing a New Standard-Setting Instrument for the Safeguarding of Intangible Cultural Heritage: Elements for Consideration*. CLT-2001/WS/8. Paris: UNESCO.

———. 2009. "UNESCO's 2003 *Convention on Intangible Cultural Heritage*: The Implications of Community Involvement in 'Safeguarding.'" In *Intangible Heritage*, ed. Laurajane Smith and Natsuko Akagawa. London: Routledge. 45–73.

Boddy, Janice. 1989. *Wombs and Alien Spirits: Women,Men, and the Zar Cult in Northern Sudan*. New Directions in Anthropological Writing. Madison: University of Wisconsin Press.

Bonniers Folklexikon. 1951–53. Ed. Axel Elvin. Stockholm: Nordiska Uppslagsböcker.

Born, Georgina, and David Hesmondhalgh. 2000. "Introduction: On Difference, Representation, and Appropriation in Music." In *Western Music and Its Others: Difference, Representation, and Appropriation in Music*, ed. Georgina Born and David Hesmondhalgh. Berkeley: University of California Press. 1–58.

Bortolotto, Chiara. 2008. "Il processo di definizione del concetto di 'patrimonio culturale immateriale': Elementi per una riflessione." In *Il patrimonio immateriale secondo l'Unesco: Analisi e prospettive*, ed. Chiara Bortolotto. Rome: Istituto Poligrafico e Zecca dello Stato. 7–48.

———. 2009. "The Giant Cola Cola in Gravina: Intangible Cultural Heritage, Property, and Territory Between Unesco Discourse and Local Heritage Practice." *Ethnologia Europaea: Journal of European Ethnology* 39 (2): 81–94.

Bouissac, Paul. 2009. "Hot Signs." *Semiotix* 15 (September).

Bowcott, Owen. 2006. "Orange Parades 'Could Become Carnivals.'" *Guardian*, June 23.

Bowen, John R. 2007. *Why the French Don't Like Headscarves: Islam, the State, and Public Space*. Princeton, N.J.: Princeton University Press.

Bowman, Marion. 1996. "Cardiac Celts: Images of Celts in Paganism." In *Paganism Today*, ed. Graham Harvey and Charlotte Hardman. San Francisco: HarperCollins. 242–51.

Bratich, Jack Z., Jeremy Packer, and Cameron McCarthy, eds. 2003. *Foucault, Cultural Studies and Governmentality*. Albany: State University of New York Press.

BDRC. 2009. "Research into Issues Surrounding Human Bones in Museums." Prepared for English Heritage. http://www.english-heritage.org.uk/content/imported-docs/k-o/opinion-survey-results.

Breglia, Lisa. 2006. *Monumental Ambivalence: The Politics of Heritage*. Austin: University of Texas Press.

Brennan, Teresa. 2004. *The Transmission of Affect*. Ithaca, N.Y.: Cornell University Press.

Briggs, Charles. 1996. "The Politics of Discursive Authority in Research on the 'Invention of Tradition.'" *Cultural Anthropology* 11 (4): 435–69.

"British Archaeologists Urge Rethink on Reburial Law." 2010. *Observer*, October 10.

"British Govt Slammed over Parade Funding." 2006. *RTÉ News Online*, June 30.

Brown, Michael. 2004a. "Heritage as Property." In *Property in Question: Value Transformation in the Global Economy*, ed. Katherine Verdery and Caroline Humphrey. Oxford: Berg. 49–68.

———. 2004b. *Who Owns Native Culture?* Cambridge, Mass.: Harvard University Press.

Brownell, Ginanne, and Amber Haq. 2007. "The World Embraces Gypsy Culture." *Newsweek International*, July 30.

Brumann, Christoph. 2009. "Outside the Glass Case: The Social Life of Urban Heritage in Kyoto." *American Ethnologist* 36 (2): 276–99.

Buchanan, Donna. 1996. "Wedding Musicians, Political Transition, and National Consciousness in Bulgaria." In *Returning Culture: Musical Change in Eastern Europe*, ed. Mark Slobin. Durham, N.C.: Duke University Press, 200–230.

———. 2006. *Performing Democracy: Bulgarian Music and Musicians in Transition*. Chicago: University of Chicago Press.

Burchell, Graham, Colin Gordon, and Peter Miller, eds. 1991. *The Foucault Effect: Studies in Governmentality*. Chicago: University of Chicago Press.

Butler, Jenny. 2005. "Druidry in Contemporary Ireland." In *Modern Paganism in World Cultures: Comparative Perspectives*, ed. Michael Strmiska. Santa Barbara, Calif.: ABC Clio. 87–125.

Cantwell, Robert. 2003. *Bluegrass Breakdown: The Making of the Old Southern Sound*. 2nd ed. Urbana: University of Illinois Press.

———. 2009. "Twang: Striking the Southern Note." Lecture in series "Race and Memory in American Vernacular Music." Center for Folklore Studies, Ohio State University, May.

Carr Gomm, Philip, ed. 2003. *The Rebirth of Druidry*. San Francisco: Thorsons.

Castaño, Joan et al. 1998. *El misterio de Elche: La festa d'Elx*. Elche: Ayuntamiento de Elche.

Castells, Manuel. 1997. *The Network Society*. Oxford: Blackwell.

Chittick, William C. 1989. *The Sufi Path of Knowledge: Ibn Al Arabi's Metaphysics of Imagination*. Albany: State University of New York Press.

Christia, Fotini, and Thalia Chantziara. 2009. "Sartorial Stumping." *New York Times*. August 18.

Church of England and English Heritage. 2005. *Guidance for Best Practice for Treatment of Human Remains Excavated from Christian Burial Grounds in England*. Text comp. Simon Mays. Swindon: English Heritage, 2005. www.english-heritage.org.uk.

Claessen, Henri J. M. 2002. Comment on "Masterpieces of Oral and Intangible Culture: Reflections on the UNESCO World Heritage List" by Peter J. M. Nas. *Current Anthropology* 43 (1): 144.

Clifford, James. 1997. *Routes: Travel and Translation in the Late Twentieth Century*. Cambridge, Mass.: Harvard University Press.

———. 2003. *On the Edges of Anthropology (Interviews)*. Chicago: Prickly Paradigm Press.

———. 2004. "Traditional Futures." In *Questions of Tradition*, ed. Mark Phillips and Gordon Schochet. Toronto: University of Toronto Press. 152–68.

Collis, Stephen. 2005. "Another Duncan Etude: Empire and Anarchy." *W10: A Duncan Delirium*. 35–47. http://www.kswnet.org/editables/pdfsANDscans-WMAG/w10.pdf#page=35, accessed January 3, 2013.

"Colombia Aid Failed to Halve Drug Making, Report Finds." 2008. Associated Press, November 6.

Colson, Elizabeth, and Conrad Kottak. 1996. "On Linkages Methodology for the Study of Multi-Level Systems." In *Transforming Societies, Transforming Anthropology*, ed. Emilio Moran. Ann Arbor: University of Michigan Press.

Community Arts Forum of Belfast. 2007. Seminar on the Future of Orangefest. Northern Visions Television, June 25. http://www.caf.ie/orangefest.asp.

Community Heritage Partners. n.d. "Building New Life for Old Places." http://www.chpartners.net/

Coole, Diana, and Samantha Frost. 2010. *New Materialisms: Ontology, Agency, and Politics*. Durham, N.C.: Duke University Press.

Copeland, Larry. 2009. "Tennessee Residents Fear Impact of Sludgy Ash Spill." *USA Today*. January 1.

Council of British Druid Orders (CoBDO). 2008. "Request for the Reburial of Human Remains and Grave Goods, Avebury." http://www.english-heritage.org.uk/content/imported-docs.

———. 2009. Official CoBDO Official Statement on Reburial. http://www.cobdo.org.uk/html/reburial_statement.html.

Cousin, Saskia, 2008. "L'Unesco et la doctrine du tourisme culturel: Généalogie d'un 'bon' tourisme." *Civilisations* 57: 41–56.

Cowan, Jane, Marie-Bebdicte Dembour, and Richard Wilson. 2000. *Culture and Rights: Anthropological Perspectives*. Cambridge: Cambridge University Press.

Crick, Anne P. 2002. "Smile, You're a Tourism Employee! Managing Emotional Displays in Jamaican Tourism." In *Tourism and Change in the Caribbean and Latin America*, ed. Ian Boxill, Orville Taylor, and Johannes Maerck. Kingston: Arawak. 162–78.

———. 2003. "Internal Marketing Attitudes in Caribbean Tourism." *International Journal of Contemporary Hospitality Management* 15 (3): 161–66.

Cupid, John. 1994. "Trinidad Carnival Traditional Characters." In *1st Carnival King and Queen of the World Magazine* 1 (1): 16–17.

Curtis, Maria. 2007. "Sound Faith: Nostalgia, global Spirituality, and the Making of the Fes Festival of World Sacred Music." Ph.D. dissertation, Department of Anthropology, University of Texas at Austin.

DaCosta Holton, Kimberly. 2005. *Performing Folklore: Ranchos Folcloricos from Lisbon to Newark*. Bloomington: Indiana University Press.

Danforth, Loring. 1982. *The Death Rituals of Rural Greece*. Princeton, N.J.: Princeton University Press.

Das, Veena. 1999. "Communities as Political Actors: The Question of Cultural Rights." In *Gender and Politics in India*, ed. Nivedita Menon. New Delhi: Oxford University Press. 441–71.

Daun, Åke. 2003. *Med rörligt sökarljus: Den nya etnologins framväxt under 1960- och 1970-talen*. Stockholm/Stehag: Brutus Östlings.

Davies, Paul. 1997. "Respect and Reburial." *Druid's Voice: The Magazine of Contemporary Druidry* 8: 12–13.

———. 1998/99. "Speaking for the Ancestors: the Reburial Issue in Britain and Ireland." *Druid's Voice: The Magazine of Contemporary Druidry* 9: 10–12.

Davis, Donald Edward. 2000. *Where There Are Mountains: An Environmental History of the Southern Appalachians.* Athens: University of Georgia Press.

Daye, Marcella, Donna Chambers, and Sherma Roberts. 2008. *New Perspectives in Caribbean Tourism.* New York: Routledge.

Deleuze, Gilles, and Félix Guattari. 1987. "1837: Of the Refrain," trans. Brian Massumi. In *A Thousand Plateaus: Capitalism and Schizophrenia.* Minneapolis: University of Minnesota Press. 310–50.

Deloria, Vine, Jr. 1969. *Custer Died for Your Sins.* New York: Macmillan.

Department for Culture, Media and Sport (DCMS). 2005. *Guidance for the Care of Human Remains in Museums.* http://webarchive.nationalarchives.gov.uk/+/http://www.culture.gov.uk.

Department of Statistics to the Government of the Republic of Lithuania. 2005. *Lithuanian Census: Population by Ethnicity.* Updated December 1. http://www.stat.gov.lt/en/pages/view/?id=1731.

Derrida, Jacques. 1988. "Signature Event Context." In Derrida, *Limited Inc.* Chicago: Northwestern University Press.

———. 2007. "A Certain Impossible Possibility of Saying the Event." *Critical Inquiry* 33 (2): 441–61.

Dewan, Shaila. 2008a. "Water Supplies Tested After Tennessee Spill." *New York Times,* December 23.

———. 2008b. "At Plant in Coal Ash Spill, Toxic Deposits by the Ton." *New York Times,* December 30.

———. 2009. "Clash in Alabama over Tennessee Coal Ash." *New York Times,* August 30.

Dickey, James. 1970. *Deliverance.* Boston: Houghton Mifflin.

Dirlik, Arif. 2000. *Postmodernity's Histories: The Past as Legacy and Project.* Lanham, Md.: Rowman and Littlefield.

Djordjević, Tihomir. 1984 [1910]. "Cigani i muzika u Srbiji" [Gypsies and Music in Serbia]. *Naš Narodni Život* 7:32–40.

Dorian, Nancy C. 1987. "The Value of Language-Maintenance Efforts Which Are Unlikely to Succeed." *International Journal of the Sociology of Language* 68: 57–67.

Doubleday, Veronica. 2007. "The Role of Women and Children's Music-Making in Afghanistan and the Afghan Diaspora: Considering Continuity and Change." Paper presented at the Conference on Music in the World of Islam, Asilah, Morocco, August 8–13.

Douglas, Mary. 1966. *Purity and Danger.* London: Routledge and Kegan Paul.

Dreyfus, Hubert L., and Paul Rabinow. 1983. *Michel Foucault: Beyond Structuralism and Hermeneutics.* Chicago: University of Chicago Press.

Duffield, Mark. 2007. *Development, Security, and Unending War: Governing the World of Peoples.* Cambridge: Polity Press.

Dundes, Alan. 1965. *The Study of Folklore.* Englewood Cliffs, N.J.: Prentice-Hall.

———. 1969. "The Devolutionary Premise in Folklore Theory." *Journal of the Folklore Institute* 6: 5–19.

———. 1980. "Who Are the Folk?" In *Interpreting Folklore.* Bloomington: Indiana University Press. 1–19.

———. 1985. "Nationalistic Inferiority Complexes and the Fabrication of Fakelore: A Reconsideration of Ossian, the *Kinder- und Hausmärchen,* the *Kalevala,* and Paul Bunyan." *Journal of Folklore Research* 22 (1): 5–18.

Eberstadt, Fernanda. 2006. "The Anti-Orientalist." *New York Times Magazine,* April 16.

Eidheim, Harald 1997. "Ethno-Political Development Among the Sami After World War II: The

Invention of Selfhood." In *Sami Culture in a New Era: The Norwegian Sami Experience*, ed. Harald Gaski. Kárasjohka, Norway: Davvi Girji. 29–61.

Einarsbøl, Elisabeth. 2005. "Reindeer Herding Rights: Norway." In *The Saami: A Cultural Encyclopaedia*, ed. Ulla-Maija Kulonen, Irja Seurujärvi-Kari, and Risto Pulkkinen. Suomalaisen Kirjallisuuden Seuran toimituksia 925. Helsinki: Finnish Literary Society. 307–10.

El Hamel, Chouki. 2008. "Constructing a Diasporic Identity: Tracing the Origins of Gnawa Spiritual Group in Morocco," *Journal of African History* 49 (2): 241–60.

———. 2013. *Black Morocco: A History of Slavery, Race, and Islam*. African Studies. Cambridge: Cambridge University Press.

Eller, Ronald D. 1982. *Miners, Millhands, and Mountaineers: Industrialization in the Mountain South, 1880–1930*. Knoxville: University of Tennessee Press.

———. 2008. *Uneven Ground: Appalachia Since 1945*. Lexington: University Press of Kentucky.

English Heritage. 2010. "Human Remains in Avebury Museum Will Stay." Press release, April 6. http://www.honour.org.uk/system/files/EH%20Press%20Release.pdf,

———. n.d. "Avebury Reburial Request—Results of Consultation." http://www.english-heritage.org.uk/professional/advice/advice-by-topic/heritage-science/archaeological-science/avebury-reburial-result.

Eriksen, Anne. 1993. "Den nasjonale kulturarven: En del av det moderne." *Kulturella Perspektiv* 1: 16–25.

Erixon, Sigurd. 1947. *Svensk byggnadskultur: Studier och skildringar belysande den svenska byggnadskulturens historia*. Stockholm: Aktiebolaget Bokverk.

Erlmann, Veit. 2003. "Communities of Style: Musical Figures of Black Diasporic Identity." In *The Black Diaspora: A Musical Perspective*, ed. Ingrid Monson. New York: Routledge. 83–102.

"Europe's Roma: Bottom of the Heap." 2008. *Economist*, June 19.

"Expert Criticises Copyright Bill." 2005. *Ghanamusic.com*. April 19. http://www.ghanamusic.com/artman/publish/article_1736.shtml.

Fabian, Johannes. 1983. *Time and the Other: How Anthropology Makes Its Object*. New York: Columbia University Press.

Farahani, Fataneh. 2007. *Diasporic Narratives of Sexuality: Identity Formation Among Iranian-Swedish Women*. Stockholm Studies in Ethnology 2. Stockholm: Acta Universitatis Stockholmiensis.

Feld, Steven. 1994. "From Schizophonia to Schismogenesis: On the Discourses and Commodification Practices of 'World Music' and 'World Beat.'" In *Music Grooves*, ed. Charles Keil and Steven Feld. Chicago: University of Chicago Press.

———. 1996. "Pygmy POP: A Genealogy of Schizophonic Mimesis." *Yearbook for Traditional Music* 28 (1996): 1–35.

———. 2000. "A Sweet Lullaby for World Music." *Public Culture* 12 (1): 145–71.

Feld, Steven, and Keith H. Basso, eds. 1996. *Senses of Place*. Santa Fe, N.M.: School of American Research.

Ferguson, James. 2007. *Global Shadows: Africa in the Neoliberal World Order*. Durham, N.C.: Duke University Press.

Fernandez, James W. 1986. *Persuasions and Performances: The Play of Tropes in Culture*. Bloomington: Indiana University Press.

Ferrell, Ann. 2009. "'Replacing' Tobacco on Kentucky Farms: Discourses of Tradition, Heritage, and Agricultural Diversification." Ph.D. dissertation, Ohio State University.

Fonseca, Isabel. 1995. *Bury Me Standing: The Gypsies and Their Journey*. New York: Random House.

Forero, Juan. 2006. "Colombia's Coca Survives U.S. Plan to Uproot It." *New York Times*, August 19.

Foucault, Michel. 1970. *The Order of Things: An Archaeology of the Human Sciences*. New York: Pantheon.

———. 1972. *The Archaeology of Knowledge and the Discourse on Language*. Trans. Sheridan Smith. New York: Pantheon.

———. 1977. *Discipline and Punish: The Birth of the Prison*. Trans. Sheridan Smith. New York: Vintage.

———. 1991. "Governmentality." In *The Foucault Effect: Studies in Governmentality*, ed. Graham Burchell, Colin Gordon, and Peter Miller, trans. David Macey. Chicago: University of Chicago Press.

———. 2003. *Society Must Be Defended: Lectures at the Collège de France, 1975–1976*. New York: Picador.

———. 2007 [1983]. *Security, Territory, Population: Lectures at the Collège de France 1977–1978*. New York: Palgrave Macmillan.

Fraser, Angus. 1992. *The Gypsies*. Oxford: Blackwell.

Friedman, Jonathan. 2000. "Des racines et (dé)routes: Tropes pour trekkers." *L'Homme* 156: 187–206.

———. 2002. "Transnationalization, Socio-Political Disorder, and Ethnification as Expressions of Declining Global Hegemony." In *The Anthropology of Politics: A Reader in Ethnography, Theory, and Critique*, ed. Joan Vincent. Oxford: Blackwell. 285–300.

Frykman, Jonas, and Billy Ehn, eds. 2007. *Minnesmärken: Att tolka det förflutna och besvärja framtiden*. Stockholm: Carlssons.

Frykman, Jonas, and Orvar Löfgren. 1986 [1979]. *Culture Builders: An Historical Anthropology of Middle Class Life*. Trans. Alan Crozier. New Brunswick, N.J.: Rutgers University Press.

Gall, Carlotta, and David E. Sanger. 2007. "Civilian Deaths Undermine Allies' War on Taliban." *New York Times*, May 13.

Gaski, Harald. 1997. "Introduction: Sami Culture in a New Era." In *Sami Culture in a New Era: The Norwegian Sami Experience*, ed. Harald Gaski. Kárasjohka, Norway: Davvi Girji. 9–61.

Gates, Henry Louis, Jr. 1993. *Loose Canons: Notes on the Culture Wars*. New York: Oxford University Press.

Geoghegan, Peter. 2009. "Belfast's Twelfth Celebrations Get a Radical Overhaul." July 8. *Culture Northern Ireland.com*.

Gheorghe, Nicolae, and Thomas Acton. 2001. "Citizens of the World and Nowhere: Minority, Ethnic, and Human Rights for Roma." In *Between Past and Future: The Roma of Central and Eastern Europe*, ed. Will Guy. Hatfield: University of Hertfordshire Press. 54–70.

Ghodsee, Kristen. 2008. "Left Wing, Right Wing, Everything: Xenophobia, Neototalitarianism, and Populist Politics in Bulgaria." *Problems of Post-Communism* 55 (3): 26–39.

Giguère, Hélène. 2005. "Le son, l'arôme et l'image: Patrimonialisation des sens et spectacularisation marchande de la culture à Jerez de la Frontera (Espagne)." Thèse de Doctorat, École des Hautes Études en Sciences Sociales et Séville, Université de Séville.

———. 2006. "Vues anthropologiques sur le patrimoine culturel immatériel: Un ancrage en basse Andalousie." *Anthropologie & Sociétés* 30 (2): 107–27.

———. 2008a. "Intervista a Antonello Bardeglinu (*Cante a tenore*)." In *Il patrimonio culturale immateriale: Analisi e prospettive*, ed. Chiara Bortolotto. Milan: Istituto Poligrafico e Zecca dello Stato. 207–9.

———. 2008b. "Intervista a Giovanni Cossu (*Cante a tenore*)." In *Il patrimonio culturale immateriale: Analisi e prospettive*, ed. Chiara Bortolotto. Milan: Istituto Poligrafico e Zecca dello Stato. 211–15.

———. 2008c. "Intervista a Mimmo Cuticchio (*Puparo*)." In *Il patrimonio culturale immateriale: Analisi e prospettive*, ed. Chiara Bortolotto. Milan: Istituto Poligrafico e Zecca dello Stato. 173–78.

———. 2008d. "Musique ethnique ou musique internationale? Diversité, *vivencia* et esthétique d'un patrimoine flamenco." In *Il patrimonio culturale immateriale: Analisi e prospettive*, ed. Chiara Bortolotto. Milan: Istituto Poligrafico e Zecca dello Stato. 129–43.

Gilroy, Paul. 1993. *The Black Atlantic: Modernity and Double Consciousness*. Cambridge, Mass.: Harvard University Press.

Gojković, Adrijana. 1977. "Romi u Muzičkom Životu Naših Naroda" [Roma in the Musical Life of Our People]. *Zvuk* 3: 45–50.

Goldman, Michael. 2005. *Imperial Nature: The World Bank and Struggles for Social Justice in the Age of Globalization*. New Haven, Conn.: Yale University Press.

Goldwasser, Michele. 1997. "Review of *The Toured: The Other Side of Tourism in Barbados*." *Western Folkore* (Winter).

Goodman, Jane. 2005. *Berber Culture on the World Stage: From Village to Video*. Bloomington: Indiana University Press.

Gordon, Colin. 1991. "Governmental Rationality: An Introduction." In *The Foucault Effect: Studies in Governmentality*, ed. Graham Burchell, Colin Gordon, and Peter Miller. Chicago: University of Chicago Press. 1–52.

Goytisolo, Juan. 1997. "Jemaa-el-Fna: Patrimoine oral de l'humanité." *Le Monde Diplomatique* 519 (June).

———. 2001. "Defending Threatened Cultures." Speech at Opening of the Meeting of the Jury, Proclamation of the Masterpieces of the Oral and Intangible Heritage of Humanity, May 15. http://www.unesco.org/bpi/intangible_heritage/goytisoloe.htm.

———. 2003. *Cinema Eden: Essays from the Muslim Mediterranean*. London: Eland Press.

———. 2008. *Makbara*. Trans. Helen Lane. Urbana, Ill.: Dalkey Press.

Green, Garth, and Philip W. Scher, eds. 2007. *Trinidad Carnival: The Cultural Politics of a Transnational Festival*. Bloomington: Indiana University Press.

Greenwood, Susan. 2005. *The Nature of Magic: An Anthropology of Consciousness*. Oxford: Berg.

Grossberg, Lawrence, Toby Miller, and Jeremy Packer. 2003. "Mapping the Intersection of Foucault and Cultural Studies: An Interview with Lawrence Grossberg and Toby Miller, October 2000." In *Foucault, Cultural Studies, and Governmentality*, ed. Jack Z. Bratich, Jeremy Packer, and Cameron McCarthy. Albany: State University of New York Press. 23–46.

Groth, Stefan. 2010. "Perspectives on Differentiation: Negotiating Traditional Knowledge." *Journal of Folkloristics and Ethnology* 4 (1): 7–24.

———. 2012. *Negotiating Tradition: The Pragmatics of International Deliberations on Cultural Property*. Göttingen: Universitätsverlag Göttingen.

Guss, David M. 2001. *The Festive State: Race, Ethnicity, and Nationalism as Cultural Performance*. Berkeley: University of California Press.

Guy, Will, ed. 2001. *Between Past and Future: The Roma of Central and Eastern Europe*. Hatfield: University of Hertfordshire Press.

Hafstein, Valdimar. 2003. "Bodies of Knowledge: Ole Work and Collecting in Late Renaissance Scandinavia." *Ethnologia Europea* 33 (1): 5–20.

———. 2004a. "The Making of Intangible Cultural Heritage: Tradition and Authenticity, Community and Humanity." Ph.D. dissertation, University of California, Berkeley.

———. 2004b. "The Politics of Origins: Collective Creation Revisited." *Journal of American Folklore* 117 (465): 300–315.

———. 2009. "Intangible Heritage as a List: From Masterpieces to Representation." In *Intangible Heritage*, ed. Laurajane Smith and Natsuko Akagawa. Key Issues in Cultural Heritage. London: Routledge. 93–111.

Hagu, Paul. 1995. "Setukaisten identiteetin ongelmat." In *Koltat, karjalaiset ja setukaiset: Pienet kansat maailmojen rajoilla*, ed. Tuija Saarinen and Seppo Suhonen. Kuopio: Snellman-instituutti. 169–81.

———. 1999. "Setukaiset: Raja-alueen ortodoksivähemmistö." In *Uskonto ja identiteetti: Suomalais-ugrilaisten kokemuksia ja vaiheita Venäjällä ja Neuvostoliitossa*, ed. Teuvo Laitila and Tuija Saarinen. Helsinki: Suomaisen Kirjallisuuden Seura. 82–95.

Hajjar, Lisa. 2000. "Human Rights in Israel/Palestine: The History and Politics of a Movement." *Journal of Palestine Studies* 30 (4) (Summer): 21–38.

Haley, Brian D., and L. R. Wilcoxon. 1997. "Anthropology and the Making of Chumash Tradition." *Current Anthropology* 38 (5): 761–94.

Hálfdánarson, Guðmundur. 2001. *Íslenska þjóðríkið: Uppruni og endimörk*. Reykjavík: Hið íslenska bókmenntafélag og ReykjavíkurAkademían.

Hall, Stuart. 1996. "Who Needs 'Identity'?" In *Questions of Cultural Identity*, ed. Stuart Hall and Paul du Gay. London: Sage. 1–17.

Hammoudi, Abdellah. 1997. *Master and Disciple: The Cultural Foundations of Moroccan Authoritarianism*. Chicago: University of Chicago Press.

Hancock, Ian. 1987. *The Pariah Syndrome*. Ann Arbor, Mich.: Karoma.

———. 1997. "The Struggle for the Control of Identity." *Transitions* 4 (4): 36–44.

———. 2002. *We Are the Romani People*. Interface Collection. Hatfield: University of Hertfordshire Press.

Handler, Richard. 1988. *Nationalism and the Politics of Culture in Quebec*. Madison: University of Wisconsin Press.

———. 2006. "Hansen's 'Orangefest' More like 'Bigotfest." *Sinn Fénn Online*, June 30.

Handler, Richard, and Jocelyn Linnekin. 1984. "Tradition, Genuine or Spurious." *Journal of American Folklore* 97 (385): 273–76.

"Hansen's 'Orangefest' More like 'Bigotfest.'" 2006. *Sinn Féin Online*, June 30. http://www.sinnfein.ie/contents/6987.

Hanson, Allan. 1982. *Ours Once More: Folklore, Ideology, and the Making of Modern Greece*. Austin: University of Texas Press.

———. 1989. "The Making of the Maori: Culture Invention and Its Logic." *American Anthropologist* 91: 890–902.

Haraway, Donna. 1991. "A Cyborg Manifesto: Science, Technology, and Socialist-Feminism in the Late Twentieth Century." In Donna Haraway, *Simians, Cyborgs, and Women: The Reinvention of Nature*. New York: Routledge, 149–81.

Hardt, Michael, and Antonio Negri. 2000. *Empire*. Cambridge, Mass.: Harvard University Press.

Hartigan, John, Jr. 1997. "Name Calling: Objectifying 'Poor Whites' and 'White Trash' in Detroit." In *White Trash: Race and Class in America*, ed. Matt Wray and Annalee Newitz. New York: Routledge. 41–56.

Harvey, Graham. 2005. *Animism: Respecting the Living World*. London: Hurst.

Harvey, Graham, and Charlotte Hardman, eds. 1995. *Paganism Today*. San Francisco: Thorsons.

Hemme, Dorothee, Markus Tauschek, and Regina Bendix, eds. 2007. *Prädikat "Heritage": Wertschöpfungen aus kulturellen Ressourcen*. Münster: Lit Verlag.

Herold, Marc W. 2006. “Hat Trick: Selling Brand Karzai.” *Afghanistan as an Empty Space*. http://cursor.org/stories/emptyspace3.html.

Herzfeld, Michael. 1982. *Ours Once More: Folklore, Ideology, and the Making of Modern Greece*. Austin: University of Texas Press.

———. 1992. *The Social Production of Indifference*. Chicago: University of Chicago Press.

———. 1997. *Cultural Intimacy: Social Poetics in the Nation-State*. London: Routledge.

Hill, Jane A. 2002. “‘Expert Rhetorics’ in Advocacy for Endangered Languages: Who Is Listening and What Do They Hear?” *Journal of Linguistics Anthropology* 12 (2): 119–33.

———. 2008. *The Everyday Language of White Racism*. Maldan, Mass.: Wiley-Blackwell.

Hobsbawm, Eric. 1983. “Introduction: Inventing Traditions.” In *The Invention of Tradition*, ed. Eric Hobsbawm and Terence Ranger. Cambridge: Cambridge University Press. 1–14.

Hobsbawm, Eric, and Terence Ranger, eds. 1983. *The Invention of Tradition*. Cambridge: Cambridge University Press.

Holmes, Douglas. 2000. *Integral Europe: Fast-Capitalism, Multiculturalism, Neofascism*. Princeton, N.J.: Princeton University Press.

Honko, Lauri. 2001. “Copyright and Folklore.” Paper read at National Seminar on Copyright Law and Matters, Mangalore University, Mangalore, Karnataka, India, February 9, 2001. *FF Network* 21: 8–10.

Honouring the Ancient Dead (HAD). 2009. “Had’s Response to the English Heritage/National Trust Consultation on the Request for Reburial of Human Remains.” Avebury, Wiltshire. Press Release, February.

hooks, bell. 1990. *Yearning: Race, Gender, and Cultural Politics*. Boston: South End.

Hopf, Ted. 2002. “Making the Future Inevitable: Legitimizing, Naturalizing and Stabilizing the Transition in Estonia, Ukraine and Uzbekistan.” *European Journal of International Relations* 8: 403–36.

Hõrn, Aare 2008. “Seto Kongressi’ läbi aoluu Setomaa piirkonna eloh.” *Setomaa* 21 (175): 6–7.

———. 2009. “Mida arvate Setomaa jagamisest?” *Setomaa* 6 (184): 1.

Hõrn, Aare, and Helen Alumäe. 2004. “Vana tiidmine ja loodusõ usk hoitvaq Setomaa loodust.” *Eesti Loodus*, Erinumber 2004 (55): 56–59.

Howes, David. 2003. *Sensual Relations: Engaging the Senses in Culture and Social Theory*: Ann Arbor: University of Michigan Press.

Hufford, Mary. 2000. “Tending the Commons: Folklife and Landscape in Southern West Virginia.” American Folklife Center, Library of Congress.

———. 2002 “Reclaiming the Commons: Narratives of Progress, Preservation, and Ginseng.” In *Culture, Environment, and Conservation in the Appalachian South*, ed. Benita J. Howell. Urbana: University of Illinois Press. 100–120.

———. 2004. *Waging Democracy in the Kingdom of Coal: OVEC and the Movement for Social and Environmental Justice in Central Appalachia, 2002–2003*. Philadelphia: Center for Folklore and Ethnography, University of Pennsylvania with New York University Robert Wagner School of Public Service.

———. 2006. “Folklore and Folklife in Appalachia: An Overview.” In *Encyclopedia of Appalachia*, ed. Rudy Abramson and Jean Haskell. Knoxville: University of Tennessee Press.

“Human Rights at the Heart of UNESCO Programming.” 2005. *SHS Newsletter* 10 (September–November).

Hutcheon, Linda. 1987. *A Poetics of Postmodernism: History, Theory, Fiction*. London: Routledge.

———. 1988. *The Politics of Postmodernism*. London: Routledge.
———. 1995. *Irony's Edge: The Theory and Politics of Irony*. London: Routledge.
———. 1998. *The Canadian Postmodern*. Toronto: Oxford University Press.
Hutton, Ronald. 1999. *Triumph of the Moon: A History of Modern Pagan Witchcraft*. Oxford: Oxford University Press.
———. 2003. *Witches, Druids and King Arthur*. London: Hambledon.
———. 2007. *The Druids*. London: Hambledon.
———. 2008a. "Druids, Witches and Hippies." Unpublished.
———. 2008b. "Modern Pagan Festivals: A Study in the Nature of Tradition." *Folklore* 119 (3): 251–73.
———. 2009. *Blood and Mistletoe: The History of the Druids in Britain*. New Haven, Conn.: Yale University Press.
Hylton, Forrest, and Sinclair Thomson. 2007. *Revolutionary Horizons: Popular Struggle in Bolivia*. New York: Verso.
ICOMOS. 1999. The 8th Draft of the International Cultural Tourism Charter. Adopted at 12th General Assembly, Mexico City, October 1999.
Inda, Jonathan Xavier, and Renato Rosaldo. 2002. "Introduction: A World in Motion." In *The Anthropology of Globalization: A Reader*, ed. Jonathan Xavier Inda and Renato Rosaldo. Malden, Mass.: Blackwell. 1–34.
"Is God Green?" 2006. *Moyers on America*. PBS. First aired October 11.
Istanbul Declaration—Final Communiqué. 2002. UNESCO. Third Round Table Meeting of Ministers of Culture. http://portal.unesco.org/en/ev.php-URL_ID=6209&URL_DO =DO_TOPIC&URL_SECTION=201.html.
Ivey, Bill. 2008. *Arts, Inc.: How Greed and Neglect Have Destroyed Our Cultural Rights*. Berkeley: University of California Press.
Ivy, Marilyn. 1995. *Discourses of the Vanishing: Modernity, Phantasm, Japan*. Chicago: University of Chicago Press.
Jääts, Indrek. 1998. *Setude etniline identiteet*. Studia Ethnologica Tartuensia 1. Tartu: Estonian National Museum.
Jacobs, Jordan. 2009. "Repatriation and the Reconstruction of Identity." *Museum Anthropology* 32 (2): 83–98.
Jaggi, Maya. 2000. "Scourge of the New Spain." *Guardian*, August 11.
Jakobsen, Janet R., and Ann Pellegrini, eds. 2008. *Secularisms*. Durham, N.C.: Duke University Press.
Jamaica Information Service (JIS). 2008. "Branding Key Initiative to Give Country Competitive Edge—Gregory." October 1.
Jameson, Fredric. 1994. *The Seeds of Time*. New York: Columbia University Press.
Joas, Hans. 2005. "The Sacralization of the Person: The History, Philosophy, and Sociology of Human Rights." Lecture at Cassirer Summer School, Helsinki Collegium for Advanced Studies, August.
Jokilehto, Jukka, and Joseph King. 2001. "Authenticity and Conservation: Reflections on the Current State of Understanding." In *Authenticity and Integrity in an African Context: Expert Meeting—Great Zimbabwe, Zimbabwe, 26–29 May 2000*, ed. Galia Saouma-Forero. Paris: UNESCO. 33–39.
Jones, Carleton. 2007. *Temples of Stone*. West Link Park, Ireland: Collins Press.
Jones, D. Gareth, and Robyn J. Harris. 1998. "Archeological Human Remains: Scientific, Human and Ethical Considerations." *Current Anthropology* 39 (2): 253–64.

Jones, Simon. 1988. *Black Youth, White Culture: The Reggae Tradition from JA to UK*. Basingstoke: Macmillan.

Kansoussi, Jaafar, and Hamid Triki. 1999. *Place Jema' el Fna: Patrimoine oral*. Marrakech: UNESCO. Reprinted from *Horizons Maghrébins: Le droit à la mémoire* 23/24 (1994).

Kapchan, Deborah. 1996. "Performance." *Journal of American Folklore* 108 (430): 479–508.

———. 2005. "Performance in Culture." In *Encyclopedia of Language and Linguistics*, ed. Keith Brown et al. 2nd ed. Amsterdam: Elsevier.

———. 2007. *Traveling Spirit Masters: Moroccan Gnawa Trance and Music in the Global Marketplace*. Middletown, Conn.: Wesleyan University Press.

———. 2008. "The Promise of Sonic Translation: Performing the Festive Sacred in Morocco." *American Anthropologist* 110 (4): 467–83.

Kaplan, Jeffrey. 1996. "The Reconstruction of the Ásatrú and Odinist Traditions." In *Magical Religions and Modern Witchcraft*, ed. James R. Lewis. Albany: State University of New York Press. 193–236.

Karp, Ivan, and Corinne Kratz. 2006. "Preface: Museum Frictions: A Project History." In *Museum Frictions: Public Cultures, Global Transformations*, ed. Ivan Karp, Corinne A. Kratz, Lynn Szwaja, and Tomás Ybarro-Frausto. Durham, N.C.: Duke University Press. xv–xxii.

Karp, Ivan, Corinne A. Krantz, Lynn Szwaja, and Tomás Ybarra-Frausto, eds., with Gustavo Buntinx, Barbara Kirshenblatt-Gimblett, and Ciraj Rassool. 2006. *Museum Frictions: Public Cultures/Global Transformations*. Durham, N.C.: Duke University Press.

Keil, Charles, and Steven Feld, eds. 1994. *Music Grooves*. Chicago: University of Chicago Press.

Kennaway, Brian. 2006. "Book Aims to Bring Orangism Back to Core Principles." *Irish Times*, May 5.

Kharmawphlang, Desmond et al. 2004. "Conversation 2: Folklore and Identity." *Indian Folklife: A Quarterly Newsletter from National Folklore Support Centre* 3 (2): 18–20.

Kirshenblatt-Gimblett, Barbara. 1988. "Mistaken Dichotomies." *Journal of American Folklore* 101 (400): 140–55.

———. 1996. "Topic Drift: Negotiating the Gap Between Our Field and Our Name." *Journal of Folklore Research* 33:245–54.

———. 1998a. *Destination Culture: Tourism, Museums, and Heritage*. Berkeley: University of California Press.

———. 1998b. "Folklore's Crisis." *Journal of American Folklore* 111 (431): 281–327.

———. 1998c. "Objects of Ethnography." In *Destination Culture: Tourism, Museums, and Heritage*. Berkeley: University of California Press. 17–78.

———. 2004. "Intangible Heritage as Metacultural Production." *Museum International* 56 (1–2): 52–65.

———. 2006a. "Exhibitionary Complexes." In *Museum Frictions: Public Culture/Global Transformations*, ed. Ivan Karp, Corinne A. Kratz, Lynn Szwaja, and Tomás Ybarra-Frausto. Durham, N.C.: Duke University Press. 35–45.

———. 2006b. "World Heritage and Cultural Economics." In *Museum Frictions: Public Culture/Global Transformations*, ed. Ivan Karp, Corinne A. Kratz, Lynn Szwaja, and Tomás Ybarra-Frausto. Durham, N.C.: Duke University Press. 161–202.

———. 2007. "From Ethnology to Heritage: The Role of the Museum." In *Entre autres: Rencontres et conflits en Europe et en Méditerranée*. Proceedings of the 8th Conference of the Société Internationale d'Ethnologie et de Folklore (SIEF), Marseille, April 26–30, 2004. Marseille: Musée des Civilisations de l'Europe et de la Méditerranée.

Klak, Thomas, ed. 1998. *Globalization and Neoliberalism: The Caribbean Context*. Lanham, Md.: Rowman and Littlefield.

Klak, Thomas, and Garth Myers. 1998. "How States Sell Their Countries and Their People." In *Globalization and Neoliberalism: The Caribbean Context*, ed. Thomas Klak. Lanham, Md.: Rowman and Littlefield. 87–110.

Klein, Barbro. 2000a. "Foreigners, Foreignness, and the Swedish Folklife Sphere." *Ethnologia Scandinavica* 30: 5–23.

———. 2000b. "The Moral Content of Tradition: Homecraft, Ethnology, and Swedish Life in the Twentieth Century." *Western Folklore* 59 (Spring): 171–95.

———. 2001. "More Swedish Than in Sweden, More Iranian Than in Iran: Folk Culture and World Migrations." In *Upholders of Culture: Past and Present*, ed. Bo Sundin. Stockholm: Royal Swedish Academy of Engineering Sciences. 67–80.

———. 2006. "Cultural Heritage, the Swedish Folklife Sphere, and the Others." *Cultural Analysis* 5: 57–80.

———. 2007. "Folklore Archives, Heritage Politics, and Ethical Dilemmas: Notes on Writing and Printing." In *Research Ethics in Studies of Culture and Social Life*, ed. Bente Gullveig Alver, Tove Ingebjørg Fjell, and Ørjar Øyen. FF Communications 292. Helsinki: Suomalainen Tiedeakatemia; Academia Scientiarum Fennica. 114–36.

———. 2008. "La folkloristique, une discipline mère?" *Ethnologie Française* 38 (2): 223–32.

Kličkova, Vera. 1996 [1951]. *Ethnographic Study of a Galičnik Wedding*. Skopje: NIP Nova Makedonia.

Klimova-Alexander, Ilona. 2005. *The Romani Voice in World Politics: The United Nations and Non-State Actors*. Aldershot: Ashgate.

Kockel, Ullrich. 2007. "Looking for Europe in the Frontier: Eco-Ethnological Reflections on Sense of Place and Historicity." *Lietuvos Etnologija* 7 (16).

Kratz, Corinne A., and Ivan Karp. 2006. "Introduction: Museum Frictions: Public Cultures/Global Transformations." In *Museum Frictions: Public Cultures, Global Transformations*, ed. Ivan Karp, Corinne A. Kratz, Lynn Szwaja, and Tomás Ybarro-Frausto. Durham, N.C.: Duke University Press. 1–32.

Krugman, Paul. 2009. "All the President's Zombies." *New York Times*, August 23.

Kulonen, Ulla-Maija, Irja Seurujärvi-Kari, and Risto Pulkkinen, eds. 2005. *The Saami: A Cultural Encyclopaedia*. Suomalaisen Kirjallisuuden Seuran toimituksia 925. Helsinki: SKS.

Kurin, Richard. 2004. "Les problématiques du patrimoine culturel immatériel." *L'internationale de l'imaginaire: "Le patrimoine culturel immatériel: Les enjeux, les problématiques, les pratiques"* n.s. 17: 59–67.

———. 2005. "Regulating Culture?" *Anthropology News* 46 (9): 28.

———. 2007. "Safeguarding Intangible Cultural Heritage: Key Factors in Implementing the 2003 Convention." *International Journal of Intangible Cultural Heritage* 2: 10–20.

Kurkiala, Mikael. 2002. "Business as Usual? Critical Remarks on the Trivialization of Difference and Diversity." *LBC Newsletter* 2 (January): 22–25.

Kuutma, Kristin. 2005. "Vernacular Religions and the Invention of Identities Behind the Finno-Ugric Wall." *Temenos: Nordic Journal of Comparative Religion* 41 (1): 51–76.

———. 2006. *Collaborative Representations: Interpreting the Creation of a Sámi Ethnography and a Seto Epic*. FF Communications 289. Helsinki: Academia Scientiarum Fennica.

———. 2007. "The Politics of Contested Representation: UNESCO and the Masterpieces of Intangible Cultural Heritage." In *Prädikat "Heritage": Wertschöpfungen aus kulturellen Ressourcen*, ed. Dorothee Hemme, Markus Tauschek, and Regina Bendix. Göttingen: LIT Verlag. 177–95.

———. 2008. "The Making of Sami Ethnography: Contested Authorities and Negotiated Representations." *Journal of Ethnology and Folkloristics* 2 (1): 55–65.

———. 2009. "Who Owns Our Songs: Authority of Heritage and Resources for Restitution." *Ethnologia Europaea* 39 (2): 26–40.

———. 2012. "Communities and the Contested Politics of Representation." Paper presented at ICH Researchers Forum—The Implementation of UNESCO's Intangible Heritage Convention, Paris, June 3.

Kuutma, Kristin, and Tiiu Jaago, eds. 2005. *Studies in Estonian Folkloristics and Ethnology: A Reader and Reflexive History*. Tartu: Tartu University Press.

LaBelle, Brandon. 2010. *Acoustic Territories: Sound Culture and Everyday Life*. London: Continuum.

Laclau, Ernesto, ed. 1994. *The Making of Political Identities*. London: Verso.

Leach, Robert. 2008. *Theatre Studies: The Basics*. New York: Routledge.

Lee, Benjamin, and Edward LiPuma. 2002. "Cultures of Circulation: The Imaginations of Modernity." *Public Culture* 14 (1): 191–213.

Lee, Ken. 2000. "Orientalism and Gypsylorism." *Social Analysis* 44 (2): 129–56.

Lehtola, Veli-Pekka. 1997. *Saamelaiset: Historia, yhteiskunta, taide*. Jyväskylä: Kustannus-Puntsi.

Lewy, Guenter. 2000. *The Nazi Persecution of the Gypsies*. New York: Oxford University Press.

Li, Tania Murray. 2001. "Boundary Work: Community, Market, and State Reconsidered." In *Communities and the Environment: Ethnicity, Gender, and the State in Community-Based Conservation*, ed. Arun Agrawal and Clark C. Gibson. New Brunswick, N.J.: Rutgers University Press. 157–79.

Lindvall, Karin, and Birgitta Johansen, eds. 2003. *Agenda kulturarv: Inspiration, diskussion*. Stockholm: Riksantikvarieämbetet.

Lipsitz, George. 1994. *Dangerous Crossroads: Popular Music, Postmodernism and the Poetics of Place*. London: Verso.

Löfgren, Orvar. 1989. "Nationalization of Culture." *Ethnologia Europaea: Journal of European Ethnology* 19: 5–25.

López, Raimundo. 2004. "El Condor Pasa: Patrimonio Cultural de la Nacion de Peru." *Argenpress.info*. http://www.argenpress.info/nota.asp?num=010267.

Low, Setha M. 1994. "Embodied Metaphors: Nerves as Lived Experience." In *Embodiment and Experience: The Existential Ground of Culture and Self*, ed. Thomas J. Csordas. Cambridge: Cambridge University Press. 139–62.

Lowenthal, David. 1985. *The Past Is a Foreign Country*. Cambridge: Cambridge University Press.

———. 1998. *The Heritage Crusade and the Spoils of History*. Cambridge: Cambridge University Press.

Lowthorp, Leah. 2007. "The Cultural Politics of UNESCO's Intangible Cultural Heritage in India: Kutiyattam Sanskrit Theatre." Paper delivered at Annual Meeting of the American Folklore Society and the Folklore Studies Association of Canada, Quebec City.

Luhrman, Tanya. 2012. *When God Talks Back: Understanding the American Evangelical Relationship with God*. New York: Vintage.

Lundström, Inga, and Marja-Leena Pilvesmaa. 1996. *Kunskap som krgsprogram för hur museerna med sitt arbete kan motverka främlingsfientlighet och rasism*. Stockholm: Statens historiska museum.

Magliocco, Sabina. 2004. *Witching Culture: Folklore and Neo-Paganism in America*. Philadelphia: University of Pennsylvania Press.

Mahmood, Saba. 2005. *Politics of Piety: Islamic Revival and the Feminist Subject*. Princeton, N.J.: Princeton University Press.

Martin, Luther H., Huck Gutman, and Patrick H. Hutton. 1988. *Technologies of the Self: A Seminar with Michel Foucault.* Amherst: University of Massachusetts Press.

Marushiakova, Elena, and Vesselin Popov. 1995. "The Romani Anthem." In *Studii Romani*, vol. 2. Sofia: Club '90. 10–21.

———. 2001. "Historical and Ethnographic Background: Gypsies, Roma, Sinti." In *Between Past and Future: The Roma of Central and Eastern Europe*, ed. Will Guy. Hatfield: University of Hertfordshire Press. 33–53.

Mathisen, Stein R. 2009. "Narrated Sámi Siedis: Heritage and Ownership in Ambiguous Border Zones." *Ethnologia Europaea: Journal of European Ethnology* 39 (2): 11–25.

May, Clifford D. 2009. "The Taliban: A Brief History." *National Post* (Canada), July 17.

McDermott, Melanie Hughes. 2001. "Invoking Community: Indigenous People and Ancestral Domain in Palawan, the Philippines." In *Communities and the Environment: Ethnicity, Gender, and the State in Community-Based Conservation*, ed. Arun Agrawal and Clark C. Gibson. New Brunswick, N.J.: Rutgers University Press. 32–62.

McDonald, Henry. 2006. "Orangemen 'Frightened Away Tourists.'" *Observer*, July 16.

McFate, Montgomery, and Andrea Jackson. 2005. "An Organizational Solution for DODs Cultural Knowledge Needs." *Military Review* (July–August): 18–21.

McKittrick, David. 2009. "Belfast Immigrants Warned: 'Get Out by Tomorrow—or You Die.'" *London Independent*, July 10.

McSherry, J. Patrice. 2005. *Predatory States: Operation Condor and Covert War in Latin America.* Lanham, Md.: Rowman and Littlefield.

Meintjes, Louise. 1990. "Paul Simon's *Graceland*, South Africa, and the Mediation of Musical Meaning." *Ethnomusicology* 34 (1) (Winter): 37–73.

Merali, Isfahan, and Valerie Oosterveld, eds. 2001. *Giving Meaning to Economic, Social, and Cultural Rights.* Philadelphia: University of Pennsylvania Press.

Merry, Sally Engle. 2006. *Human Rights and Gender Violence: Translating International Law into Local Justice.* Chicago: University of Chicago Press.

Mertus, Julie. 2008. *Human Rights Matters: Local Politics and National Human Rights Institutions.* Stanford, Calif.: Stanford University Press.

Messer, Ellen. 1993. "Anthropology and Human Rights." *Annual Review of Anthropology* 22:221–49.

———. 1997. "Pluralist Approaches to Human Rights." *Journal of Anthropological Research* 53:293–315.

———. 2002. "Anthropologists in a World With and Without Human Rights." In *Exotic No More: Anthropology on the Front Lines*, ed. Jeremy MacClancy. Chicago: University of Chicago Press. 319–37.

Miller, Daniel. 1991. "Absolute Freedom in Trinidad." *Man* 26: 323–41.

———. 1998. *A Theory of Shopping.* Cambridge: Polity.

Miller, Toby. 2006. "Comentario." *Cultural Analysis* 5: 107–15.

Mirga, Andrzej, and Nicolae Gheorghe. 1997. *The Roma in the Twenty-First Century: A Policy Paper.* Princeton, N.J.: Project on Ethnic Relations.

Moran, Emilio, ed. 1996. *Transforming Societies, Transforming Anthropology.* Ann Arbor: University of Michigan Press.

Moreno, Anthony. n.d. "El cóndor pasa (si pudiera): Comentario." *Literatura . . . ¡y algo más!* http://canto.elbajio.com/canto/condor.html.

Morris, Steven. 1998. "Unplanned Results of a Planned Community." Paper written for English 577, The Festival, Ohio State University.

Morvaridi, Behrooz. 2004. "Resettlement, Rights to Development, and the Ilisu Dam, Turkey." *Development and Change* 35: 719–41.

Mouawad, Jad, and Kate Galbraith. 2009. "By Degrees: Plugged-In Age Feeds a Hunger for Electricity." *New York Times,* September 19.

Munjeri, Dawson. 2001. "The Notions of Integrity and Authenticity: The Emerging Patterns in Africa." In *Authenticity and Integrity in an African Context: Expert Meeting—Great Zimbabwe, Zimbabwe, 26–29 May 2000*, ed. Galia Saouma-Forero. Paris: UNESCO. 17–19.

Mutua, Makau. 2002. *Human Rights: A Political and Cultural Critique.* Philadelphia: University of Pennsylvania Press.

Nas, Peter J. M. 2002. "Masterpieces of Oral and Immaterial Culture: Reflections on the UNESCO World Heritage List." *Current Anthropology* 43 (1): 139–43.

National Initiative for Service Excellence (NISE). 2008. "Building Excellence the Barbadian Way." http://www.nisebarbados.org/.

———. 2010. "Company Statement."

Nilsson, Bo G. 2004. "Framtidens salt: Om museernas och folklivsforskarnas bidrag till folkhemsbygget." In *Samhällsideal och framtidsbilder: Perspektiv på Nordiska museets dokumentation och forskning*, ed. Cecilia Hammarlund-Larsson, Bo G. Nilsson, and Eva Silvén. Stockholm: Carlssons. 67–139.

Noyes, Dorothy. 2003. "Group." In *Eight Words for the Study of Expressive Culture*, ed. Burt Feintuch. Urbana: University of Illinois Press. 7–41.

———. 2006. "The Judgment of Solomon: Global Protections for Tradition and the Problem of Community Ownership." *Cultural Analysis* 5: 27–56.

———. 2007. "Cultural Warming? Brazil in Berlin." In *Kulturpolitik und Politik der Kultur: Festschrift für Alexander Stephan*, ed. Helen Fehervary and Bernd Fischer. German Life and Civilization 47. Bern: Peter Lang. 55–76.

———. 2009. "Culture as Cover: Imperial Self-Expression in the Neoliberal Moment." Paper at The Race in Culture: Twentieth Century Ethnology and Empire in Comparative Perspective conference, Mershon Center for International Security Studies, Ohio State University. May 2.

Noyes, Dorothy. 2003. "Group." In *Eight Words for the Study of Expressive Culture*, ed. Burt Feintuch. Urbana: University of Illinois Press, 7–41.

———. 2006. "The Judgement of Solomon: Global Protections for Tradition and the Problem of Community Ownership." *Cultural Analysis* 5: 27–56.

———. 2007. "Cultural Warming? Brazil in Berlin." In *Kulturpolitik und Politik der Kultur: Festschrift für Alexander Stephan*, ed. Helen Fehervary and Bernd Fischer. German Life and Civilization47. Bern: Peter Lang, 55–76.

———. 2009. "Culture as Cover: Imperial Self-Expression in the Neoliberal Moment." Paper presented at The Race in Culture: Twentieth Century Ethnology and Empire in Comparative Perspective. Mershon Center for International Security Studies, Ohio State University, May 2.

Nuti, Paul J. 2005. "UNESCO and Cultural Diversity: An Unconventional Approach?" *Anthropology News* 46 (9): 25.

O'Connell, Mary Ellen. 2008. *The Power and Purpose of International Law.* Oxford: Oxford University Press.

"Ó Cuív Grants €250,000 to Promote Orange Order." 2008. *Irish Times.* February 2.

Ó Giolláin, Diarmuid. 2000. *Locating Irish Folklore: Tradition, Modernity, Identity.* Cork: Cork University Press.

Olwig, Karen Fog. 1999. "The Burden of Heritage: Claiming a Place for a West Indian Culture." *American Ethnologist* 26 (2): 370–88.

Ong, Aihwa. 2007. *Neoliberalism as Exception: Mutations in Citizenship and Sovereignty*. Durham, N.C.: Duke University Press.

"Orangefest Aims to Bridge the Gap." 2009. *Sunday Business Post Online* (Belfast), July 12.

"Orange Order Marches On, But Now It's a Festival." 2007. *London Independent*, July 8.

Ortiz, Carmen. 1999. "The Uses of Folklore by the Franco Regime." *Journal of American Folklore* 112 (446): 479–96.

Ortner, Sherry. 1995. "Resistance and the Problem of Ethnographic Refusal." *Comparative Studies in Society and History* 37 (1): 173–93.

———. 1999. "Thick Resistance: Death and the Cultural Construction of Agency in Himalayan Mountaineering." In *The Fate of Culture: Geertz and Beyond*, ed. Sherry Ortner. Berkeley: University of California Press. 136–63.

Osborne, Virginia Nickles. 2007. " 'Let's Go to the Woods, Boys': Reading *Deliverance* as a Cold War Novel." *James Dickey Newsletter* 24: 1–20.

Ots, Thomas. 1994. "The Silenced Body—The Expressive *Leib*: On the Dialectic of Mind and Life in Chinese Cathartic Healing." In *Embodiment and Experience: The Existential Ground of Culture and Self*, ed. Thomas J. Csordas. Cambridge: Cambridge University Press. 116–36.

Pagans for Archaeology. 2008. "What We Stand For." June 7. http://archaeopagans.blogspot.com/2008/06/what-we-stand-for.html.

Paine, Robert. 1994. *The Herds of the Tundra: A Portrait of Saami Reindeer Pastoralism*. Washington, D.C.: Smithsonian Institution.

Panagia, Davide. 2009. *The Political Life of Sensation*. Durham, N.C.: Duke University Press.

Paques, Viviana.1991. *La religion des esclaves: Recherches sur la confrerie marocaine des Gnawa*. Bergamo: Moretti and Vitali.

Patemen, Carole. 1988. *The Sexual Contract*. Stanford, Calif.: Stanford University Press.

———. 2002. "Self Ownership and Property in the Person: Democratization and a Tale of Two Concepts." *Journal of Political Philosopphy* 10 (10): 20–53.

Penley, Constance. 1997. "Crackers and Whackers: The White Trashing of Porn." In *White Trash: Race and Class in America*, ed. Matt Wray and Annalee Newitz. New York: Routledge. 89–112.

Petrova, Dimitrina. 2003. "The Roma: Between a Myth and a Future." *Social Research* 70 (1): 111–61.

Portelli, Alessandro. 1991. "No Neutrals There: The Cultural Class Struggle in the Harlan Miners' Strike of 1931–32." In Portelli, *The Death of Luigi Trastulli and Other Stories: Form and Meaning in Oral History*. SUNY Series in Oral and Public History. Albany: State University of New York Press. 216–40.

Poulot, Dominique. 1997. *Musée, nation, patrimoine*. Paris: Gallimard-Jeunesse.

———. 2001. *Patrimoine et musées: L'institution de la culture*. Paris: Hachette.

Powell, Shirley, Christine E. Garza, and Aubrey Hendricks. 1993. "Ethics and Ownership of the Past: The Reburial and Repatriation Controversy." *Archeological Method and Theory* 5: 1–42.

Pressouyre, Léon. 2001. "Cultural Heritage and the 1972 Convention: Definition and Evolution of a Concept." In *African Cultural Heritage and the World Heritage Convention: Second Global Strategy Meeting*, ed. Bertrand Hirsch, Laurent Lévi-Strauss, and Galia Saouma-Forero. Paris: UNESCO. 56–64.

Purvis, Andrew. 2002. "Roma Rule." *Time*, June 24, 70–71.

Quirante Santacruz, Luis. 2001. *Del teatro del Misteri al misterio del teatro.* Valencia: Universitat de Valéncia.

Ramcharitar, Raymond. 2008. "Tourist Nationalism in Trinidad and Tobago." In *New Perspectives on Caribbean Tourism*, ed. Marcella Daye, Donna Chambers and Sherma Roberts, 79–93. London: Routledge.

Rancière, Jacques. 2010. *Dissensus: On Politics and Aesthetics.* Ed. and trans. Steven Corcoran. New York: Continuum.

Rastrick, Ólafur. 2007. "Menningararfur í fjölmenningarsamfélagi: Einsleitni, fjölhyggja, tvíbendni." In *Þriðja íslenska söguþingið 18.–21. maí 2006. Ráðstefnurit*, ed. Benedikt Eyþórsson and Hrafnkell Lárusson. Reykjavík: Sagnfræðingafélag Íslands. 333–41.

Raun, Toivo. 1991. "The Petseri Region of the Republic of Estonia." *Jahrbücher für Geschichte Osteuropas* 39 (4): 514–32.

Reich, Robert. 2012. "Why BP Isn't a Criminal." *Huffington Post*, November 16.

Republic of Bolivia, Ministry of Foreign Affairs and Religion. 1973. Letter to the Director-General of UNESCO, April 24. Ref. No. D.G.O.I.1006-79.

Rice, Timothy. 1994. *May It Fill Your Soul: Experiencing Bulgarian Music.* Chicago: University of Chicago Press.

———. 1996. "The Dialectics of Economics and Aesthetics in Bulgarian Music." In *Returning Culture: Musical Change in Eastern Europe*, ed. Mark Slobin. Durham, N.C.: Duke University Press. 176–99.

Ringold, Dena. 2000. *Roma and the Transition in Central and Eastern Europe: Trends and Challenges.* Washington, D.C.: World Bank.

Ringold, Dena, Mitchell Orenstein, and Erica Wilkins. 2004. *Roma in an Expanding Europe: Breaking the Poverty Cycle.* Washington, D.C.: World Bank.

Robin, Marie-Monique. 2008. *Le monde selon Monsanto: De la dioxine aux OGM, une multinationale qui vous veut du bien.* Paris: Broché.

Rose, Nikolas. 1999. *Powers of Freedom: Reframing Political Thought.* Cambridge: Cambridge University Press.

Rosenblum, Amalia. 2009. "Prisoners of Conscience: Public Policy and Contemporary Repatriation Discourse." *Museum Anthropology* 20 (3): 58–71.

Russo, Mary J. 1995. *The Female Grotesque: Risk, Excess, and Modernity.* New York: Routledge.

Said, Edward. 1978. *Orientalism.* New York: Vintage.

Sarv, Maarja. 2009. "Kiä' mi olõ? Seto identiteet Eesti, Euroopa ja Soome-ugri kultuuriruumis." *Setomaa* 13 (191): 6.

Sarv, Õie. 1997. "Ei saa me läbi Setota ja Venemaa meelest ei lähe . . ." In *Lee 4: Ümin.* Tartu: Eesti Rahva Muuseumi Sõprade Selts. 96–99.

———. 2008. "Läämi' vasta Seto Kongressilõ." *Setomaa* 15–16 (169–70): 11.

———. 2009. "Mida arvate Setomaa jagamisest?" *Setomaa* 6 (184): 1.

Sarv, Vaike. 1997. "Üheksa nimega hõim." *Setomaa* 2 (11): 1–2.

Scheper-Hughes, Nancy. 1992. *Death Without Weeping: The Violence of Everyday Life in Brazil.* Berkeley: University of California Press.

Scher, Philip W. 1998. "Confounding Categories: The Global and the Local in the Process of a Caribbean Art." *Small Axe* 6: 37–56.

———. 2002. "Copyright Heritage: Preservation, Carnival and the State in Trinidad." *Anthropological Quarterly* 75 (Summer): 453–84.

———. 2012. "Uneasy Heritage: Ambivalence and Ambiguity in Caribbean Heritage Practices." In

Heritage Regimes and the State, ed. Regina Bendix, Aditya Eggert, and Arnika Peselmann . Gottingen Studies in Cultural Property 6. Göttingen: Göttingen University Press. 79–96.

Scott, David. 1991. "That Event, This Memory: Notes on the Anthropology of African Diasporas in the New World." *Diaspora* 1 (3): 261–84.

———. 2001. "The Government of Freedom." In *New Caribbean Thought: A Reader*, ed. Brian Meeks and Folke Lindahl. Kingston: University of the West Indies Press. 428–50.

———. 2005. "Colonial Governmentality." In *Anthropologies of Modernity: Foucault, Governmentality, and Life Politics*, ed. Jonathan Xavier Inda. Malden, Mass.: Blackwell. 23–49.

Scott, James C. 1990. *Domination and the Arts of Resistance*. New Haven, Conn.: Yale University Press.

———. 1998. *Seeing like a State: How Certain Schemes to Improve the Human Condition Have Failed*. New Haven: Yale University Press.

———. 2009. *The Art of Not Being Governed: An Anarchist History of Upland Southeast Asia*. New Haven, Conn.: Yale University Press.

Seremetakis, C. Nadia. 1994. *The Senses Still: Perception and Memory as Material Culture in Modernity*. Boulder, Colo.: Westview Press.

Serres, Michel. 2011. *Malfeasance: Appropriation Through Pollution*. Stanford, Calif.: Stanford University Press.

Seto Kongress. 1994. Kolmas Seto Kongress, September 10, 1993. Värskas. Tartu.

Seurujärvi-Kari, Irja. 2005a. "Convention Concerning Indigenous and Tribal Peoples in Independent Countries (ILO No. 169)." In *The Saami: A Cultural Encyclopaedia*, ed. Ulla-Maija Kulonen, Irja Seurujärvi-Kari, and Risto Pulkkinen. Suomalaisen Kirjallisuuden Seuran toimituksia 925. Helsinki: SKS. 50–53.

———. 2005b."Cultural Autonomy." In *The Saami: A Cultural Encyclopaedia*, ed. Ulla-Maija Kulonen, Irja Seurujärvi-Kari, and Risto Pulkkinen. Suomalaisen Kirjallisuuden. Seuran toimituksia 925. Helsinki: SKS. 58–59.

———. 2005c. "National Identity: 'Saaminess.'" In *The Saami: A Cultural Encyclopaedia*, ed. Ulla-Maija Kulonen, Irja Seurujärvi-Kari, and Risto Pulkkinen. Suomalaisen Kirjallisuuden Seuran toimituksia 925. Helsinki: SKS. 234–36.

———. 2005d. "Saami Council." In *The Saami: A Cultural Encyclopaedia*, ed. Ulla-Maija Kulonen, Irja Seurujärvi-Kari, and Risto Pulkkinen. Suomalaisen Kirjallisuuden Seuran toimituksia 925. Helsinki: SKS. 344–46.

———. 2005e. "World Council of Indigenous Peoples (WCIP)." In *The Saami: A Cultural Encyclopaedia*, ed. Ulla-Maija Kulonen, Irja Seurujärvi-Kari, and Risto Pulkkinen. Suomalaisen Kirjallisuuden Seuran toimituksia 925. Helsinki: SKS. 437–40.

Shaw, Denise. 2005. "Rape, Murder, and Masculinity in *Deliverance*." *James Dickey Newsletter* 22: 33 45.

Sherkin, Samantha. 2001. "A Historical Study on the Preparation of the 1989 Recommendation on the Safeguarding of Traditional Culture and Folklore." In *Safeguarding Traditional Cultures: A Global Assessment*, ed. Peter Seitel. Washington, D.C.: Center for Folklife and Cultural Heritage, Smithsonian Institution. 42–56.

Shoup, Daniel. 2006. "Can Archaeology Build a Dam? Sites and Politics in Turkey's Southeast Anatolia Project." *Journal of Mediterranean Archaeology* 19: 231–58.

Silverman, Carol. 1989. "Reconstructing Folklore: Media and Cultural Policy in Eastern Europe." *Communication* 11 (2): 141–60.

———. 1996. "Music and Marginality: Roma (Gypsies) of Bulgaria and Macedonia." In *Returning*

Culture: Musical Changes in Central and Eastern Europe, ed. Mark Slobin. Durham, N.C.: Duke University Press, 231–53.

———. 1999. "Rom (Gypsy) Music." In *Garland Encyclopedia of World Music*, Europe volume, ed. Timothy Rice, James Porter, and Christopher Goertzen. New York: Garland, 270–93.

———. 2007a. "Bulgarian Wedding Music Between Folk and Chalga: Politics, Markets, and Current Directions." *Musicology* 7: 69–97.

———. 2007b. "Trafficking in the Exotic with 'Gypsy' Music: Balkan Roma, Cosmopolitanism, and 'World Music' Festivals." In *Balkan Popular Culture and the Ottoman Ecumene: Music, Image, and Regional Political Discourse*, ed. Donna Buchanan. Lanham, Md.: Scarecrow Press. 335–61.

———. 2012. *Romani Routes: Cultural Politics and Balkan Music in Diaspora*. New York: Oxford University Press.

Silverman, Helaine, and D. Fairchild Ruggles, eds. 2007. *Cultural Heritage and Human Rights*. New York: Springer.

Skounti, Ahmed. 2009. "The Authentic Illusion: Humanities Intangible Cultural Heritage, the Moroccan Experience." In *Intangible Heritage*, ed. Laurajane Smith and Natsuko Akagawa. Key Issues in Cultural Heritage. London: Routledge. 74–92.

Skounti, Ahmed, and Ouidad Tebbaa (2005). *Place Jemaâ El Fna. Patrimoine culturel Immatériel de Marrakech, du Maroc et de l'humanité*. Rabat: Bureau de l'UNESCO.

Skounti, Ahmed, and Ouidad Tebbaa. 2011. *De l'immatérialité du patrimoine culturel*. Actes du colloque de juin 2009. Publications de la Faculté des lettres et des sciences humainse de l'Universitè Cadi Ayyad et du Bureau d l'UNESCO à Rabat. Marrakech: Imprimerie Walili.

Skrydstrup, Martin. 2009. "Theorizing Repatriation." *Ethnologia Europaea: Journal of European Ethnology* 39 (2): 54–66.

Slyomovics, Susan. 2005. *The Performance of Human Rights in Morocco*. Philadelphia: University of Pennsylvania Press.

Small, Christopher. 1998. *Musicking: The Meanings of Performing and Listening*. Hanover, n.H.: University Press of New England.

Smith, Bonnie G., ed. 2000. *Global Feminisms Since 1945*. Series on Rewriting Histories. New York: Routledge.

Smith, Geoffrey. 2009. "Behind the Post-Industrial: Red, White, and Blue; Blood Red; or Just Black." Paper written for English 694, American Regional Cultures and Global Transition: Appalachia, Louisiana, and the Texas Border Country. Ohio State University.

Smith, Laurajane. 2006a. "Empty Gestures? Heritage and the Politics of Recognition." In *Cultural Heritage and Human Rights*, ed. Helaine Silverman and D. Fairchild Ruggles. New York: Springer. 159–71.

———. 2006b. *Uses of Heritage*. London: Routledge.

Smith, Martin. 2009. "Balancing Interests: Making Decisions Regarding Prehistoric Human Remains." Presentation at Pagans and Archaeology conference, University of Bristol, June 27.

"Soldiers in Barracks for Twelfth." 2006. *BBC News Online*. July 12.

Solon, Olivia. 2011. "Academics Claim Reburial Legislation Is Stifling Archaeology." *Wired*, February 8.

Spivak, Gayatri. 1988. *In Other Worlds: Essays in Cultural Politics*. New York: Routledge.

———. 1999. *A Critique of Postcolonial Reason: Toward a History of the Vanishing Present*. Cambridge, Mass.: Harvard University Press.

Statens Offentliga Utredningar (SOU). 1994. *Minne och bildning: musseernas uppdrag och organisation*. Stockholm: Norstedts.

St. George, Robert Blair. 1998. *Conversing by Signs: Poetics of Implication in Colonial New England.* Chapel Hill: University of North Carolina Press.

Stein, Rebecca, and Ted Swedenburg, eds. 2005. *Palestine, Israel, and the Politics of Popular Culture.* Durham, N.C.: Duke University Press.

Stenou, Katérina. 2003. *UNESCO and the Issue of Cultural Diversity: Review and Strategy, 1946–2003.* Rev. ed. Paris: UNESCO Division of Cultural Policies and Intercultural Dialogue.

Stewart, Kathleen. 1996. "Mimetic Excess in an Occupied Place." In *A Space on the Side of the Road: Cultural Poetics and Politics in an "Other" America.* Princeton, N.J.: Princeton University Press. 41–66.

———. 2007. *Ordinary Affects.* Durham, N.C.: Duke University Press.

Stracansky, Pavol. 2009. "Europe: The Right Rises." Inter Press Service, May 5.

Strmiska, Michael. 2005. "Modern Paganism in World Cultures: Comparative Perspectives." In *Modern Paganism in World Cultures: Comparative Perspectives*, ed. Michael Strmiska. Santa Barbara, Calif.: ABC Clio. 1–53.

Ströbele-Gregor, Juliana. 1996. "Culture and Political Practice of the Aymara and Quechua in Bolivia: Autonomous Forms of Modernity in the Andes." *Latin American Perspectives* 23 (2): 72–90.

Strzelewicz, Willy. 2004 (1983). *De mänskliga rättigheternas historia: Från den amerikanska oavhängighetsförklaringen till våra dagar.* Stockholm: Ordfront. In German, *Der Kampf um die Menschenrechte.* Frankfurt am Main: Societäts-Verlag, 1968.

Swain, Hedley. 2007. "The Value of Human Remains in Museum Collections." *Public Archaeology* 6 (3): 193–97.

"Taliban, Opium in Afghanistan Difficult to Contain." 2007. NPR *Morning Edition*, December 31.

Tauschek, Markus. 2009. "Cultural Property as Strategy: The Carnival of Binche, the Creation of Cultural Heritage and Cultural Property." *Ethnologia Europaea: Journal of European Ethnology* 39 (2): 67–80.

"Tennessee County Wants Millions to Fix Image After Ash Spill." 2009. Associated Press, September 13.

Thompson, Krista. 2006. *An Eye for the Tropics: Tourism, Photography, and Framing the Caribbean Picturesque.* Durham, N.C.: Duke University Press.

Thompson, Michael. 1979. *Rubbish Theory: The Creation and Destruction of Value.* Oxford: Oxford University Press.

Thompson, Tok. 2006. "Heritage Versus the Past." In *The Past in the Present: A Multidisciplinary Approach*, ed. Fabio Mugnaini, Pádraig Ó Héalaí, and Tok Thompson. Catania: Edit Press. 197–208.

"Thousands March in Orange Parades." 2006. *BBC News Online*, July 12.

Tiersma, Peter Meijas. 1999. *Legal Language.* Chicago: University of Chicago Press.

Tilden, Freeman. 1957. *Interpreting Our Heritage.* Chapel Hill: University of North Carolina Press.

Timmo, Margus. 2006. "Tegelemiq võimaluisigaq!" *Peko Helü.* Suvi (01): 5.

Todorova, Maria. 1997. *Imagining the Balkans.* New York: Oxford University Press.

Tornatore, Jean-Louis. 2011. "Du patrimoine ethnologique culturel immatériel: Suivre la voie politique de l'immatérialité culturelle." In *Le patrimoine culturel immatériel: Enjeux d'une nouvelle catégorie*, ed. Chiara Bortolo. Paris: Maison des Sciences de l'Homme. 75–91.

"Toxic Waters." 2009. *New York Times*, August 22, September 12, 17, October 12.

Trinidad Express Newspaper. 1993. February 19, Letters to the Editor, 4

Trumpener, Katie. 1992. "The Time of the Gypsies: A 'People Without History' in the Narratives of the West." *Critical Inquiry* 18: 843–84.

Tsing, Anna. 1993. *In the Realm of the Diamond Queen*. Princeton, N.J.: Princeton University Press.

———. 2002. "Conclusion: The Global Situation." In *The Anthropology of Globalization: A Reader*, ed. Jonathan Xavier Inda and Renato Rosaldo. Malden, Mass.: Blackwell. 453–85.

———. 2005. *Friction: An Ethnography of Global Connection*. Princeton, N.J.: Princeton University Press.

Tucker, Willard. 2009. MFA thesis. Ohio State University.

Tunbridge, J. E., and Gregory John Ashworth. 1996. *Dissonant Heritage: The Management of the Past as a Resource in Conflict*. Chichester: Wiley. Turino, Thomas. 1988. "The Music of Andean Migrants in Lima, Peru: Demographics, Social Power, and Style." *Latin American Music Review* 9 (2): 127–50.

Turino, Thomas. 1988. "The Music of Andean Migrants in Lima, Peru: Demographics, Sockal Power, and Style." *Latin American Music Review* 9 (2): 127–50.

Turner, Ted. 1997. "Human Rights, Human Difference: Anthropology's Contribution to an Emancipatory Politics." *Journal of Anthropological Research* 53: 273–91.

Turner, Victor. 1969. *The Ritual Process: Structure and Anti-Structure*. Lewis Henry Morgan Lectures. Chicago: Aldine.

Turtinen, Jan. 2006. *Världsarvets villkor: Intressen, förhandlingar och bruk i internationell politik*. Stockholm Studies in Ethnology 1. Stockholm: Acta Universitatis Stockholmiensis.

"TVA Buys 71 Properties Affected by Coal Ash Spill." 2009. Associated Press, April 10.

UNESCO. 1971. Possibility of Establishing an International Instrument for the Protection of Folklore. Document B/EC/IX/11-IGC/XR.1/15.

———. 1977. Letter from the Ministry of Foreign Affairs and Religion, Republic of Bolivia, April 24, 1973. Document FOLK/I/3, Annex. Paris.

———. 2001. *Proclamation of Masterpieces of the Oral and Intangible Heritage of Humanity*. Paris: UNESCO.

———. 2002. Istanbul Declaration—Final Communiqué, Third Round Table Meeting of Ministers of Culture. http://portal.unesco.org/en/ev.php-URL_ID=6209&URL_DO=DO_TOPIC&URL_SECTION=201.html.

———. 2003a. Convention pour la sauvegarde du patrimoine culturel immatériel. Paris: UNESCO.

———. 2003b. Intersessional Working Group of Government Experts on the Preliminary Draft Convention for the Safeguarding of the Intangible Cultural Heritage. Report. Document CLT-2003/CONF.206/3. Paris.

———. 2004. Address by Mr. Koïchiro Matsuura, Director General of UNESCO, on the Convention for the Safeguarding of the Intangible Cultural Heritage, June 1, Copenhagen. Document DG/2004/079.

———. 2006. *Chefs-d'œuvre du patrimoine oral et immatériel de l'humanité. Proclamations 2001, 2003 et 2005*. Paris: UNESCO.

———. 2009. Tourisme culturel. http://portal.unesco.org/culture/fr/ev.php-URL_ID=36700&URL_DO=DO_TOPIC&URL_SECTION=201.html.

Urciuoli, Bonnie. 2008. "Skills and Selves in the New Workplace." *American Ethnologist* 35: 211–28.

U.S. Army/Marine Corps. 2006. *Field Manual No. 3-24: Counterinsurgency*. Washington, D.C. *www.usgcoin.org/library/doctrine/COIN-FM3-24.pdf*.

U.S. English Foundation. n.d. Republic of Lithuania Law on the Principles of State Protection of

Ethnic Culture. http://www.usenglish.org/foundation/research/olp/viewLegislation.asp?CID=46&LID=72.

Vananurm, Ilmar, ed. 2005. *Petserimaa külad I.* Võru: Kirjastus Hilanamoro. *Mu Setomaa.* Võru: Setomaa Valdade Liit.

Vibraek, Janne. 2008. "Il Museo internazionale delle marionette Antonio Pasqualino." In *Il patrimonio culturale immateriale: Analisi e prospettive*, ed. Chiara Bortolotto. Milan: Istituto Poligrafico e Zecca dello Stato. 189–95.

Viel, Annette. n.d. "When the Spirit of the Site Breathes Life: Nature and Culture in Tune with Perpetuity." In *Musées et écologie culturelle, perspectives canadiennes, Museums and Sustainable Communities.* Patrimoine Canada, ICOM, Musée de la civilisation, Québec. www.chin.gc.ca/Resources/Icom/English/Collection/e_tabledes.html.

Vincent, Joan. 2002. "Law." In *Encyclopedia of Social and Cultural Anthropology*, ed. Alan Barnard and Jonathan Spencer. London: Routledge. 330–32.

Walcott, Derek. 1999. *What the Twilight Says: Essays.* New York: Farrar, Straus and Giroux.

Wallis, Robert J. and Jenny Blain. 2001. 'A British Reburial Issue? Statement by the Sacred Sites, Contested Rights/Rites Project." www. sacredsites.org.uk.

Weintraub, Andrew, and Bell Yung. 2009. *Music and Cultural Rights.* Urbana: University of Illinois Press.

Werbner, Pnina. 1997. "Essentialising Essentialism, Essentialising Silence: Ambivalence and Multiplicity in the Constructions of Racism and Ethnicity." In *Debating Cultural Hybridity: Multi-Cultural Identities and the Politics of Anti-Racism*, ed. Pnina Werbner and Tariq Modood. London: Zed. 226–54.

Whisnant, David E. 2008. *All That Is Native and Fine: The Politics of Culture in an American Region.* 2nd ed. Chapel Hill: University of North Carolina Press.

Whitehead, Alfred North. 1968. *Essays in Science and Philosophy.* Westport, Conn.: Greenwood.

Wilce, James. 2003. *Eloquence in Trouble: The Poetics and Politics of Complaint in Rural Bangladesh.* London: Oxford University Press.

Wilk, Richard. 1995. "Learning to Be Local in Belize." In *Worlds Apart: Modernity Through the Prism of the Local*, ed. Daniel Miller. London: Routledge. 110–33.

Willemont, Jacques, prod. 2011 *Un village picard.* Film.

Williams, Gareth. 2002. *The Other Side of the Popular: Neoliberalism and Subalternity in Latin America.* Durham, N.C.: Duke University Press.

Williams, Raymond. 1977. *Marxism and Literature.* Oxford: Oxford University Press.

———. 1984 [1961]. *The Long Revolution.* Harmondsworth: Penguin.

Wilson, John, and Karyn Stapleton. 2007. "Narratives on Lesser-Used Languages in Europe: The Case of Ulster Scots." In *The Discourse of Europe: Talk and Text in Everyday Life*, ed. Sharon Millar and John Wilson. Amsterdam: Benjamins. 173–96.

Wilson, Richard A. 1997. *Human Rights, Culture, and Context: Anthropological Perspectives.* London: Pluto Press.

Wilson, William A. 1973. "Herder, Folklore and Romantic Nationalism." *Journal of Popular Culture* 6 (4): 819–35.

———. 1976. *Folklore and Nationalism in Modern Finland.* Bloomington: Indian University Press.

WIPO Lex. 2010: Law on the Principles of State Protection of Ethnic Culture VIII-1328 of September 21, 1999 (as amended on January 9, 2006). WIPO Lex No. LT042. http://www.wipo.int/wipolex/en/details.jsp?id=5572, viewed July 23, 2013.

Wittrock, Björn. 2004. "The Making of Sweden." *Thesis Eleven* 77 (May): 4–63.

Wright, Julie Pritchard, prod. 1992. *The Toured: The Other Side of Tourism in Barbados*. Film. Berkeley: Distr. University of California Extension Center for Media and Independent Learning.

Yoder, Don. 1963. "The Folklife Studies Movement." *Pennsylvania Folklife* 13 (3): 43–56. Reprinted in Don Yoder, *Discovering American Folklife: Studies in Ethnic, Religious, and Regional Culture*. Ann Arbor, Mich.: UMI Research Press, 1990.

Young, Toby, and Tom Vanderbilt. 1994. "The End of Irony?" *Modern Review* 1 (14) (April–May): 6–7.

Yudice, George. 2003. *The Expediency of Culture: Uses of Culture in the Global Era*. Durham, N.C.: Duke University Press.

Contributors

Valdimar Tr. Hafstein is Associate Professor of Folkloristics/Ethnology at the University of Iceland. He has been a visiting professor at Berkeley and the Georg-August Universität, Göttingen, a research fellow at New York University, and has taught at Edinburgh University and the Icelandic Academy for the Arts. He chaired the Icelandic UNESCO Commission in 2011–2012. He helped found the open access journal *Cultural Analysis* in 2000 and served as its co-editor until 2007. He serves on the editorial board for *Ethnologia Europaea* as well as *Cultural Analysis*. He is author of some 20 articles in English and 15 articles in Icelandic on topics from copyright to heritage theory, and from traditional wrestling to CCTV surveillance, and has co-edited two special issues in English and three book volumes in Icelandic. His work has been translated into French, Italian, Portuguese, Croatian, and Danish. His recent work includes book chapters on "Cultural Heritage," "Europe at the Crossroads of Rights and Culture" (with Martin Skrydstrup), "Célébrer les différences, renforcer la conformité," and "Intangible Heritage as a List: From Masterpieces to Representation."

Deborah Kapchan writes on aesthetics, poetics, and sound/listening practices in Moroccan art and performance. She is author of *Gender on the Market: Moroccan Women and the Revoicing of Tradition* (University of Pennsylvania Press), as well as *Traveling Spirit Masters: Moroccan Trance and Music in the Global Marketplace*. Her third book, *Poetic Justice: Translating Art and Ideology in Morocco* is in progress; an edited volume, *Theorizing Sound Writing*, is under review. She has been a Guggenheim Fellow, a Fulbright-Hays recipient, and a grantee of the American Institute of Maghreb Studies, the Wenner-Gren Foundation for Anthropological Research, and the Social Science Research Council. She is currently Associate Professor of Performance Studies at New York University.

Barbro Klein is Director Emerita of the Swedish Collegium for Advanced Study, Uppsala, and Professor Emerita of Ethnology at Stockholm University. She has taught at a number of institutions, among them University of California, Berkeley. She is a Fellow of the American Folklore Society and a Member of the Royal Gustavus Adolphus Academy in Uppsala; the latter awarded her a major prize in 2006. In 2000, she received the festschrift, *Folklore, Heritage Politics, and Ethnic Diversity*, edited by Pertti Anttonen. She has written extensively on oral narration, rituals, and other forms of expressive culture in diverse settings. Her books include *Legends and Folk Beliefs in a Swedish American Community: A Study in Folklore and Acculturation*, *Från erfarenhet till text: om kulturvetenskaplig reflexivitet* ("From experience to text: on reflexivity in the cultural sciences") with Billy Ehn, *Swedish Folk Art: All Tradition Is Change* (edited with Mats Widbom), *Creating Diversities: Folklore, Religion, and the Politics of Heritage* (edited with Stein Mathisen and Anna-Leena Siikala), and *The Benefit of Broad Horizons* (edited with Hans Joas). Her recent articles include "Women and the Formation of Swedish Folklife Research."

Sabina Magliocco is Professor of Anthropology at California State University, Northridge. A recipient of Guggenheim, National Endowment for the Humanities, Fulbright, and Hewlett fellowships, and an honorary Fellow of the American Folklore Society, she has published on religion, folklore, foodways, festival, and witchcraft in Europe and the United States, and is a leading authority on the modern Pagan movement. She is author of numerous books and articles, including *The Two Madonnas: The Politics of Festival in a Sardinian Community*, *Witching Culture: Folklore and Neo-Paganism in America*, and *Neopagan Sacred Art and Altars: Making Things Whole*. With filmmaker John M. Bishop she produced the documentary film series *Oss Tales*, on a May Day custom in Cornwall and its reclamation by American Pagans. Her current research is on animals in the spiritual imagination.

Dorothy Noyes is Professor and Director of the Center for Folklore Studies at the Ohio State University. Elected a Fellow of the American Folklore Society in 2005, she has held fellowships at the Camargo Foundation, the Davis Center for Historical Studies at Princeton, and the Lichtenberg-Kolleg of Georg-August Universität, Göttingen. She studies the collective representations of plural societies. Her book *Fire in the Plaça: Catalan Festival Politics After Franco* (University of Pennsylvania Press) was named a Choice Outstanding

Academic Title and won the 2005 Book Prize of the Fellows of the American Folklore Society. Other articles on the heritage turn include "Traditional Culture: How Does it Work?" "Hardscrabble Academies: Toward a Social Economy of Vernacular Invention," and "The Judgment of Solomon: Global Protections for Tradition and the Problem of Community Ownership."

Philip W. Scher is Associate Professor of Anthropology at the University of Oregon. A recipient of Guggenheim and Fulbright Senior Scholar Fellowships, his primary research interests lie in the politics of cultural heritage, popular and public culture, tourism, and globalization. His geographical area of focus has been the Caribbean and Caribbean diaspora. He is author of *Carnival and the Formation of a Caribbean Transnation*, co-editor of *Trinidad Carnival: The Cultural Politics of a Transnational Festival*, and editor of *Perspectives on the Caribbean: A Reader in Representation, Culture and History*. Other recent publications include "Copyright Heritage: Preservation, Carnival and the State in Trinidad," "The Devil and The Bedwetter," "Heritage Tourism in The Caribbean," and "Uneasy Heritage: Ambivalence and Ambiguity in Caribbean Heritage Practices." His latest work concerns the politics of Heritage at UNESCO World Heritage Sites.

Carol Silverman, Professor of Anthropology and Folklore at the University of Oregon, has been involved with Balkan culture for over 25 years as a researcher, teacher, activist, and performer. Focusing on Roma in Bulgaria and Macedonia and the American diaspora, her research explores the intersection of politics, music, human rights, gender, and state policy with a focus on issues of representation. Her current project, supported by the Guggenheim Foundation, examines the issue of appropriation in the globalization of Gypsy music. Among her recent publications are *Romani Routes: Cultural Politics and Balkan Music in Diaspora*, "Global Balkan Gypsy Music: Issues of Migration, Appropriation, and Representation," "Education, Agency, and Power Among Macedonian Muslim Romani Women in New York City," "Gypsy Music, Hybridity, and Appropriation: Balkan Dilemmas of Postmodernity," and "Music, Emotion, and the 'Other': Balkan Roma and the Negotiation of Exoticism."

Index